D1568249

Caribbean Migration to Western Europe and the United States

Caribbean Migration to Western Europe and the United States

Essays on Incorporation, Identity, and Citizenship

Edited by

MARGARITA CERVANTES-RODRÍGUEZ,
RAMÓN GROSFOGUEL, AND ERIC MIELANTS

TEMPLE UNIVERSITY PRESS
Philadelphia

Temple University Press
1601 North Broad Street
Philadelphia PA 19122
www.temple.edu/tempress

☉ The paper used in this publication meets the requirements of the American National Standard for Information Sciences—Permanence of Paper for Printed Library Materials, ANSI Z39.48-1992

Library of Congress Cataloging-in-Publication Data

Caribbean migration to Western Europe and the United States : essays on incorporation, identity, and citizenship / edited by Margarita Cervantes-Rodríguez, Ramón Grosfoguel, and Eric Mielants.
    p.   cm.
Includes bibliographical references and index.
ISBN 978-1-59213-954-5 (hardcover : alk. paper)
    1. Caribbean Area—Emigration and immigration.   2. West Indians—
Migrations.   3. West Indians—Europe, Western—Social conditions.   4. West Indians—
United States—Social conditions.   5. Europe, Western—Emigration and immigration.
6. United States—Emigration and immigration.   I. Cervantes-Rodríguez, Margarita,
1957–   II. Grosfoguel, Ramón.   III. Mielants, Eric.

    JV7321.C376   2009
    304.8'40729—dc22   2008027195

2   4   6   8   9   7   5   3   1

Contents

Caribbean Migration
to Western Europe
and the United States

Introduction

Caribbean Migrations to Western Europe and the United States

RAMÓN GROSFOGUEL, MARGARITA CERVANTES-RODRÍGUEZ, AND ERIC MIELANTS

This edited volume is the result of the colloquium "Caribbean Migrations to Western Europe and the United States" held on June 20–21, 2002, at the Maison des Science de l'Homme in Paris. To the best of our knowledge, this was the first post-9/11 conference held on Caribbean migration. The post-9/11 period is marked by "Islamophobia"—overt discrimination against Muslim people—and the invisibility of ongoing racist discrimination against old colonial/racialized subjects of empire within the metropolitan centers (Grosfoguel and Mielants 2006a). "Islamophobia" and racism toward Arabs and Muslim people are not new. Orientalist discourses have existed for at least two hundred fifty years (Said 1978). The entanglement of Orientalist discourses with the stereotype of the "Arab terrorist" is not new, either. For the past thirty years, in Western media and public discourses, Arabs and Muslims who fight for national liberation have been construed as "terrorists" (Said 1981). What is novel is the entanglement of "Islamophobia" with a new discourse about "national security," by which the civil rights of immigrant and minority groups are further threatened by harsher law-enforcement measures. Some of these measures lead to detention without due process and deportation for criminal activities that previously did not receive such an extreme penalty. Meanwhile, the case for Western states' military aggression against non-European populations is made in the name of "a safer world."

Today, metropolitan public discourse and the media's focal points include the globalization of "Islamic terrorism," geopolitics in the Middle East, and

Muslims. To be sure, there are a number of fundamentalist groups shaping the agendas of transnational terrorist groups. What is perverse, however, is the use of this threat to further jeopardize—and in some cases, even nullify—civil rights, the mere recognition of which took years of political struggle in the West and to increase state terrorism across the world. As shown in this volume, Caribbean migrants in the United States and Western Europe have been vulnerable to policy changes in the realms of civil rights and welfare that tend to reinforce the social distance between citizens and non-citizens. This trend predates 9/11, but it is being reinforced and has acquired new dimensions in relation to the post-9/11 wave of turmoil in world politics, which has complex entanglements with the geopolitics of migration and natural resources.

The essays presented here on Caribbean migrations—their demographic, socioeconomic, political, and cultural impact on the United States and Western Europe, as well as their role in the development of transnational social fields—makes this volume timely and relevant. This volume also examines how contrasting discourses of democracy and racism, the openness of borders and xenophobia, and globalization and pro-nativism shape issues pertaining to incorporation, citizenship, and identity formation among immigrants who move between a geopolitically strategic, albeit subordinated, area of the world and core zones. These analytical axes make this volume timely and relevant for both Caribbean studies and comparative migration studies from a global perspective.

Caribbean migrants are among the groups with the longest presence in areas associated with colonization and the emergence of a corresponding global "colonial pattern of power" (Quijano 2000) that has relied on the concepts of culture and race as tools of domination over colonial subjects. The Caribbean was the first peripheral region to be colonized by Europe in the construction of what Ramón Grosfoguel (2004) elsewhere has called the "modern/colonial capitalist/patriarchal world-system" and the last peripheral region to formally eliminate colonial administrations."[1] Even today, there are many non-independent countries in the Caribbean: Dutch, French, American, and British Caribbean territories such as Aruba, Curaçao, Bonaire, Martinique, Guadeloupe, Turks and Caicos, the Cayman Islands, Puerto Rico, the British Virgin Islands, St. Maarten/Saint Martin, the U.S. Virgin Islands, for example, do not have an independent status vis-à-vis the United States or European powers. The analysis of issues pertaining to incorporation, citizenship, and identity formation among Caribbean migrants in Western Europe and the United States sheds light on global threads that have been operating since the origins of the formal colonial period and that continue to shape the incorporation of racialized subjects from subordinated, peripheral areas of the world system.

Caribbean migration is not a new subject in the field of international migration. However, this volume has unique scholarly features that merit attention. First, many edited volumes on Caribbean migration tend to cover the migratory circuits toward only one or two metropolitan centers. In this volume, we have included all of the contemporary circuits of Caribbean migration to the metropoles—that is, migration to France, Spain, the United States, the Netherlands, and the United Kingdom. To understand the different circuits of Caribbean migration and the migrants' modes of incorporation into the metropoles, it is important to understand this history and the particular relationship (colonial, neocolonial, independent, non-independent) between the country of origin and the metropolitan center. Second, this volume addresses the different metropolitan cultural, political, and economic processes that shape Caribbean migration and the incorporation process. A major rationale guiding this compilation is that it is impossible to understand the incorporation of immigrants and particular forms of social exclusion related to the multiple processes of incorporation, and particularly the location of Caribbean migrants in the metropolitan racial/ethnic and class hierarchies, without addressing the socio-historical contexts of the metropolitan political economy and cultural/national ideologies and transnational social fields related to them. A number of essays in this volume address the transnational linkages between country of origin and the metropoles in relation to metropolitan political, economic, and cultural processes. And third, this compilation calls attention to the complex material and symbolic dimensions of the migration experience and the processes of incorporation of Caribbean migrants in Western Europe and the United States. Based on case studies, it offers an assessment of how such dynamics currently unfold. A general pattern of power related to geopolitical relationships that in many cases can be traced to colonialism frames Caribbean migration to Western Europe and the United States, yet it does so in everyday life through specific dynamics pertaining to labor markets, state policies, approaches to citizenship, sources of meaning and identity formation, and specific family and household strategies that migrants employ either to cope with the shrinking avenues of social mobility or to resist forms of exclusion.

In what follows, we contextualize Caribbean migrations to the metropoles historically in light of current theoretical approaches while introducing the main contents of the anthology chapter by chapter.

Colonial Legacies and the Coloniality of Power Argument

The Caribbean massively imported people from different regions of the world for centuries. The relation between European colonizers and African and Asian populations started in the Caribbean sugar plantations and was marked by the demand for and supply of colonial labor. African slaves arrived in the Caribbean in the late sixteenth century after the enslavement and genocide of thousands of indigenous people (Tainos and Caribs), while Asian indentured labor started arriving in significant numbers in the late nineteenth century after the global demise of slavery and its imminent collapse in those areas of the Americas where it was still practiced. Immigrants from metropolitan areas also arrived in the Caribbean, more so after formal independence was achieved, while a circuit of intra-Caribbean migration evolved in the first half of the twentieth century as the big sugar enterprises and other capitalist corporations, the most profitable of which (such as Cuba and the Dominican Republic) were operating under the control of the United States, pulled cheap labor from the region. From the second half of the nineteenth century and throughout the first decades of the twentieth century, there was an expansion of transnational social fields (including transatlantic ones) involving migration to, within, and to some extent from the Caribbean. At that time, transnationalism was framed by the continuing use of the region as an epicenter of surplus value extraction in the world-economy through the multiplication of the global labor flows that involved the area, and the expansion of the transnational faction of the capitalist class directly linked to it. These developments went hand-in-hand with the continuing use of the Caribbean as the target of geopolitical designs, which shaped migration through two dynamics that were often interrelated; the development of large-scale accumulation schemas and the rise of violent conflicts, which often led to life-threatening scenarios (Baez Everetz 1986; Bovenkerk 1975; Cervantes-Rodríguez 2009; de la Riva 1979; Grosfoguel 2003; Portes and Walton 1981; Rich 1986).

Transnationalism related to Caribbean migration since the second half of the twentieth century, however, has been marked by the fact that the Caribbean has emerged as a region of "emigration." After World War II, tens of thousands of Caribbean workers migrated to metropolitan centers. The postwar economic boom produced a labor shortage at the bottom of the labor market in the core of the capitalist world economy. This labor shortage was supplied by the mass-recruitment of cheap labor that to a great extent came from the non-independent colonial territories of the Western empires. Thousands of workers from the British, Dutch, French, and American Caribbean territories were recruited to work in the United Kingdom, the Netherlands, France, and the United States. Global economic restructuring (which led to the rearticulation of the Caribbean to the world economy through several intermediate processes, such as the rise of export-processing zones and the feminization of the job market), combined with political turmoil generated within the Cold War context, would further reinforce the late-twentieth-century pattern of Caribbean migration to Western Europe and the United States. Although specific market trends, policies, and even legislation, such as the British government's Commonwealth

Immigration Act of 1961, have severely curbed immigration from specific Caribbean islands to Western Europe and the United States at certain junctures, the Caribbean has remained a labor-exporting and refugee-generating region while dense cultural, political and socioeconomic transnational fields have been formed in relation to migration.

Although Caribbean migration is inscribed within a global pattern and there are some particularities that pertain to the region, this volume also demonstrates that the migratory fields between the French Caribbean and France, the British Caribbean and Great Britain, the Dutch Caribbean and the Netherlands, and the U.S. Caribbean and the United States have some distinct features. It is important to distinguish Caribbean migrations from "non-independent" territories from Caribbean migrations from formally "independent" territories (Grosfoguel 2003). The metropoles' mass-recruitment of colonial labor from the Caribbean during the 1950s and 1960s has four common characteristics.[2]

First, it was an organized labor migration from non-independent territories. Each metropolitan center used the labor available in the Caribbean colonies to satisfy its labor demands during the postwar period. The United States underwent an economic boom because it was the sole industrial economy in the world without competition from other core countries, while the boom of the Western European economies was due to the process of reconstruction after World War II. Puerto Ricans were among the first colonial groups to be massively recruited to work in the manufacturing and agrarian enterprises of the U.S. Northeast. The formation of the Migration Division within the colonial administration on the island was the institutional mechanism used to massively recruit Puerto Rican labor to the United States, and it served as a model for the rest of the region. West Indians from the British colonies were also recruited to work in the United Kingdom as cheap labor in public services and manufacturing. The British Migration Office in Barbados was an imitation of the Puerto Rican Migration Division Office; similar to the Puerto Rican case, this office recruited labor directly from Barbados to the United Kingdom. In other British colonies, such as Jamaica and Trinidad, institutional mechanisms were in place to foster labor migration, such as job advertisement, social workers, and direct recruitment from the British public administration and private companies. Dutch Caribbean labor from Suriname and the Netherlands Antilles (Curaçao, Aruba, and others) was also recruited to work in the Netherlands. In Curaçao during the 1960s, social workers were instrumental in the recruitment of labor. Similar to the Puerto Rican case, the French state organized the BUMIDOM (Le Bureau pour le développement des migrations dans les départements d'outre-mer, or Bureau for the Development of Migration in the Overseas Departments) to recruit labor from Martinique, Guadeloupe, and French Guiana to work in the French public administration. The contribution by Monique Milia-Marie-Luce in this volume compares the organized migration from Puerto Rico to the United States with the organized migration from Martinique, Guadeloupe, and French Guiana to France. She examines the similarities and differences of the Migration Division Office in Puerto Rico and the BUMIDOM in France, and, based on archival work, shows how the Migration Division Office in Puerto Rico served as a showcase for the whole Caribbean region and, in particular, for the French Overseas Department after World War II. It was through the Caribbean Commission, an organization created by Western colonial powers in the Caribbean to coordinate their policies in the region during the early years of the Cold War, that the migration model used by the United States in Puerto Rico was exported to the rest of the region. Milia-Marie-Luce's work invites the production of more comparative historical research in Caribbean migration studies. In sum, one common feature of all of these migrations from non-independent territories is that several state institutional mechanisms were in place to recruit colonial labor or to foster colonial labor migration as a way to supply cheap workers to serve the needs of the metropolitan labor market.

Second, colonial labor migrants from the Caribbean were all legal citizens of the metropole. After World War II, colonial reforms in the Caribbean led by the Caribbean Commission (an international organization of Western powers in the Caribbean) extended metropolitan citizenship rights to the colonies. This facilitated the massive transfer of labor from the colonies to the metropole. No institutional barriers such as visa procedures or work permits were present to prevent massive labor migration from the Caribbean colonies. Moreover, the legal status of Caribbean colonial laborers as metropolitan citizens gave them access to welfare-state policies and social rights enjoyed by all metropolitan citizens. This supplemented their incomes and helped meet the cost of reproducing their labor force, given their low salaries compared with those of European and Euro-American workers.

Third, colonial migrations from non-independent territories have included a larger representation of the lower classes than that from formally independent territories (Grosfoguel 2003). Without metropolitan citizenship, members of the lower classes would face many obstacles to migrating. Most of the migrants from independent Caribbean countries, who do not have such citizenship rights, thus come from the most educated and the middle sectors of the working classes. There are important exceptions to this pattern: migrants from Haiti to southern Florida, from the Dominican Republic to New York via Puerto Rico, and from Cuba to Miami who overcome institutional barriers to migration by crossing the oceans on rafts or boats; particular types of workers sought by "host countries" to do jobs that the metropolitan populations are not willing to do, such as Dominican domestic workers in Spain (see the chapter by Laura Oso Casas in this volume); and immigrants who make use of family-reunification programs, such as recent Jamaican immigrants to the United States (Jones 2007). Such state institutional arrangements facilitate the direct recruitment of lower-class migrants from independent Caribbean countries.

Fourth, despite their legal status as metropolitan citizens, Caribbean colonial migrants experience racist discrimination, creating what is usually regarded as "second-class citizenship" inside the metropoles (Grosfoguel 1999). Consequently, the racial/colonial hierarchies that were put in place on a world scale during the European colonial expansion are now reproduced within the metropolitan global cities, which in turn leads to questions about continuities and discontinuities of colonial legacies in the present.

One of the central contemporary Eurocentric myths since World War II has been that, with the demise of colonial administrations in the periphery of the capitalist world economy, we are living in a "postcolonial," "post-imperial" world (Grosfoguel 1999). The question is not whether colonialism, understood as the presence of colonial administrations, ended: the answer to that question is obvious, and from that point of view we would be living in a so-called postcolonial world. The question is whether colonial relations of exploitation and domination between Europeans and Euro-Americans and non-European people finished with the end of colonial administrations. The answer to that question is more complex. The global hierarchies put in place during more than four hundred fifty years (1492–1945) of colonial administrations articulating the relationship between European and Euro-American metropoles and non-European peripheries did not disappear with the end of colonial administrations. Today, despite some anomalous cases, it is obvious that most of the non-European periphery is organized into "independent" states. However, the global hierarchies created during the four hundred fifty years of European colonial expansion, such as the international division of labor (core–periphery), the racial/ethnic hierarchy (European/Euro-American and non-Europeans), the gender hierarchy, the epistemic hierarchy, and the interstate system (military and political power) are still with us, even though colonial administrations have ended (Grosfoguel 2004). This is what the Peruvian sociologist Anibal Quijano refers to as "coloniality of power" (Quijano 2000). Power structures at the global and national levels are still informed by colonial ideologies and structures that go back in time several centuries.[3]

Coloniality of Power, Transnationalism, and Migrants' Incorporation

What is the relevance of "coloniality" to discussions of Caribbean migrants inside the metropoles? To understand the transnational processes of migrants' incorporation into metropolitan societies, it is important to make conceptual distinctions among diverse migration experiences. The application of the "coloniality of power" perspective to migration studies allows us to open new spaces of reflection and invites an alternative conceptualization on the subject. Migrants do not arrive in an empty or geopolitically neutral space. Migrants arrive in metropolitan spaces that are always "polluted" by colonial history—that is, a colonial imaginary, colonial knowledges, a racial/ethnic hierarchy linked to a history of dominance, and subordination in the interstate system that can be traced directly to empire building and colonial relations. Migrants arrive in a space of power relations that is always already informed and constituted by coloniality. There is no geopolitically neutral space of migrant incorporation.

The reconceptualization of migration studies in light of the coloniality of power argument invites critical assessment of the widely held perception, mainly in U.S. academia, that non-European immigrants will eventually follow the path of European immigrants in the incorporation process. Migration studies in the United States tend to take as a point of reference the mainstream European migration experience when trying to predict what the future holds for the incorporation path of non-European immigrants. Large-scale immigration of non-European groups has brought to the forefront debates on the issue of cultural assimilation and Anglo supremacy. Based on the European experience, mainstream research on incorporation is often rooted in the assimilation framework, which has systematically portrayed the United States as a society where language acquisition begins the process of assimilation. This perspective holds that assimilation occurs over generations along with the depreciation of ethnicity as a meaningful source of identification. What is perceived as the "largely symbolic" nature of ethnicity by the third generation points to a path of acculturation and acceptance into U.S. society.[4]

There have been some reactions to the oversimplification of the canonical assimilation argument. Scholars following the "segmented-assimilation" perspective (cf. Portes and Zhou 1993; Portes and Rumbaut 2001), for example, address the link between assimilation and social mobility and suggest that the assumption that full assimilation is a precondition of successful incorporation is problematic. Other sociological works (e.g., Massey 1995) bring to our attention important differences in the social contexts of immigrants' incorporation in the "post-1960 immigration regime" as compared with previous ones and conclude that, at least in the case of migration from Latin America, it is incommensurable with the European experiences in many aspects. Linguistic and geographical concentrations, the continuing nature of the migration process, and even involvement in transnational activities are cited as important points of rupture with the European models.

However, these critiques are biased by what has been called "methodological nationalism," or the propensity to conflate the concepts of society and nation-state (Wimmer and Glick Schiller 2003). Furthermore, the canonical assimilation argument has been associated with a reduction of the Durkheimian conceptualization of "socialization" to the issue of cultural assimilation. However, these arguments neglect the fact that cultural assimilation is seen as a process that comes "from within"—that is, a process in which the nation-state is the repository of social relations and conflicts. What is missing from the outlined critiques of the canonical assimilation argument is the role of transnational racial constructs in the process of incorporation and ultimately how the incorporation of the migrants is shaped by the re-enactment of racist and culturalist constructs that can be traced to colonial and neocolonial designs, including territorial and political annexation or domination, in which European powers and the United States have been directly involved. Lack of success, defined in terms of European assimilation on U.S. soil, is usually accounted for by a "cultural" problem inside the migrant community (Glazer and Moynihan 1963). By homogenizing the diverse incorporation experiences of migrant groups, the group that is dominant within the racial/ethnic hierarchy avoids confronting the legacy of racist discrimination that is rooted in colonial legacies. This is usually left unexplored in accounts that rely on the concept of assimilation.

The coloniality of power perspective to migration studies and the transnational approach share a critical positionality toward canonical statements of the mainstream assimilation perspective. By focusing on transnational activities from a methodological stance that challenges what has been called "methodological nationalism" (Wimmer and Glick Schiller 2003), current developments in the transnational approach shed light on the complex matrix of social relations that shapes issues pertaining to identity formation, labor-market incorporation, and political loyalties and participation. Specific research on migration and transnationalism that has focused on non-European groups (e.g., Basch et al. 1994; Glick Schiller and Fouron 1999; Ong 1999) has advanced our understanding of such process as mediated by racial constructs, capital-accumulation strategies, and the Eurocentric project of modernity. Although the literature on transnationalism does not address the issue of the "immigrant analogy" based on the early European migration to the United States, it fosters a more complex understanding of the experiences of incorporation as shaped by dynamics of race, class, and gender related to global hierarchies. The transnational perspective has challenged the static models of migration that focus on migration in terms of unidirectional mobility from "sending" to "host society" and incorporation as a process that encompasses the "host society" exclusively. It examines immigrants' multidirectional interaction between country of origin and country of arrival and the circulation of capital, money, material goods, ideologies, symbols, and political projects that the migration process conveys under conditions of capitalist expansion in an unequal and hierarchical international system. It also calls attention to families and households as key units in understanding such dynamics.

The coloniality of power argument allows us to distinguish between migrants based on their colonial experiences, or lack thereof. From this perspective, the main difference between Western European migrants (to the United States and other areas of the world) and Caribbean migrants does not rely primarily on the timing of their experience but on the fact that Caribbean populations had been colonized/racialized as inferior others and now migrate to their respective metropolitan and neo-metropolitan areas. Western Europeans historically have moved (and have been perceived as moving) from centers of wealth and influence in the global hierarchies and have been racialized as superior. Migrants from colonial and former colonial areas, however, are not just another group of immigrants; they are subjected to treatment as "colonial/racialized subjects of empire"—that is, subjects inside the empire as part of a long colonial history (Grosfoguel 2003). The metropolitan colonial imaginary, racial/ethnic hierarchy, and racist discourses are frequently constructed in relation to these subjects. A long history of racialization and inferiorization of "colonial/racial subjects of the empire" informs, constitutes, and determines present power relations. The coloniality of power of the metropolitan country is organized around and against these colonial subjects; they are frequently at the bottom of the racial/ethnic hierarchy. And migrants from peripheral locations who were never directly colonized by the metropolitan countries to which they have migrated are racialized in ways similar to the "colonial racial subjects of empire" that were there for a longer time (Grosfoguel 2003, 2004).

To avoid culturalist explanations about the failure or success of one particular migrant group, it is crucial to understand that conquest and colonization shape migration in important ways beyond creating the turmoil and unrest that they induce, which frequently lead to displacement, if not mass-migration. Culturalist explanations are part of transnational hegemonic ideologies that are very popular in the new forms of "antiracist racisms" in the core of the capitalist world economy and that, together with other ideological positions, such as the ideology of competitiveness, justify the supremacy of certain groups and states vis-à-vis the majority of the world's population. This is linked to what has been called "new racism" or "cultural racism" as we witness the reproduction of the old colonial/racial hierarchies of Europeans versus non-Europeans and the hegemony of racist ideologies inside each metropolitan center. To understand this process, we need to link the present racial/ethnic hierarchy to the colonial history of each empire. Otherwise, it makes no sense to question why Caribbean people remain at the bottom of the social structures and the targets of metropolitan racism. It is not an accident that in London, Amsterdam, Paris, and New York, colonial Caribbean minorities share the bottom of racial/ethnic hierarchy with other colonial/racialized subjects (Grosfoguel 1999). In London, West Indians, Pakistanis, and Bangladeshis are at the bottom of the racial/ethnic hierarchy. In Amsterdam, Dutch Antilleans and Surinamese share with Moroccans and Turks the experience of racist oppression. Eric Mielants's contribution to this volume discusses the colonial legacy of the Dutch empire in relation to Caribbean migrants in the Netherlands. After describing the history of the migration processes from Suriname and the Dutch Antilles, Mielants shows how both Surinamese and Dutch Antilleans have a long history of colonization/racialization with the Netherlands that is reproduced inside the metropole. He shows how the use of culturalist arguments contributes to justify the racialization of these communities and provides an insightful discussion of the racialization of these Dutch citizens in housing, the labor market, and public schools.

In Paris, French Caribbeans share with Algerians the discrimination produced by French colonial racism. Michel Giraud's crucial intervention shows the history and perverse effects of French colonial legacies in contemporary France. While acknowledging that French Republican ideology assumes an abstract notion of equality that serves to conceal racial discrimination in today's France, Giraud also submits the liberal forms of multiculturalism that end up reproducing extreme forms of "identity politics" to an in-depth critique while pointing out the links between French colonial history and contemporary French racist discourses. According to Giraud, racism toward migrants coming from a direct colonial history with the metropole, such as Martinicans, Guadeloupeans, and French Guianese migrants, cannot be de-linked from colonial history. As he states, "The difficulties in integration shared by French Caribbean immigrants and certain foreign nationals highlight the fact that ... the discrimination suffered by these 'immigrants' depends less on the dividing-line between nationals and non-nationals set forth by law, and more than on a social image of immigrants from the former colonies and their descendants that presents them as an alien element in society, one that threatens the 'integrity' of national identity."

By bridging the coloniality of power argument and the transnational approach to migration studies, we can produce a more nuanced understanding of the racial/ethnic inequalities inside various metropolitan centers. The transnational approach to migration studies allows us to understand the complex global networks of interaction produced by trans-migrants between the country of origin and its metropolitan centers. The coloniality of power argument allows us to understand how racism and colonial legacies affect social relations and networks related to the migration experience and, especially, the transnational networks between a peripheral country of origin and a core center, as well as those involving Europeans and Euro-Americans and non-Europeans inside metropolitan centers.

Moreover, the coloniality of power argument sheds light on how a global pattern of power that emerged during the colonization of indigenous groups in the Americas, and which that conveys the use of "culture" and "race" as powerful "concepts of control" and instruments of domination, currently shape not only migration patterns, but also migrants' everyday lives, including the reasons why and the ways in which they construct transnational social fields. Through the Caribbean experience, this volume shows how macro-interventions and processes such as militarism and economic restructuring that are historically rooted in a colonial relationship currently continue to shape forms of labor control, ethnic (usually employed as a code language hiding to hide forms of racism) and gender relations, among other and other social dynamics that are permeated by racial and cultural constructs. Such constructs have placed Caribbean groups in a disadvantaged position in the process of incorporation into the societies of U.S. and Western European societies and the United States.

Recent developments in the transnational perspective to migration studies (Basch et al. 1994; Glick Schiller 1999; Glick Schiller and Fouron 1999) have led to a better grasp of the transnational continuum that shapes the migration experience, for which the key concept of "simultaneous incorporation" (Wimmer and Glick Schiller 2003) has been critical. However, as Nina Glick Schiller points out in this volume, analyses of transnationalism can generate their own limitations: "transnational studies, while it takes us beyond methodological nationalism, can produce new silences. Transnational Studies may even obstruct the analysis of imperialism."

Pointing out how migrants tend to face and circumvent societal constraints by using transnational strategies, Laura Oso Casas's contribution calls attention to the important role of Dominican women who have emigrated to Spain as heads of transnational households and the constraints they face in both Spain and the Dominican Republic in achieving social mobility. Oso's chapter shows how different social agents and their respective (sometimes conflicting) interests shape Dominican women's strategies of incorporation in Spain, including transnational ones. The chapter by John R. Logan and Wenquan Zhang focuses on Cubans and Dominicans in their main settlement areas in Miami and New York. They examine Cubans and Dominicans against the backdrop of the Latino experience. The chapter reveals significant contrasts in these groups' socioeconomic characteristics and residential patterns, which reflect differences in their immigration contexts. However, the authors argue, there are also similarities that create a foundation for describing what is the "typical" Latino experience. Such similarities refer to the fact that Cubans and Dominicans, like most Latinos, are predominantly first-generation immigrants, and the two groups tend to live in neighborhoods where co-ethnics and Latinos are greatly over-represented. Further, they indicate that for the two cases their ethnic neighborhoods are disadvantaged, compared to other neighborhoods where group members live, and upward residential mobility generally requires moving to mainstream zones of the metropolis.

Critical Thinking, Critical Border Thinking, and Migration Studies

The discussion of the importance of the coloniality of power perspective to transnational migration studies is linked to epistemological questions. Migration studies tend to reproduce one of the most pervasive myths of Eurocentric social science: that of a neutral, universalist, objective point of view. There is no neutrality in knowledge production. We always speak from a location in the gender, racial, class, and sexual hierarchies of the European modern/colonial capitalist/patriarchal world system (Grosfoguel 2004; Lee and Wallerstein 2004). In the case of international migration, because of its relation to colonial legacies and the reproduction in the present of colonial situations between migrants and "host populations," we always speak from a location in the "colonial difference" produced by the coloniality of power. The "colonial difference" is a concept articulated in Latino postcolonial critique (Mignolo 2000) as a further elaboration of Quijano's coloniality of power. It refers to the coloniality of power at the epistemic level, to the loci of enunciation, to the epistemological relation between colonizer and colonized that creates tensions and conflicts in the process of knowledge production. The way knowledge is produced is a constitutive element of the "colonial difference." Migration studies speak from a non-neutral location in the colonial divide. They reproduce the perspectives of either the colonizer or the colonized or a complex fluid and antagonistic combination of the two. To be sure, migration studies have tended to reproduce the colonizers' point of view, a point of view that frequently justifies the domination, marginalization, or poverty of the migrant population in terms of a claim to a neutral, universalistic, and objective culturalist or economic reductionist argument. According to this literature, migrants have "difficulties" due to "objective" factors, such as their cultural background (attitudes, behavior, mentality, values) or economics (class origin, economic crisis, market constraints). Issues such as discrimination, xenophobia, and racism are rarely addressed in these studies (cf. Grosfoguel and Mielants 2006b).

This compilation has been produced from a multiplicity of approaches and locations that challenge canonical discourses on assimilation, immigrant incorporation, and identity formation while avoiding essentialist notions about the migrants' identity and their experiences. Although the voices of migrants are heard throughout most of the chapters in one way or another, those focused on sources of meaning, identity construction, cultural resistance, and emotional development make it a clear point that immigrants are not just passive recipients of imposed constraints and epistemologies. Mary Chamberlain's chapter on contemporary Caribbean migration to England traces the role of family strategies and cultural codes intended to provide support to the extended Caribbean family. Using the case-study technique, Chamberlain lets two Caribbean families speak about their own experiences while exploring their narratives and how they describe their transnational lives. She argues, "The similarities and repetitions in the accounts of family and migration conform to, and reinforce, 'cultural templates': patterns of response through which accounts may be stereotyped, and in which values and priorities are encoded, and transmitted." As such, she argues, these narratives constitute feedback to the transnational experience, a sort of discursive practice that "provide[s] important clues in understanding the nature and meaning of Caribbean transnational family life, and [is] increasingly powerful as [an] expression of, and foci for, a Caribbean cultural identity."

Elizabeth Aranda's chapter on Puerto Ricans in Florida examines how Puerto Ricans' identities shape their understanding and social constructions of "home" and explores what such constructions reveal about the impact of transnational patterns of living on migrants' emotional and cultural livelihoods. Aranda's contribution focuses on exploring the emotional implications of the transnational space that Puerto Ricans arriving in Florida from both the island and the Northeast have developed. She shows that Puerto Ricans coming from the island and those coming from New York ("Nuyoricans") to Florida find an ethnoscape where they can "nurture their ethnic identities without having to return to their country of origin." In a critical assessment of the influence of the increasing Latinization of Florida in Puerto Ricans' decision to settle there, she contends that, while such ethnic social constructions sometimes result in marginalization within the Puerto Rican community, they also lead to greater solidarity among islanders and Nuyoricans, as those who find themselves on the fringes of multiple groups often reach out to those who are marginalized. The proximity to both the island and New York, she argues, shapes a transnational identity that affects constructions of home as not bounded to a particular place, but to particular feelings. She explores how such feelings, embedded in a sense of rootedness, help in coping with exclusion and displacement associated with their migration experience and being Puerto Ricans in the United States.

Lisa Maya Knauer's contribution focuses on the social spaces of the racially marked practices of "traditional" Afro-Cuban music and religion—rumba and Santería—in the New York area and Havana. She explores how these cultural practices help shape a translocal counter-public—made up of "multi-directional flows of money, goods, practices, and people, and where varied social actors in both places craft identities through intra- and intercultural negotiation and contestation." Her main locus of observation is the weekly rumba performances in the New York City area. She demonstrates that, more than mere cultural expressions of a minority group, such performances point to "competing claims of authenticity and ownership and racialized, gendered, and class-based conflicts over public space and public culture." Livio Sansone's contribution calls attention to the emergence of Amsterdam as a major city of the Black Atlantic region and the centrality that mass-immigration of people of African descent from Suriname, the Dutch Antilles, and a variety of African countries, particularly Ghana, has had in this development. While previous research has emphasized the making of a Dutch black culture with an epicenter in Amsterdam, Sansone's chapter sheds light on the mutual influences of cultural trends and lifestyles of the "host society" and the societies of origin in remaking both the cultural landscapes of Amsterdam and those of the "Dutch black culture" through the shaping of "traditional [aspects] of Surinamese Creole community life in the Netherlands."

"Critical border thinking" is the epistemology that emerges in colonial situations where the hegemonic perspective is subverted from the cosmologies, languages, and epistemologies of the subaltern (Mignolo 2000). It is a form of epistemology that emerges in the "in-betweenness" of two languages, two cosmologies, two epistemologies, where the subversion of hegemonic knowledge is brought about by the geopolitics of knowledge of the subaltern. This anthology does not address the issue of critical border thinking and migration directly, but some essays refer to the centrality of the migration process in Caribbean border cultural expressions, language asymmetries, and border thinking as permeated by the colonial difference. The works compiled in this anthology show that the interplay of colonialism, coloniality, capitalism, and international migration has profoundly shaped the transnational spaces in which Caribbean migrants are embedded. It invites us to think of their links to the flow of commodities, ideologies, cultural expressions, and geopolitical projects in relation to colonization and the advancement of capitalism and how such projects continue to inform the migration experience and affect migrants' everyday lives, the mechanisms that sustain them, and the strategies employed to subvert them.

Notes

1. The notion of the "European modern/colonial capitalist/patriarchal world system" is a reinterpretation of the work of Gloria Anzaldúa, Walter Mignolo, Anibal Quijano, and Immanuel Wallerstein. For a detailed discussion, see Grosfoguel 2004.
2. For a comprehensive discussion, see Grosfoguel 2003.
3. For a comprehensive discussion, see Grosfoguel and Cervantes-Rodríguez 2002.
4. A detailed critical assessment can be found in Cervantes-Rodríguez and Lutz 2003.

References

Basch, Linda, Nina Glick Schiller, and Cristina Szanton Blanc. 1994. *Nations Unbound: Transnational Projects, Postcolonial Predicaments, and Deterritorialized Nation-States.* Langhorne, Penn.: Gordon and Breach.

Bovenkerk, Frank. 1975. *Emigratie uit Suriname.* Antropologisch-Sociologisch Centrum, University of Amsterdam.

Cervantes-Rodríguez, Ana Margarita, and Amy Lutz. 2003. "Coloniality of Power, Immigration and the English-Spanish Asymmetry in the United States." *Nepantla* 4, no. 3: 494–523.

Cervantes-Rodríguez, Margarita. 2009. *International Migration in Cuba: Accumulation, Imperial Designs and Transnational Social Fields.* University Park: Pennsylvania State University Press, forthcoming.

de la Riva, Juan Perez. 1979. "Cuba y la migracion antillana 1930–31." Annuario Estadistico, Havana, Cuba.

Everetz, Franz Baez. 1986. *Braceros Haitianos en la Republica Dominicana.* Santo Domingo: Instituto Dominicano de Investigaciones Sociales.

Glazer, Nathan, and Daniel Patrick Moynihan. 1963. *Beyond the Melting Pot: The Negroes, Puerto Ricans, Jews, Italians, and Irish of New York City.* Boston: MIT Press.

Glick Schiller, Nina. 1999. "Transmigrants and Nation-States: Something Old and Something New in the U.S. Immigrant Experience." Pp. 95–119 in *The Handbook of International Migration,* ed. Charles Hirschman, Philips Kasinitz, and Josh DeWind. New York: Russell Sage Foundation.

Glick Schiller, Nina, and Georges Fouron. 1999. "Transnational Lives and National Identities: The Identity Politics of Haitian Immigrants." Pp. 64–100 in *Transnationalism from Below,* ed. Luis E. Guarnizo and Michael P. Smith. Comparative Urban and Community Research, no. 6. New Brunswick, N.J.: Transaction Publishers.

Grosfoguel, Ramón. 1999. "Cultural Racism and Colonial Caribbean Migrants in the Core of the Capitalist World-Economy." *Review* 22, no. 4: 409–434.

Grosfoguel, Ramón. 2003. *Colonial Subjects: Puerto Rico in a Global Perspective.* Berkeley: University of California Press.

Grosfoguel, Ramón. 2004. "The Implications of Subaltern Epistemologies for Global Capitalism: Transmodernity, Border Thinking and Global Coloniality." Pp. 283–293 in *Critical Globalization Studies: Continued Debates, Neglected Topics, New Directions,* ed. William I. Robinson and Richard Appelbaum. New York: Routledge.

Grosfoguel, Ramón, and Ana Margarita Cervantes-Rodríguez, eds. 2002. *The Modern/Colonial/Capitalist World-System in the Twentieth Century: Global Processes, Antisystemic Movements, and the Geopolitics of Knowledge.* Westport, Conn.: Greenwood Press.

Grosfoguel, Ramón, and Eric Mielants. 2006a. "The Long-Durée Entanglement between Islamophobia and Racism in the Modern/Colonial Capitalist/Patriarchal World-System." *Human Architecture* 5, no. 1: 1–12.

Grosfoguel, Ramón, and Eric Mielants. 2006b. "Introduction: Minorities, Racism and Cultures of Scholarship." *International Journal of Comparative Sociology* 47, nos. 3–4: 179–189.

Jones, Terry. 2007. *Jamaican Immigrants in the United States and Canada.* New York: LFB Scholarly Publishing.

Lee, Richard, and Immanuel Wallerstein, eds. 2004. *Overcoming the Two Cultures: Science versus the Humanities in the Modern World-System.* Boulder, Colo.: Paradigm Press.

Massey, Douglas. 1995. "The New Immigration and Ethnicity in the United States." *Population and Development Review* 21: 631–652.

Mignolo, Walter. 2000. *Local Histories/Global Designs: Coloniality, Subaltern Knowledges and Border Thinking.* Princeton, N.J.: Princeton University Press.

Ong, Aihwa. 1999. *Flexible Citizenship: The Cultural Logics of Transnationality.* Durham, N.C.: Duke University Press.

Portes, Alejandro, and Rubén Rumbaut. 2001. *Legacies: The Story of the Immigrant Second Generation.* Berkeley: University of California Press.

Portes, Alejandro, and John Walton. 1981. *Labor, Class, and the International System.* New York: Academic Press.

Portes, Alejandro, and Min Zhou. 1993. "The New Second Generation: Segmented Assimilation and its Variants." *Annals* 503: 74–96.

Quijano, Anibal. 2000. "Coloniality of Power, Eurocentrism and Latin America." *Nepantla* 1, no. 3: 533–580.

Rich, Paul. 1986. *Race and Empire in British Politics.* Cambridge: Cambridge University Press.

Richardson, Bonham. 1983. *Caribbean Migrants.* Knoxville: University of Tennessee Press.

Said, Edward. 1978. *Orientalism.* New York: Vintage.

Said, Edward. 1981. *Covering Islam.* New York: Vintage.

Wimmer, Andreas, and Nina Glick Schiller. 2003. "Methodological Nationalism, the Social Sciences, and the Study of Migration: An Essay in Historical Epistemology." *International Migration Review* 37, no. 7: 576–610.

1

Theorizing about and beyond Transnational Processes

Nina Glick Schiller

In this chapter, I provide an overview of the developing field of transnational studies and the place of migration studies within it. I begin by examining the barriers that initially blocked the emergence of transnational studies. Briefly noting the emergence of four subfields, I suggest several distinctions that move us beyond some of the conceptual confusion that marked the euphoria of the emergence of a new paradigm and allow for the theory building that is now necessary. The new paradigm can facilitate the analysis of structures of power that legitimate social inequalities. At the same time, transnational studies can generate its own forms of obfuscation. Concluding on this note, I caution that transnational studies, while it takes us beyond methodological nationalism, can produce new silences. Transnational studies may even obstruct the analysis of imperialism.

Throughout, I speak from my perspective as a scholar of the Caribbean and highlight the seminal role of Caribbean scholarship in documenting and theorizing transnational processes. Globe-spanning connections, cultural syncretism, and cultural flows have been the substance of Caribbean history and society for more than five hundred years, and transnational processes that exist everywhere but have been obscured by national historiography have long been visible in the Caribbean.

Factors Obstructing Transnational Studies

If we look back, we can see that there have been several conceptual roadblocks on the path toward transnational studies. Among the factors that impeded the development of a transnational perspective were (1) a bounded and a-historical concept of culture and society; (2) methodological nationalism; and (3) migration studies that were mired in assimilationist or multicultural paradigms. Please note that in discussing the history of social science thinking about transnational processes, I use a set of terms that includes "nationalism," "ethnicity," and "identity" as they are commonly used in the migration literature in English. Different national traditions of scholarship have deployed these terms in different way, so that the terms cannot be readily translated and assumed to have the same meanings. These different national traditions, each with their own historical trajectories, also impede the development of a transnational paradigm and deserve in-depth discussion. My purpose here is not to impose Anglo-American understandings but to begin the work of a dialogue about transnational processes that includes migration.

Unbounding Concepts of Culture and Society

Despite talk of the current fluidity of borders and boundaries, and although capital, goods produced by multinational corporations, arms and armies, and media messages flow more freely than in the recent past, we are all today enmeshed in an increasingly impermeable regime of passports that stands as a barrier to migration. In the midst of these contradictions, in which borders seem almost by definition to be linked to the power of the state to limit migration, we often forget that the sanctity of borders and boundaries is rather new in both human history and social science theory. In the previous period of globalization, which we can place in general terms between 1880 and 1914, migrants entered a new state with few impediments. There was a general understanding that tying people to the land was a remnant of feudal society that was rendered archaic with the growth of industrial capitalism and new modes of transportation such as railroads and steamships (Torpey 2000).[1] In general, this was a period when not even passports and entry documents were required.[2] After France took the lead in eliminating such barriers to the free movement of labor in 1861, most European countries abolished the passport and visa system, which they had installed previously in efforts to retain rather than exclude labor. By 1914, all such documents had been virtually eliminated in Europe (Torpey 2000). Labor migration spanned the globe, with little or no restrictions in most states. Poles and Italians migrated to northern France;

Switzerland welcomed diverse populations; England saw influxes from the continent; and German industrial development fuelled migrations from the east and south. Brazil welcomed migrants from Europe, the Middle East, and Japan. Indians and Chinese laborers went to the Caribbean and to southern and eastern Africa. Mexicans, Turks, Syrians, and populations from Southern Europe and Eastern Europe migrated to the United States (Wyman 1993).[3] Workers migrated into regions in which there was industrial development and returned home or went elsewhere when times were bad. Switzerland, France, England, Germany, the United States, Brazil, and Argentina built industrialized economies with the help of billions of labor migrants who worked in factories, fields, mills, and mines. West Indians, primarily Barbadian, who migrated to Panama to build the canal, and Haitians and other Caribbean laborers who left for the industrialized sugar plantations of Cuba were part of this vast dispersal of people. A considerable number of these migrants retained home ties; some even became circular migrants as they moved to perform activities seasonally. It was during this period that Randolph Bourne (1916) spoke of a "Transnational America."

In this context of globalization and the movement of capital, technology, and ideas, as well as people, scholars developed concepts of culture and society that were not confined to the borders of nation-states. Brought to greatest prominence by various theories of cultural diffusion, this unbounded approach to the study of social processes maintained some influence until World War II. Diffusionists understood that migration has been the norm through human history, including the history of the modern state, and that ideas as well as objects could travel long distances and not be associated with a specific territory. Today, the British diffusionist school of anthropology, which read the entire history of cultures as one of migration, is often rightly used as an illustration of theory gone awry and as an example of the manner in which European scholars tried every possible means to dismiss indigenous creativity around the world. But diffusionists were aware that cultural flows and social relationships are not limited by political boundaries; there are longstanding connections between disparate regions and localities. Transnational studies have now begun to recover and reinterpret the strengths of diffusionist perspectives.

To do so, it has been important to set aside the organic, territorially embedded view of culture popularized by British functionalist and structural-functionalist anthropology. This scholarship failed to examine social and economic relationships that shaped the history and political economy of a particular locality. It overlooked the influence of colonialism and capitalism on the subject peoples. Beginning in the 1940s, U.S. anthropologists adopted a similar mindset by studying "communities," as if they were discrete units subject only to local historical developments and divorced from larger social, political, and economic processes. The popularization of Clifford Geertz's influential work on culture as localized text continued this bounded approach to culture in anthropology long after the demise of community studies and forms of functionalism.

Even when social science began to examine transnational processes, the legacy of this bounded theory that approached culture as a discrete, stable, and historically specific local system of meanings continued to impede historical analysis. Those scholars, including the founders of cultural studies, who worked within the Geertzian tradition of cultures as discrete webs of signification spoke as if transnational processes were novel and transgressive, occurring in response to dramatic changes in communication technology and global capitalism. They framed the outcome of transnational processes as hybridity, which implicitly defined a previous stage of cultural production unblemished by diffusion. In the new "post-national moment," the borders and structures of nation-states, they predicted, would become increasingly meaningless.

Anthropologists who developed a transnational paradigm for the study of migration began with a very different approach to culture. Many of us deployed a broader and older Tylerian concept of culture that encompasses social relations, social structure, and trans-generationally transmitted patterns of action, belief, and language. We also used a body of theory, methodology, and data that did not privilege place-bound or territorially based identities. Especially important were the ethnographies of Southern Africa and the Copperbelt and the methodological approaches to complex societies and colonial relationships developed by Max Gluckman (1967), A. L. Epstein, J. Clyde Mitchell, and others whose work came to be known as the "Manchester School."

The Manchester School researchers gave us a conceptual and methodological toolkit appropriate for the study of transnational processes. Because their research on urban life included the ongoing home ties of urban labor migrants, their observations of social relations extended across time and space. Manchester School anthropologists approached the study of networks and social situations as a study of dynamic processes. In fact, these scholars were taking important steps in documenting the effects of globalization, although they described it as an industrial urban social system or in terms of colonialism.

Other anthropological studies of migration, dating from the 1950s to the 1980s, while less engaged in relations of power, also pointed to the significance of the rural–urban connections of urban migrants and provided an intellectual and ethnographic foundation for transnational studies. However, the significance of this work was lost during the heyday of area studies that fixed culture to territory. The Caribbean was treated as an anomaly. Its scholarship was ignored in theory building in anthropology and other disciplines. Yet the Caribbean experience provided an important conceptual base that allowed both scholars and political actors to think beyond a concept of bounded culture, because from the moment of conquest, Caribbean culture was openly hybrid, and its trans-border connections were apparent. Repeatedly, Caribbean researchers described migrations that connected people across borders and sought to conceptualize culture flows. At various times, Caribbean ethnographies and discussions of Caribbean life spoke of transculturation, creolization, circular migration, remittance societies, and return migration (Ortiz 1995 [1940]; Rubenstein 1983; Thomas-Hope 1985; Wood and McCoy 1985). Long-term patterns of migration that stretched across generation, investments in landholdings and businesses from abroad, and continuing home ties were widely reported. In 1971, Father Joseph Fitzpatrick noted that it was best to see Puerto Ricans as "commuters" rather than immigrants because of their circulation between Puerto Rico and the United States. Building on this history, Constance Sutton and Susan Makiesky-Barrow (1992 [1975]: 114) spoke of a "transnational sociocultural and political system." During the 1980s, studies of immigrants in the Caribbean routinely noted transnational connections (Georges 1982; Gonzales; 1988; Pessar 1985; Wiltshire et al. 1990). Nancy Gonzales (1988: 10) raised the question of how the "individual segments of a transnational ethnic group can sustain a sense of unity" and spoke of the "Garifuna" forming "part societies within several countries" Yet this work was not brought to the level of theory to challenge the dominant understanding of culture and society. Even those scholars who drew on world systems in discussion migration in the Caribbean and Latin America, and who stressed the importance of migrant networks (such as Portes and Bach 1985) were constrained in their thinking by the limitations of dominant social theory with its bounded concepts of culture and society.

Methodological Barriers to Envisioning Transnational Processes

Methodological nationalism has been a potent barrier to the study of transnational processes. Methodological nationalism is an intellectual orientation that assumes national borders to be the natural unit of study, equates society with the nation-state, and conflates national interests with the purposes of social science (Wimmer and Glick Schiller 2002). If we shed the assumptions of methodological nationalism, it is clear that nation-state building was from the beginning a trans-border process. While nation-states are always constructed within a range of activities that strive to control and regulate territory, discipline subjects, and socialize citizens, these processes and activities do not necessarily occur within a single national territory. However, if you accept the prevailing paradigm that divides a state's affairs into internal, national matters and international affairs that have to do with state-to-state relations, the history of trans-border and transnational nation-state building becomes invisible. The writing of national histories compounds this invisibility by confining the national narrative within the territorial boundaries of the state. This restricted view of national history became increasingly marked after World War I and continued until the end of the Cold War.

Within this growth of scholarship colored by methodological nationalism, there was no conceptual space to examine the way in which the forging of each nation-state was not confined to its territorial borders but took place in a complex dialectic between a state and its colonies or between the population within a national territory and its political exiles and transmigrants living abroad. Only recently has the scholarship on colonialism begun to illustrate the way in which the nation-state building of France, England, and even the United States (as it took on colonies and began to police the Caribbean) was shaped by distinctions drawn between colonizer and colonized or between immigrants and natives (Gilroy 1991; Glick Schiller 1999a, 1999b; Lebovics 1992; Rafael 1995; Stoler 1989). These distinctions served to homogenize and valorize the national culture of the colonizing country and popularize the notion that it was a unitary and bounded society, distinguishable from the subordinated peoples by the racial divide.

Again, Caribbean historians and scholars of Caribbean descent were often pioneers, insisting that economies of imperialism were central to understanding the history of regions and the wealth of specific nation-states. They traced the relationship between colonized regions and the development of Europe (Mintz 1985; Williams 1994 [1944]). Caribbean scholars have understood that colonial "structures implanted in these societies served the economic requirements of the metropolitan systems which controlled Caribbean territories. Their economies were designed neither for self-sufficient nor independent growth" (Wiltshire 1984; Mintz 1985: 1, quoted in Basch et al. 1994: 57). From the perspective of the Caribbean, it was possible to develop the concept of part societies that could be understood only in relationship to distant locations. In the United States, where nation-state building is older and the state is much more powerful, methodological nationalism had imposed greater constraints on historical analysis. Frank Thistlewaite (1964) combated this tendency by calling for a revisionist historiography that documented transatlantic connections that included migrant linkages, but this perspective gained a foothold only slowly.[4]

While global histories developed, including Immanuel Wallerstein's world-systems perspective and Eric Wolf's historically informed anthropology, most historical writing about states until the 1990s approached them as discrete entities. This continues to be the dominant perspective in the newly revived historiography, art history, and archaeology of many Eastern and Southern European academics (Karakasidou 1994). When anthropologists worked in industrialized Western countries, methodological nationalism again shaped what they saw. The anthropology of "immigrant communities" within modernizing or industrial nation-states tended to describe ethnic groups as culturally different from the "majority" population because of their varying historical origin, including their history of migration. Rarely were these differences understood to be a consequence of the politicization of ethnicity in the context of nation-state building. Yet it was a central part of the nation-state project to define all those populations not thought to represent the "national culture" as racially and culturally different, producing an alterity that contributed to efforts to build unity and identity (Glick Schiller 1999a, 1999b; Hall 1977; Williams 1989; Wimmer 2002).

In the 1970s and early 1980s, large corporations and financial institutions, aided and abetted by national and local governments, began a massive restructuring of capitalism around the globe. During the same period, social scientists noted aspects of this transformation, studying the global assembly line, rural–urban migration, the international division of and feminization of labor, and the continuing and deepening dependence of peripheral states (Nash and Fernandez-Kelly 1983). However, neither anthropologists nor other social scientists developed a term or a theory to address the totality of the changes that link economic restructuring to global cultural processes. Even when they looked globally, researchers identified nationally and could not develop paradigms that took them beyond the interests of their own state because of methodological nationalism.

Migration Studies and Immigrant Identities: Assimilation, Multiculturalism, and the Return to Assimilation

The history of migration studies serves as an example of the effects of methodological nationalism on research paradigms. Scholars in both the United States and Europe looked at migration processes only through the political agendas of their own states and their particular migration policies. Although migration studies had an early effervescence in the social sciences, until the 1960s immigrants were expected to assimilate by abandoning their own cultures and identities and merging into or helping to forge the mainstream culture. This process was thought to take several generations. Ethnic communities might be formed along the way, but assimilation was the ultimate outcome and political goal.

Looking back at earlier scholarship, especially studies produced before World War II, it is interesting to note that many scholars actually documented the transnational ties of European and Asian immigrants—their patterns of sending home remittances, continuing family ties, and political engagement with homeland politics. Writing in 1949, R. A. Schermerhorn used the term "home country nationalism" for the transnational political activities of immigrants. As late as 1954, Nathan Glazer noted that many immigrants maintained their home ties, observing that

> In America, great numbers of German immigrants came only with the intention of fostering the development of the German nation-state in Europe . . . the Irish, the second most important element in the earlier immigration, were also a nation before they were a state and, like the Germans, many came here with the intention of assisting the creation of an Irish state in Europe. On one occasion they did not hesitate to organize armies in America to attack Canada. (Glazer 1954: 161)

Many of these earlier researchers also understood that many immigrants left home with only very local or regional identities and dialects and actually learned to identify with their ancestral land only after they had settled in the United States. However, the home-country nationalism and transnational ties of immigrants were portrayed as short-lived because migration theory took assimilation to be an inevitable process. In the postwar years in the United States, even an acknowledgment of the home ties of migrants tended to disappear with the popularization of Oscar Handlin's highly influential *The Uprooted* (1973 [1954]) and his concept of immigrants as "uprooted"—that is, without transnational ties. Forgotten was that even in his book, Handlin had a chapter on return migration. Also unremarked was that fact that, while he spoke of uprooting and his methodological nationalism led him to center his attention on the U.S. social fabric, Handlin was not an assimilationist. He documented the discrimination faced by immigrants such as the Irish and noted that they responded by maintaining Irish institutions and an Irish identity.

Cultural and ethnic persistence among immigrants became a subject of scholarship only with the development of "cultural pluralist" theory in the United States in the 1960s.[5] However, it was not until the multiculturalist turn that scholars in Canada, Australia, England, and the United States generally acknowledged and celebrated the fact that generations after a migration, cultural differences and distinct identities remained among some sectors of the immigrant population. This acknowledgment did not lead to a theory of transnational connection in migration studies. Instead, methodological nationalism prevailed, and cultural diversity became an alternative narrative for celebrating national identity. Most recently, some U.S. sociologists have resurrected the term "assimilation," critiquing multicultural theory and transnational migration studies with evidence that most immigrants become well incorporated into U.S. daily life (Alba and Nee 1997, 2003; Barkin 1995; Morawska 2003).[6]

Transnational Studies Appears on the Scene

It is now clear that the development of transnational studies reflected both objective changes in the global structuring of capitalism and the subjective development of new ways to think about the world. To discuss transnational studies coherently, we must distinguish between the terms "global" and "transnational" (Glick Schiller 2004).[7] Transnational processes take place across the borders of nation-states. States shape but do not contain these ongoing cross-border interconnections or flow of people, ideas, objects, and capital. As a field, transnational studies examines the exercise of political power by governments. It notes the presence of specific national forms of "governmentality" that make up people's daily lives as they live within transnational social fields, and it examines the nation-state building that occurs within transnational cultural processes.

The term "global" carries us into a different level of analysis, one deployed by theorists such as those concerned with world systems or worldwide environmental processes. Here the concern is with phenomena that affect the planet. Capitalism, for example, is now a global system of economic relations that has extended across the entire planet and has become the context and medium of human relationships, although with differential effects. Consequently, the term "globalization" allows us to refer to periods of intensified and unequal integration of the world through capitalist systems of production, exchange, distribution, and communication.

When it first emerged as a field of study in about 1990, globalization studies was primarily the domain of geographers and focused on the rescaling and governance of territorial units within global flows of capital, labor, and symbolic representations. Soon researchers broadened the discussion and made it more historically grounded, looking at various periods in world history when transformations in capitalism led to various forms of economic and cultural integration. A focus on globalization may frame various forms of transnational studies, but these fields of research ask different questions and address a different set of problems. The link between the two was the publication in 1989 of David Harvey's *The Conditions of Postmodernity: An Enquiry into the Conditions of Cultural Change*. The excitement with which Harvey's book was received was an indicator of a fundamental change in thinking that allowed transnational processes once again to become visible. Harvey, a geographer by training, stepped beyond disciplinary boundaries to link changing structures of capital accumulation, which he called flexible accumulation, with cultural transformations that included the development of new analytical paradigms such as postmodernism. As the interest in global connections and transnational processes flourished, scholarship went in several different directions that have emerged as distinct areas of transnational studies: culture, diaspora, and migration.

Transnational cultural studies usually does not distinguish between global and transnational cultural flows and studies both. However, recent scholarship makes it clear that the distinction is worth making, because certain cultural products must be seen as global while the movements of other goods are shaped by state processes (Caglar 2002). Films and television shows originating in India and Latin America, as well as in the United States, are disseminated globally. People in Africa, Japan, and Brazil may watch the same *telenovela* and identify with its heroes and heroines. However, certain media are transnational, organized within specific transnational social fields and oriented to publics within them. For example, English-language Caribbean newspapers and websites originating in the United States contain messages aimed at constituencies located in a transnational social field that extends between the islands and the New York metropolitan area. On its website the, *New York Liberty Star* (2004) claims that it "serves as a medium through which New Yorkers can stay abreast with the latest news and information that affects their community, the Caribbean and the rest of the world. . . . [T]he company's primary goal is to create a voice for those communities underserved by large scale media." In contrast to transnational cultural studies, diaspora studies scholars are concerned with global articulations of identity that were not geographically confined. While many people place migration within diaspora studies, keeping migration studies as a separate field makes some sense. There is a certain sense of displacement that can exist in the realm of the imagination or identity politics but is not specifically linked to either nation-state-building processes or social relations that connect individuals to state-based or territorially based institutions. People may identify with the black diaspora, and this identification may have an important bearing on their emotions as well as their political orientation. They may at the same time be part of a transnational politics that links them to a specific homeland or to a region such as the Caribbean.

In the 1990s, researchers began to conceptualize migration as a transnational process, initiating transnational migration studies. Finally, migrants' transnational familial, religious, political, and economic networks were examined without their analysis being confined by the borders of a single nation-state. It is in the domain of transnational migration studies that the heritage of

Caribbean scholarship has perhaps had its greatest influence, although certainly Stuart Hall and Paul Gilroy, among others, have brought the Caribbean lens into discussions of diasporic identities and longings.[8] Rosina Wiltshire, Winston Wiltshire, and Joyce Toney, scholars from the eastern Caribbean, working with Linda Basch, a U.S. anthropologist who had studied oil workers in Trinidad, began to speak about transnational migration in the 1980s (Basch et al. 1994; Wiltshire et al. 1990). Beginning in 1987, Basch, Cristina Szanton Blanc, and I, working together in New York, began to theorize what we called "transnationalism" and proposed that the processes of living across borders was a significant aspect of migration globally. This effort was part of a growing scholarship that sought to analyze transnational processes and globalization. I use the word "theorize" to describe our activities, although it is not formally a verb in English, to distinguish between the act of ethnographic description of people who migrate and maintain home ties and the activity of conceptualizing transnational migration as social relations that differed from the migration experience posited by the existing literature.

The new migration scholarship acknowledged not only the multiplicity of cross-border ties maintained by migrants but also sought to understand the implication of these transnational connections for all of the localities and states to which the migrants were connected. At first, many researchers in all areas of transnational studies preached a form of technological determinism. They tended to see communications technology—computers, telephones, televisions, communication satellites, and other electronic innovations—as the motor of change. Suddenly we could all visually experience the same war, the same concert, or the same commercial and share the information age. The power of the new technology, combined with the insistence of postmodern theorists that the past was stable and the present fluid, led to an emphasis on the novelty of transnational processes. This reinforced the previous hegemonic anthropological paradigm so that scholars spoke as if previously people actually lived within fixed, bounded units of tribe, ethnic group, and state. A mantra developed: the past contained homogenous cultures, while now we lived in a world of hybridity and complexity. However, more recent scholarship in all fields of transnational studies is more historically informed and nuanced and less prone to techo-determinism. Researchers also have turned their attention to reexamining state processes, noting that the current phase of globalization has been marked by the "hyper-presence" and "hyper-absence" of the state (Suárez-Orozco and Thomas 2001). States maintain the role of identity containers, formulating categories of national identity by differentiating foreigners from those who can claim the right to belong. These identity processes become the lens through which globally disseminated media, music, and commodities are experienced and consumed.

Clarifying Our Basic Concepts

To further develop research and theory in transnational studies, several points need to be developed. On my list of priorities are (1) theorizing the difference between transnational social fields and cultural flows; (2) differentiating between transnational migrants and actors who live within transnational social fields; and (3) distinguishing between transnational *ways of being* and *ways of belonging*. The failure to distinguish between the study of transnational cultural flows and transnational migration has been particularly problematic, leading to several problems that impede the development of social theory.

Theorizing the Difference between Transnational Social Fields and Transnational Cultural Flows

In the first place, I want to stress why I think that it is important to distinguish between flows and fields—the differing emphasis of transnational cultural studies and migration studies. Transnational cultural flows may include but do not depend on direct people-to-people relationships and interaction. In reading a book, newspaper, or magazine; listening to a radio; watching a film or television; or surfing the Internet, one can obtain ideas, images, and information that cross borders. In contrast, a social field can be defined as an unbounded terrain of multiple interlocking egocentric networks. "Network" is best applied to chains of social relationships that are egocentric and are mapped as stretching out from a single individual. "Social field" is a more encompassing term than "network," taking us to a societal level of analysis. However, despite this level of analysis, social fields only exist when actual individuals have social relations with others. Approaching social fields as a network of networks allows us to map the indirect connections between disparate individuals who do not know each other or even know of each other yet are shaped by and shape each other. A transnational social field is composed of interlocking networks of interpersonal connections that stretch across borders (Glick Schiller 1999a; Glick Schiller and Fouron 1999).

Why emphasize this distinction? Because in the euphoria that accompanied the ability to finally think about and study transnational processes, scholars began to speak as if every time we surf the Web or watch a soap opera produced elsewhere, we enter into some new social space that engenders transformation. The world of the imagination and the experience of social relations are different forms of human experiences, although they may ultimately be interrelated. To have flights of fancy that bring us to Jamaica, or Haiti, or Cuba, whether my imagination is fueled by an old-fashioned book or electronic media, has different life consequences than to have ongoing commitments to people located across national borders. Imagination may lead to action, social relations may be formed through the web, and this kind of interaction between transnational imaginaries and social fields must be studied. However, we cannot study the relationship between two distinct processes if we conflate them. (Of course, blogging and internet social networking bring aspects of the imaginational social relations together. However, the tensions within these new forums derive from the difference between fantasy and daily life.)

The term "transnational social space" has emerged as a means of moving transnational studies toward the study of social relationships (Faist 2000a, 2000b). In some research, the space metaphor has morphed back into a study of transnational communities, maintaining a sense of bounded culture and society, although across political borders. Thomas Faist, however, focuses on social relations and institutions, defining these spaces as "characterized by a high density of interstitial ties on informal or formal, that is to say institutional levels" (Faist 2000b: 89). When used in this way, the terms "transnational social fields" and "transnational social space" refer to the same phenomenon, one only visible outside the conceptual frameworks provided by methodological nationalism. Striving to move beyond the nation-state framework and building in part on the Dominican experience of migration, Luis Guarnizo (1997) and Patricia Landoldt (2001) refer to a "transnational social formation." Whatever the term used, it is essential, as Peggy Levitt and I point out, to distinguish between "the existence of transnational social fields and the consciousness of being embedded in them" (Levitt and Glick Schiller 2004). For years, immigrants in the United States maintained transnational networks but, in keeping with the dominant assimilationist narrative, portrayed themselves as immigrants who were busy becoming American. Most Haitians I knew in New York in research I conducted in 1969–1970 and 1985–1986 stated that they had a choice: stay exiles who planned to eventually return to Haiti or "forget about Haiti" (Basch et al. 1994; Glick Schiller et al. 1987; see also Fouron 1984). Meanwhile, they were deeply involved in transnational family networks while becoming incorporated into life in the United States.

Differentiating between Transnational Migrants and Actors Who Live within Transnational Social Fields

Because transnational social fields have been studied by scholars who work with migrants, there has been a failure to differentiate between people who cross borders and other social actors who may be live within transnational relationships but who either have never themselves migrated or, having once migrated, never return to their birthplace. It is crucial to differentiate between transnational migrants and other people embedded in transnational social fields. Some of the people in a transnational field not only migrate but also continue to circulate across borders. However, to understand the significance of transnational processes, it is also important to note that transnational social fields include individuals who migrate and never then return home and others who have never themselves crossed borders but who are linked through social relations to people in distant and perhaps disparate locations (Glick Schiller 2003). We miss much of the significance of transnational connections if we confine our study to people who frequently cross borders, as some researchers have suggested.

Today, as in the past, the vast majority of the world's people never move from their home localities, and large numbers of those who have migrated cannot or do not return to the place from which they originated. Nonetheless, because they are embedded in transnational social fields, the daily context of their lives, the resources on which they depend, and their patterns of decision making are shaped by their relations with people who are geographically distant, embedded in other nation-states and governed through diverse concepts of citizenship.

Distinguishing between Transnational
Ways of Being and Ways of Belonging

As we develop transnational theory, it is also essential that we distinguish between *ways of belonging* and *ways of being. Ways of being* refers to the actual social relations and practices that individuals engage in rather than to the identities associated with their actions Ways of being include various quotidian acts through which people live their lives. Individuals can be embedded in a social field but not identify with any label or cultural politics associated with that field. They have the potential to identify with others with whom they interact on the basis of some common identifier because they live within the social field, but not all choose to do so. In contrast, *ways of belonging* refers to identity practices that signal or enact a conscious connection to a particular group. These actions are not individually imagined identities but ones marked by visible actions that signal belonging such as flying a flag or wearing a religious symbol. Ways of belonging combine action and an awareness of the kind of identity that action signifies.

When lives are lived across borders, people experience *transnational ways of being* (Glick Schiller 2003, 2004).[9] The term refers to the life ways of people who, whether or not they themselves migrate, are shaped by their transnational relationships and interactions. They raise children, sustain families, and act out family tensions and rivalries within transnational networks. They negotiate, build, and break social relationships with sexual partners, spouses, friends, business connections, and acquaintances who live elsewhere. They engage in trade, investment, and the transfer of goods and information across borders. Their actions are shaped by gossip, rumor, and cultural production that are generated within their cross-border social relations. Because many descendants of migrants are embedded in transnational social fields, they may live transnational ways of being, whether or not they identify with a homeland or diasporic identity and whether or not they speak the native language of their ancestors. The fact that these ways of being take place in transnational social fields tells us nothing about how these activities will be represented, understood, and translated into an identity politics—that is, into a transnational way of belonging.

When we study *transnational ways of belonging*, we enter the realm of cultural representation, ideology, and identity through which people reach out to distant lands or people through memory, nostalgia, and imagination. A person who displays the Dominican flag while living in the United States may or may not be participating in a transnational way of belonging. Transnational belonging, while not rooted in social networks, is more than an assertion of origins, optional ethnicity, multiculturalism, or "roots," which are all forms of identity that place a person as a member of a single nation-state. Transnational belonging links people through their imaginative actions to those located across national boundaries. It is possible for a person to indicate transnational belonging without living within a transnational social field. It is important to note that ways of being and ways of belonging denote processes rather than fixed categories. People who adopt certain forms of cultural representation may find themselves new participants in transnational social fields and from the belonging enter into a transnational way of being.

Take, for example, Roger Carlos, a U.S. politician who speaks no Spanish. His father came from Mexico but married a non-Hispanic Texan native and did not involve his family in either a transnational social field or a Mexican identity.[10] When Carlos settled in Manchester, New Hampshire, a small city in the United States, and was elected to local office, he suddenly became the first Hispanic to hold office there. His Spanish surname led him to be identified as a representative of the "Hispanic community," although he had never been to Mexico, or anywhere else in Latin America, and had not participated in any ethnic organizations or activities. When he accepted this identity and acted on it, he accepted a particular way of belonging. It was not yet, however, transnational or linked to a way of being. Carlos began by identifying himself in terms of a U.S.-based ethnicity: Hispanic. However, as he began to explain his Mexican roots, on some level he began to define himself as someone connected to Mexico, although he had never been there. This was a transnational way of belonging. This identity claim facilitated Carlos's relationship with representatives of the Mexican government. In this way, he became a link between the

Mexican government and the Mexican migrant population in New Hampshire. As a result, Carlos began a transnational way of being as a participant in a transnational social field.

However, people who live in transnational social fields may at various times adopt different forms of cultural representation. Transnational belonging is an emotional connection to people who are elsewhere: a specific locality such as a village, a region, a specific religious formation, or a social movement. They may be geographically dispersed but are bound together within a notion of shared history and destiny. It is these myriad types of transnational belonging that some scholars wish to term "transnational communities," but more specific terms of reference seem warranted.

Building on work by Anderson (1994), I have adopted the term *long-distance nationalism* for a set of identity claims and practices that link together people who claim descent from an ancestral land (Glick Schiller 1999; Glick Schiller and Fouron 2002). These people see themselves as acting together to constitute, strengthen, overthrow, or liberate a homeland. Long-distance nationalism brings together transnational social fields and identity claims. It unites people settled in various locations abroad and those in the homeland in political processes organized within a transnational social field. It is on this basis that Dominican political parties have offices in New York and candidates for office in the Dominican Republic or in New York campaign in both locations (Grahm 2001). The first New York City councilman of Dominican birth, Guillermo Linares, was elected in a campaign conducted in both New York and the Dominican Republic, with funds coming from both locations. In 1996, the Dominican Republic elected President Leonel Fernández, who had spent significant periods of his life in both countries. Growing up in New York City in a Dominican neighborhood, he had obtained a law degree in the Dominican Republic but then returned to the United States to attend graduate school at Columbia University. As in the case of candidates running for office from throughout the Caribbean, Fernández campaigned in both New York and the Dominican Republic.

However, long-distance nationalism is not the only way in which transnational ways of being and belonging are being brought together. The growth of a Caribbean identity and the growth of organizations in the United States interested in lobbying for the development of the Caribbean region reflect the development of transnational social fields and identity claims that extend beyond nation-state identities. In 1985, I attended a meeting of political activists that included newspaper editors, a judge, academics, and longtime participants in New York City politics. All had Caribbean backgrounds. Several were better known as African Americans or Hispanics. The meeting was called to build a local-level Caribbean politics that would both serve as a constituency for local electoral politics and to ensure that U.S. development policies better served the Caribbean. Several of the actors had interests that stretched between the United States and the Caribbean and wanted to extend their influence within a transnational social field that provided a bigger terrain than their home island. The time was ripe for members of this group to assume leadership positions, the meeting convener stated, because Caribbeans were becoming one of the biggest ethnic groups in New York City. In response, one of the participants, a Panamanian, noted that most people of Caribbean descent in New York did not usually identify that way. Not to worry, the convener replied: "First you create the ethnic identity, and then you create the constituency. By speaking as Caribbean leaders, we will get Caribbean followers." Soon after that, the mayor of New York selected the head of a Haitian coalition of community organizations to be his adviser on Caribbean affairs. Mayors of New York are known to visit Caribbean islands as part of their efforts to strengthen their political base. A Caribbean identity and social field serves their interests also, generalizing their campaigns more widely than the constituency of any one island.

New Directions

Reevaluating Locality by Using the Concept of Social Fields

The concept of transnational social field also calls into question the neat divisions of connection into local, national, transnational, and global. In one sense, all are local in that near and distant connections penetrate the daily lives of individuals lived within a locale. But within this locale, a person may participate in personal networks or receive ideas and information that connect them to others in a nation-state, across the borders of a nation-state, or globally, without ever having migrated. By conceptualizing transnational social fields as crossing the boundaries of nation-states, we also note that individuals within these fields, through their everyday activities and relationships, are influenced by multiple sets of laws and institutions. Their daily rhythms and activities respond not only to more than one state simultaneously but also to social institutions, such as religious groups, that exist within many states and across their borders.

Reevaluating the Concept of Society by Using the Concept of Transnational Social Field

The concept of transnational social field challenges established notions of society, opening up new ways of understanding the structuring of social relationships. Once we put aside methodological nationalism and stop equating the boundaries of nation-states with the boundaries of normal social relationships, we need to rethink our notion of society itself. Working along similar lines, Ewa Morawska (1994) speaks of migration as "structuration," positing it as a continuing dynamic between structure and agency that extends into a transnational domain. Faist's (2001a, 2001b) use of the term "transnational social spaces" for cross-border social relations also reflects an orientation that moves us beyond an equation of society with the nation-state. But we need to go further (Levitt and Glick Schiller). If social relations exist as part of normal life across as well as within the borders of nation-states, we need to think of society as exactly this network of networks rather than as anything that has a single sense of consensus, unity, organicity, wholeness, the very starting points of all social theory since Comte.

The Concept of Simultaneity

The dominant paradigms of the past not only obscured the continuing transnational connections of immigrants but have also made it impossible to see that many migrants simultaneously become incorporated into a new land while preserving forms of transnational connection that connected them to daily life and decision making in other locations. I mean by simultaneity simply that people can live in more than one locality at the same time and be connected to the political processes of more than one state. There is no contradiction between an individual being part of one place where the person is physically located and at the same time being enmeshed in social relationships with others elsewhere. These transnational social relationships contribute to daily decision making together with other interactions that take place within national borders. People may migrate and settle into a locality so that they and their descendants become part of that new locality, its neighborhood life, its organizational activities, and its politics and economics. At the same time, their connections elsewhere may continue to shape their activities, structure their consumption, and organize their activities. My recent research on simultaneity challenges strongly held ideas about immigrant incorporation. It sets aside the argument, which has become common sense in Europe, that differing opportunity structures of particular countries are the primary factors that shape migrants' integration into the receiving nation-state. Instead I examine variations in locality and in transnational networks in order to explain different modes of local, national, and transnational incorporation that are engendered by transnational ways of being and belonging (Glick Schiller, Caglar, and Guldbrandsen 2006; Glick Schiller and Caglar 2009). Migrants tend to use their multiple transnational connectedness to become embedded in more than one state, despite public policies.

Thinking about and beyond
Transnational Processes

The exhilaration of new insights that comes from setting aside old paradigms continues to mark transnational studies. Having proclaimed its virtues, I must also warn of the weaknesses of the concept of simultaneity, weaknesses that illustrates the limits of the transnational paradigm itself. It is important to acknowledge that, as it develops, transnational studies is creating its own forms of conceptual blinders. Discussion of the balancing acts that migrants stage through simultaneous incorporation can deter us from examining the tremendous and growing imbalance between concentrations of wealth and poverty that make migration strategies and transnational families a necessity. We also may not see the degree to which migrant strategies are being undercut by worldwide economic collapse.

If we become too entrenched in the way transnational studies frames its problem, we may not be able to make the necessary connections between the transnational processes we are documenting and more global forces. Restrained by our theory, our scholarship will be limited in its contributions. Transnational studies must not lose sight of the broader global picture in its concentration on the dynamics of specific transnational processes. Transnational processes are linked to more global phenomena but are not identical to them. For example, it is important to confront the current moment of capitalism and discuss the contemporary hierarchy of global military power through which the United States dominates political processes throughout the world. Our discourse about social fields that cross state borders must not neglect the vast variations among states. A continuing weakness of the concept of social field is that it flattens our discussion of social difference including the need to analyze social class within and across states.

Therefore, while building on the strengths of the new transnational paradigm, scholars cannot be confined to it. Rather, transnational and global studies need to come together within a new analysis of imperialism and its contradictions, including the transnational social fields and cultural flows that can constitute movements for social justice and the end of global disparities in opportunities, wealth, and power. The past insights produced by scholars of the Caribbean about the "partial" nature of Caribbean "societies" as a result of the colonial appropriation of wealth maintained by military force prove relevant in our analysis of contemporary U.S. imperial power.

Notes

1. Of course, Europeans settled without impediment in their colonial territories, including the Caribbean.

2. German states rapidly vacillated during this period between imposing and eliminating passports.

3. The United States, currently portrayed as the land of immigrants, unlike European states, was actually the first and, for a time, the only state to erect significant barriers when it passed the Chinese Exclusion Act in 1882 and it was renewed in 1892.

4. Bodnar (1985), Cinel (1982), and Wyman (1993) were able to break sufficiently with U.S. methodological nationalism to document return migration and transnational connections, but they did not develop a theoretical framework to encompass this scholarship.

5. Horace Kallen used the term in the 1920s. However, U.S. nation-state building until the 1960s and the growth of the third generation focused on the assimilation of immigrants. In immigrant studies the term "ethnic group" was rarely used, and this alternative view of immigrant settlement received little attention. Caribbean discussions of "plural societies" promoted by M. G. Smith (1965) were reflections about relations within colonial empires that brought together culturally disparate peoples.

6. But see a summary of a related trend in Europe (Brubaker 2001), as well as a parallel redefinition of the term "assimilation" (Faist 2003).

7. Here I build on an article by Daniel Mato (1996).

8. In 1998, Sydney Mintz, building on a lifetime of Caribbean studies, took the emerging discussion of transnationalism to task for disregarding the long history of transnational processes and the heritage of Caribbean scholarship. However Linda Basch, Karen Olwig, Patricia Pessar, Njina Sorensen, Georges Fouron, Joyce Toney, and I, along with many others, developed studies of transnational migration and cross-border connections that built from Caribbean history and scholarship.

9. Faist (2000b) contrasts "social ties" with symbolic ties. He encompasses in his sense of social ties a commitment to a common interest or norm. My term "ways of being" decouples social ties from any sense of shared values by those who share a way of being. I focus on common practices, behavior, and action.

10. The name Roger Carlos is a pseudonym, in keeping with our research protocol.

References

Alba, Richard, and Victor Nee. 1997. "Rethinking Assimilation Theory for a New Era of Immigration." *International Migration Review* 31, no. 4: 826–874.

Alba, Richard, and Victor Nee. 2003. *Remaking the American Mainstream: Assimilation and Contemporary Immigration.* Cambridge, Mass.: Harvard University Press.

Anderson, Benedict. 1994. "Exodus." *Critical Inquiry* 20: 314–327.

Barkin, Elliot. 1995. "Race, Religion and Nationality in American Society: A Model of Ethnicity—From Contact to Assimilation." *Journal of American Ethnic History* 14 (Winter): 38–101.

Basch, Linda, Nina Glick Schiller, and Cristina Szanton Blanc. 1994. *Nations Unbound: Transnational Projects, Postcolonial Predicaments, and Deterritorialized Nation-States.* Amsterdam: Gordon and Breach.

Bodnar, John E. 1985. *The Transplanted: A History of Immigrants in Urban America.* Bloomington: Indiana University Press.

Bourne, Randolph. 1916. "Trans-National America." *Atlantic Monthly,* vol. 118, no. 1, July, 86–97.

Brubaker, Rogers. 2001. "The Return of Assimilation? Changing Perspectives on Immigration and Its Sequels in France, Germany, and the United States." *Ethnic and Racial Studies* 24, no. 4: 531–548.

Caglar, Ayse. 2002. "Mediascapes, Advertisement Industries and Cosmopolitan Transforma-
tions: Turkish Immigrants in Europe." Available online at http://www2.rz.huberlin.de/
amerika/projects/newurbanism/nu_pt_ caglar_a.html2002.
Cinel, Dino. 1982. *From Italy to San Francisco.* Stanford, Calif.: Stanford University Press.
Epstein, A. L. 1958. *Politics in an Urban African Community.* Manchester: Manchester Uni-
versity Press.
Faist, Thomas. 2000a. *The Volume and Dynamics of International Migration.* New York:
Oxford University Press.
Faist, Thomas. 2000b. "Transnationalization in International Migration: Implications for
the Study of Citizenship and Culture." *Ethnic and Racial Studies* 23, no. 2: 189–222.
Faist, Thomas. 2003. "Amalgamating Newcomers, National Minority and Diaspora—
Integration(s) of Immigrants from Poland in Germany." Pp. 205–234 in *Identity and
Integration: Migrants in Western Europe,* ed. Rosemarie Sackmann, Bernhard Peters, and
Thomas Faist. Ashgate: Aldershot.
Fouron, Georges. 1984. "Patterns of Adaption of Haitian Immigrants of the 1970s in New
York City." Ph.D. diss., Teachers College, Columbia University, New York.
Georges, Eugenia. 1990. *The Making of Transnational Community: Migration, Development,
and Cultural Change in the Dominican Republic.* New York: Columbia University Press.
Gilroy, Paul. 1991. *"There Ain't No Black in the Union Jack": The Cultural Politics of Race and
Nation.* Chicago: University of Chicago Press.
Glazer, Nathan. 1954. "Ethnic Groups in America: From National Culture to Ideology." Pp.
158–174 in *Freedom and Control in Modern Society,* ed. T. Abel Morroe Berger and
C. Page. New York: Van Nostrand.
Glick Schiller, Nina. 1999a. "Transmigrants and Nation-States: Something Old and Some-
thing New in the U.S. Immigrant Experience." Pp. 94–119 in *The Handbook of Inter-
national Migration: The American Experience,* ed. Charles Hirshman, Philip Kasinitz,
and Josh DeWind. New York: Russell Sage.
Glick Schiller, Nina. 1999b. "Who Are These Guys? A Transnational Perspective on National
Identities." In *Identities on the Move: Transnational Processes in North America and the
Caribbean Basin,* ed. Liliana Goldin. Houston: University of Texas Press.
Glick Schiller, Nina. 2003. "The Centrality of Ethnography in the Study of Transnational
Migration: Seeing the Wetland Instead of the Swamp." In *American Arrivals,* ed. Nancy
Foner. Santa Fe, N.M.: School of American Research.
Glick Schiller, Nina. 2004. "Transnationality." In *A Companion to the Anthropology of Politics,*
ed. David Nugent and Joan Vincent. Malden, Mass.: Blackwell.
Glick Schiller, Nina, Linda Basch, and Cristina Blanc Szanton. 1992. *Towards a Transnational
Perspective on Migration: Race, Class, Ethnicity and Nationalism Reconsidered.* New York:
New York Academy of Science.
Glick Schiller, Nina, and Ayse Caglar. 2009. "Towards a Comparative Theory of Locality in
Migration Studies: Migrant Incorporation and City Scale." *Journal of Ethnic and Migra-
tion Studies* 35, no. 2 (February): forthcoming.
Glick Schiller, Nina, Ayse Caglar, and Thaddeus Guldbrandsen. 2006. "Beyond the Ethnic
Lens: Locality, Globality, and Born-Again Incorporation." *American Ethnologist* 33, no.
4 (November): 612–633.
Glick Schiller, Nina, Josh De Wind, Marie Lucie Brutus, Carrolle Charles, George Fouron,
and Louis Thomas. 1987. "Exile, Ethnic, Refugee: Changing Organizational Identities
Among Haitian Immigrants." *Migration Today* 15, no. 1: 7–11.

Glick Schiller, Nina, and Georges Fouron. 2002. *Georges Woke Up Laughing: Long Distance Nationalism and the Search for Home.* Durham, N.C.: Duke University Press.

Gluckman, Max. 1967. "Introduction." Pp. xi–xx in *The Craft of Social Anthropology,* ed. A. L. Epstein. London: Tavistock.

Gonzalez, Nancie L. 1988. *Sojourners of the Caribbean: Ethnogenesis and Ethnohistory of the Garifuna.* Urbana: University of Illinois Press.

Grahm, Pamela. 2001. "Political Incorporation and Re-incorporation: Simultaneity in the Dominican Migrant Experience." Pp. 87–108 in *Transnational Communities and the Political Economy of New York in the 1990s,* ed. Hector Cordero-Guzman, Robert Smith, and Robert Ramón Grosfoguel. Philadelphia: Temple University Press.

Guarnizo, Luis Eduardo. 1997. "The Emergence of a Transnational Social Formation and the Mirage of Return Migration among Dominican Transmigrants." *Identities* 4: 281–322.

Hall, Stewart. 1977. "Pluralism, Race, and Class in Caribbean Society." Pp. 150–180 in *Race and Class in Post-Colonial Caribbean Society: A Study of Ethnic Group Relations in the English Speaking Caribbean, Bolivia, Chile, and Morocco.* Paris: United Nations Educational, Scientific and Cultural Organization.

Handlin, Oscar. 1973 (1954). *The Uprooted.* Boston: Little, Brown.

Harvey, David. 1989. *The Conditions of Postmodernity: An Enquiry into the Conditions of Cultural Change.* Cambridge, Mass.: Blackwell.

Karakasidou, Anastasia. 1994. "Sacred Scholars, Profane Advocates: Intellectuals Molding National Consciousness in Greece." *Identities* 1, no. 1: 35–61.

Landoldt, Patricia. 2001. "Salvadoran Economic Transnationalism: Embedded Strategies for Household Maintenance, Immigration Incorporation, and Entrepreneurial Expansion." *Global Networks* 3: 217–241.

Lebovics, Herman. 1992. *True France: The Wars over Cultural Identity, 1900–1945.* Ithaca, N.Y.: Cornell University Press.

Levitt, Peggy, and Nina Glick Schiller. 2004. "Transnational Perspectives on Migration: Conceptualizing Simultaneity." *International Migration Review* 39, no. 3: 1002–1039.

Mato, Daniel. 1995. "On Global and Local Agents and the Making of Transnational Identities and Related Agendas in 'Latin' America." *Identities* 4, no. 1: 167–212.

Mintz, Sidney. 1985. *Sweetness and the Place of Sugar in Modern History.* New York: Viking.

Mitchell, J. Clyde. 1969 *Social Networks in Urban Situations.* Manchester: Manchester University Press.

Morawska, Ewa. 1994. "In Defense of the Assimilation Model." *Journal of American Ethnic History* 13, no. 2 (Winter): 76–87.

Morawska, Ewa. 2003. "Immigrant Transnationalism and Assimilation: A Variety of Combinations and a Theoretical Model They Suggest." In *Integrating Immigrants in Liberal Nation-States: Policies and Practices,* ed. Christian Joppke and Ewa Morawska. London: Palgrave Press.

Nash, June, and Maria Patricia Gernandez-Kelly. 1983. *Woman, Men and the International Division of Labor.* Albany: State University of New York Press.

Ortiz, Fernando. 1995 (1940). *Cuban Counterpoint, Tobacco and Sugar.* Durham, N.C.: Duke University Press.

Pessar, Patricia. 1988. *When Borders Don't Divide: Labor Migration and Refugee Movements in the Americas.* Staten Island, N.Y.: Center for Migration Studies.

Portes, Alejandro, and Robert Bach. 1985. *Latin Journey: Cuban and Mexican Immigrants in the United States.* Berkeley: University of California Press.

Rafael, Vincent L. 1995. *Discrepant Histories: Translocal Essays on Filipino Cultures.* Philadelphia: Temple University Press.

Rubenstein, Hymie. 1983. "Remittances and Rural Underdevelopment in the English Speaking Caribbean." *Human Organization* 42, no. 4: 306.

Schermerhorn, R. A. 1949. *These Our People: Minorities in American Culture.* Boston: D. C. Heath.

Stoler, Ann L. 1989. "Making Empire Respectable: The Politics of Race and Sexual Morality in 20th Century Colonial Cultures." *American Ethnologist,* no. 16: 634–660.

Suárez-Orozco, Marcelo, and V. Thomas. 2001. "Right Moves: Immigration, Globalization, Utopia, and Dystopia." Paper presented at the School of American Research Advanced Seminar, Santa Fe, N.M.

Sutton, Constance, and Susan Makiesky-Barrow. 1992 (1975). "Migration and West Indian Racial and Ethnic Consciousness." Pp. 86–107 in *Caribbean Life in New York City: Sociocultural Dimensions,* ed. Constance Sutton and Elsa M. Chaney. New York: Center for Migration.

Thistlewaite, Frank. 1964. "Migration from Europe Overseas in the Nineteenth and Twentieth Centuries." Pp. 73–92 in *Population Movements in Modern European History,* ed. Herbert Moller. New York: Macmillan.

Thomas-Hope, Elizabeth M. 1978. "The Establishment of a Migration Tradition: British West Indian Movements to the Hispanic Caribbean in the Century after Emancipation." Pp. 68–81 in *Caribbean Social Relations,* ed. Colin G. Clark. Liverpool: University of Liverpool.

Torpey, John. 2000. *The Invention of the Passport: Surveillance, Citizenship and the State.* Cambridge: Cambridge University Press.

Williams, Brakette. 1989. "A Class Act: Anthropology and the Race to Nation across Ethnic Terrain." *Annual Reviews of Anthropology* 18: 401–444.

Williams, Eric. 1994 (1944). *Capitalism and Slavery.* Chapel Hill: University of North Carolina Press.

Wiltshire, Rosina, Linda Basch, Winston Wiltshire, and Joyce Toney. 1990. *Caribbean Transnational Migrant Networks: Implications for Donor Societies.* Ottawa: International Development Research Centre.

Wiltshire, Winston. 1984. "The Economic Impact of Caribbean Emigration on Labour Donor Societies: Grenada and St. Vincent." Unpublished ms., Research Institute for the Study of Man, New York.

Wimmer, Andreas. 2002. *Nationalist Exclusion and Ethnic Conflict Shadows of Modernity.* Cambridge: Cambridge University Press.

Wimmer, Andreas, and Nina Glick Schiller. 2002. "Methodological Nationalism and Beyond: Nation-State Building, Migration and the Social Sciences." *Global Networks* 2, no. 4: 301–334.

Wood, Charles H., and Terry L. McCoy. 1985. "Migration, Remittances and Development: A Study of West Indian Cane Cutters in Florida." *International Migration Review,* no. 19 (Summer): 251–277.

Wyman, Mark. 1993. *Round-Trip to America: The Immigrants Return to Europe, 1880–1930.* Ithaca, N.Y.: Cornell University Press.

I

State Policies and Migrants' Strategies

2

Colonial Racism, Ethnicity, and Citizenship

The Lessons of the Migration Experiences of French-Speaking Caribbean Populations

Michel Giraud

No immigration can be viewed simply either as an idyllic passage toward an El Dorado or as an apocalyptic descent into hell. The realities of immigration from the French Caribbean to mainland France have never fit in totally with the golden dreams that once nourished the myths of departure from Guadeloupe or Martinique. Neither have they totally justified the cut-and-dried judgments of those who, in the times of BUMIDOM,[1] compared it to a new slave trade. The fact, as indicated by Alain Anselin in a book offering the most illuminating analysis of these events to appear to date, is that the real situation was marked by "movement in two contrasting directions: one toward social integration and advancement, and the other, stronger, toward 'relative degradation' and 'marginalisation.'"[2] The immigrants and would-be emigrants from the French Caribbean will probably continue to weigh up the pros and cons of this twofold movement. For as long as the results inclined them to hope for a balance in their favor, the settling-down process of those who had arrived in France remained fairly stable, and the flows of migration continued to grow. Now, however, they perceive the disadvantages of migration as outweighing its advantages. As a result, those flows are tending to diminish, and the return to their own countries, which was once a mere myth, has started to become a reality in a small way.

However, there is a decisive factor in the process of the incorporation of Caribbean migrants into their adoptive societies: the racial discrimination they may face there. That is equally true for the French Caribbeans living in mainland

France and the non-French Caribbeans who have emigrated to other European countries or North America.[3] It is true for the Haitians who have settled in the Dominican Republic, the Bahamas, or even one of the three French American Departments, or DFAs (French Guiana, Guadeloupe, and Martinique); for the Dominicans from the Republic of Dominica in Guadeloupe or the Dominicans from the Dominican Republic, formerly Santo Domingo, in Puerto Rico. In these latter cases, the term "racism" may seem inappropriate. It is not. When Caribbean immigrants into Caribbean countries find their manners and life-style labeled as inherent in a particular group and inseparable from it ("Haitians are like this"; "Dominicans are like that"), they are unquestionably being treated in "racist" terms and discriminated against in consequence.

Whatever their political status in their adoptive country, all these groups encounter similar difficulties. Thus, immigrants who are marginalized in the countries of Europe and North America come from countries where immigrants from other Caribbean countries are just as clearly marginalized in their turn. This bitter paradox provides food for thought. In the first place, common sense proclaims that immigration is a thorny path to tread in any country and that the fact of suffering injustice does not render a group of people any the less capable of inflicting it. More important, we need to understand what causes this state of affairs to work out all of its implications when it comes to promoting the rights of immigrants, no matter where they come from.

With this end in view, a study of immigration and emigration in the French Caribbean countries and French Guiana is of particular interest in that they manifest, in an extreme form, the double paradox referred to earlier. On the one hand, the Guadeloupeans, French Guianese, or Martinicans who suffer discrimination in mainland France do so despite their longstanding French citizenship.[4] And on the other, those who contribute their bit to the marginalization suffered by immigrants who come from other Caribbean countries to try to earn a living in Guadeloupe, Martinique, or French Guiana have plenty in common with them. They belong to nations that have experienced the same misfortunes in the history of colonization and, culturally at least, they are close cousins.

Proletarianization and the Experience of Racism

There has been a change in the kind of people from the French Caribbean who have settled in mainland France. Until the end of the 1950s there were still relatively few of these migrants.[5] They were composed of members of the middle classes (middle- and upper-ranking civil servants, fee-earning professionals, and students) and were highly qualified. Today—and, in fact, from the 1960s onward—the overwhelming majority are employees and workmen in low-qualified jobs.[6] This proletarianization has brought them to a position that in many ways is close to that of the most frequently disparaged groups of immigrants (particularly those from Tunisia, Algeria, Morocco, and Sub-Saharan Africa), and they are often grouped together with them in practice. Meanwhile, social competition has been increased by the wide-ranging economic changes in French society. As one of the main manifestations of this competition, there has been a worsening of "anti-immigrant" racism toward people from the French Caribbean and those from Africa. This has arisen from the very fact that they are progressively putting down roots in France.

For example, in the allocation of housing, immigrants from the French Caribbean sometimes meet with the same difficulties as "foreigners," and often from the same district authorities. These difficulties stem from the carefully managed "quota" policies implemented by certain local authorities (including "left-wing" ones).[7] In such cases, immigrants from the French Caribbean and French Guiana are grouped together with foreign immigrants in the category of "*populations allogènes* (non-native populations)."[8] Or again, they are often refused employment, just like the most stigmatized of "foreign" workers. An official study commissioned to look at access to employment for young people with no qualifications and their introduction into the work environment confirms that such refusals are motivated by phenotyped views of applicants.[9] Immigrants from French Caribbean countries in search of work are heard to say that if they were not black, they would be taken on.[10] And when they do have a job, as underlined by the Lucas report in 1983, in mainland France "with an equivalent level of qualifications, a worker from the DOM [Overseas Departments] has more difficulties than a worker from France itself in accessing a job corresponding to his qualifications, or will more often be sent in the direction of a less qualified job."[11]

While they are constantly assured that they are wholly French by right, people from Guadeloupe, French Guiana, and Martinique discover, once they are in mainland France, that they are in practice, as Aimé Césaire put it, "wholly separate Frenchmen." The difficulties in integration shared by French Caribbean immigrants and certain foreign nationals highlight the fact that, as a colleague and I have suggested elsewhere, the discrimination suffered by these "immigrants" depends less on the dividing line between nationals and non-nationals set forth by law than on a social image of immigrants from the former colonies and their descendants that presents them as an alien element in society, one that threatens the "integrity" of national identity.[12] In the light of the opposition set up by this image between those who "belong" to the nation and those who "do not belong" (not just in law but also, especially, in an ineffable sense of legitimate rights), people from the French Caribbean are considered as "not completely belonging," although they are not, strictly speaking, foreigners.

The image in question, based both on a biologizing concept of nation and a racist stigmatizing of immigrants, stems directly from France's colonial experience.[13] But this inheritance is not specific to France: it is found in all immigration countries that were former colonial powers. Thus it has been noted that,

> at the global level, an overarching scale of evaluation was formed in the course of Europe's ascent to world hegemony in the age of modernity. A racialized conceptualisation was determinatively shaped by the master–slave relationship that ensued . . . racialism—involving both an essentialization of somatic variation from "whites" as it developed historically, and an ascription of genetically determined personality and cultural characteristics to the resultant groups—continues to play an important role in the evaluation of the desirability of immigrants.[14]

This picture, then, is basically only a product of the continued application, in a new context, of the old principle of separation, which, as Frantz Fanon expressed incisively in the first pages of *The Wretched of the Earth*, violently compartmentalized the colonial world into two mutually exclusive and antagonistic sub-groups, two "species" or "races."

Hence, to return to the subject under discussion, the "skin color" (or, in broader terms, the phenotype) makes "black French nationals . . . in the reality of daily life, into foreigners."[15] However, one cannot let oneself be blinded by any apparent evidence of the supreme role played by skin color, though one might be induced to do so by the notion of the "visible minority," which has recently become widespread in France. What is really expressed by the supreme role of "race" is social domination, and the supposed evidence only ends up in making a travesty of this domination, trying to legitimize it by pretending it is based on natural characteristics. Such a deceptive substitution of causes needs to be avoided. It would tend to make people believe that groups of a certain "race"—for example, people of Caribbean "extraction" living in mainland France—constitute sociological minorities because of the "visibility" of their phenotypes when, in fact, their place in the social system in which they live has been allotted to them by the history of colonization and certain current minoritizing tendencies that cause them to be particularly "seen" and discriminated against. As Stuart Hall writes concerning "Blacks" in England, "Their histories are in the past, inscribed in their skins. But it is not because of their skins that they are Black."[16] The fact is that different "skin colors" are never merely a given (after all, why should "blacks" be "visible" and "whites" not?) but a historical and social construct.

Reversing the Stigma

It took time for immigrants from Guadeloupe, French Guiana, and Martinique who settled in mainland France to see through the popular picture of "immigrants" from France's former colonies to the discrimination contained in it, veiled as such discrimination was by a certain "Republican" ideology. They then had to recognize that the fact of having French nationality did not fully protect them from the effects of that discrimination.

Thus, during the first period of Caribbean immigration to mainland France, most of these immigrants stubbornly refused to be confused with "foreign" immigrants—or to consider themselves or be regarded as immigrants at all. This reaction was all the stronger since they included a high proportion of people belonging to the middle classes. Immediately after the election of François Mitterrand as president of France in 1981, there was a great surge in the number of "free" radio stations. One of these, the "Afro-Caribbean" community's Radio Mango, ran a series of programs, to which I was a regular contributor, on the situation of people from the Francophone Caribbean who had settled in and around Paris. Even at that date, large numbers of listeners telephoned the switchboard to protest against being classed as "immigrants," saying very forcefully that they were French citizens. About fifteen years later, a certain number of people from the Francophone Caribbean questioned by Hélène Mélin, after having had job applications rejected because of their "color," declared that they found it "annoying that the French think that all Blacks are the same whether they are Caribbean or African" and that "It's unexpected and even irritating to be compared to Africans."[17] Most of them therefore made up their minds to "avoid rocking the boat" and adopted a policy of "ethnic transparency" in the society in which they were now living. Where their behavior was concerned, they played the French national identity card in an attempt to become established and rise on the social ladder in France and were sometimes successful.

In view of the heavy stigma laid on certain "foreign" groups, this attitude is understandable. That does not mean to say it should be considered an acceptable one, since it typifies the ambiguity of the situation of French Caribbeans in mainland France. To be precise, it typifies the tension existing between the two poles of that situation, as pointed out in the quotation from Césaire referred to earlier. On the one hand, for a long time their French citizenship made people from the French Caribbean living in France into relatively privileged "immigrants" compared with others (and still does now to a lesser extent), especially in terms of access to public employment. On the other hand, the specific social conditions prevailing today tend increasingly to widen the gap between them and "the French."

This separation from the mainstream society of their "country of residence," and all the racist rejection they undergo more and more frequently at that society's hands, have impelled the Francophone Caribbeans living in mainland France—or, at least, large numbers of them—to return afresh to the very "difference" that is so often thrown in their faces and to value it anew. This "reversing of the stigma" is a well-known reaction. Thus, they have begun to acquire a strong awareness of their communal identity and to mobilize around the emblems of that identity. Nevertheless, it is important to note that this mobilization cannot be seen merely in terms of an automatic reaction against the discrimination experienced or as a long-suppressed expression of cultural atavism or, still worse, of an essential otherness. Like all such mobilizations, it is first and foremost the mark of a social and political strategy. This strategy makes the open affirmation and appreciation of a particular identity—going to the lengths, where necessary, of (re)constructing it—into a means of having that identity universally recognized as legitimate and, consequently, a means of satisfying the specific claims formulated in its name. This fact enables us to understand why, through many promotional evenings or cultural days, the celebration of their own cultural heritage (music, dance, food, and, to a lesser extent, literature and theater) has become an essential note of the public presence of the Francophone Caribbeans in mainland France. It can equally be understood why that cultural presence has mostly been organized by a huge number of associations.[18] This is because the structure of an association is both the best support and the best possible instrument for effecting the strategy described above, being the only type of collective organization in France that enables mobilization on the basis of a community, in a way that neither trade unions nor political parties could do, around a wide range of problems such as those involving employment, accommodation, and cultural expression.

A large number of immigrants from the French Caribbean and French Guiana living in France have thus turned from prizing their French citizenship to placing the emphasis instead on their particular identity. This transfer came about not suddenly but in stages and is not yet complete.[19] The former attitude still holds good in many cases. Still less would it be true to say that there are no further developments to be expected. Several possible paths forward remain open, as will be explained later. Which of them will be taken depends at least in part on the change in status that each of the French Overseas Departments may shortly undergo.

The Trap of Ethnicity

To get a better idea of the elements involved in the vague prospects lying at the "crossroads" just referred to, it seems useful at this point to stop and consider one particular stage of the transformation that has taken place: the intermediate phase, which in most cases no longer obtains today. Basically, this middle phase consisted of a strong trade-union movement in the course of which, in the second half of the 1970s, many workers from the French Overseas Departments had already made very vocal demands that were particular to themselves, especially concerning paid leave in order to return regularly to their own countries and the employees' transfer to those countries. They had frequently done so, however, within the framework of the great national trade unions.

The first reason it is useful to take a closer look at this phase now is to recall that these workers had great difficulty in gaining recognition from their union authorities for the legitimacy of their demands. These authorities tended not to be very open toward particular circumstances that did not fall within the sphere of working conditions. At that time, such demands were judged to be too "particularist" or too "political" (since they concerned the present and future situation of the immigrants' countries). So it was not until they had been disappointed in their hopes of union support that the great majority of social activists among the French Caribbean immigrants began to set up community-type associations to press their collective claims.[20] The second reason for dwelling on this situation is to underline the fact that, with this disappointment, the prospect receded of combining the particular claims, which were then—and still are—being put forward by these immigrants and the universal values of citizenship. The third reason is to promote reflection about the risk of ethnic delimiting, if not actual ethnic isolationism, with a shift away from mobilization based primarily on professional or class solidarity toward mobilization in which community relations and solidarities are predominant. The "single option" of community-type associations is especially prone to this risk. Paradoxical though it may seem, the risk is still greater when the French citizenship of the members of the "community" in question, their long acquaintance with national political maneuvering, the great abilities and savoir faire of their elites (of whom there are many and who are often still to be found leading their associations) combine to give this option, via the practices of political lobbying, a discreet but real effectiveness not enjoyed by associations of "foreign" immigrants.

The particular situation of French Caribbean immigrants in mainland France needs to be taken into account to satisfy their aspirations—aspirations that, despite being particular to themselves, are generally quite legitimate in the order of natural law. This might lead to an obligation of specificity. Specificity would then be used as an a priori justification of any advantage whatsoever being taken by a particular ethnic group, even if it were likely that such an advantage would remain of very little practical importance. And this would be done in contempt of or indifference toward the bonds of solidarity necessarily linking French Caribbean immigrants not only with other immigrants, but also with the French working classes and those in every other country in the world. Thus it is to be feared that, in the words of the Tunisian-born philosopher Hélé Béji, there exists "within every proclamation of one's difference . . . an unspoken conviction of one's proven superiority, [and then] the claim to cultural difference can no longer be considered as a manifestation of one's rights, but as a masked economy of force."[21] Or, to put it in a more nuanced way, it is to be feared that the refusal to have an identity that one has neither chosen nor even accepted imposed on one—a legitimate defensive attitude in itself—may turn into the offensive and unacceptable aim of imposing on everyone else the promotion of one's own interests in the name of the specificity that one is claiming.[22]

The risk of isolationism, becoming shut in on themselves, is today far from a reality. However, it is no mere imaginary threat. To realize this, one only has to recall that the refusal to be confused with "foreign," and especially African, immigrants persists among many immigrants from the French Caribbean. More recently, this refusal has been compounded among some of them with the desire to hold themselves apart from the French, whom they have long distrusted because of the repeated discrimination they have suffered at their hands. One may also observe that French Caribbean immigrants—and, more particularly, their associations—play no part in the great social agitations that take place in France from time to time. It makes no difference whether these agitations are in defense of the rights of "foreign" immigrants, such as the recent ones concerning the *sans papiers* (undocumented migrants), the victims of the "double penalty,"[23] or families evicted from their homes; nationwide, such as those against poverty or in defense of the rights of the unemployed; or even international, such as the struggle against globalization or in solidarity with Third World nations under attack. This last even applies when the geographical, historical, and cultural proximity of the nations concerned—for example, Haiti—might lead one to look for greater involvement on their part. This being the case, I think it doubtful whether the partial relaxation of their original firm rejection of immigrant status on the part of people from the French Overseas Departments, which is attributable, as is often claimed, to a reduction of their traditional assimilationism, can be seen as a positive development. It is not very positive if at the same time their growing pride in their identity as French Caribbeans divides them just as much (or even more, though for another reason) from the other members of the society in which they are living, including "foreign" immigrants.

There is another worrying indication of the danger of isolationism springing from identity awareness. This is the discrimination and even violence suffered by workers and their families from neighboring countries (especially from Haiti and Dominica, but also, in the case of French Guiana, from Suriname, Guyana, or Brazil) who migrate into the French Caribbean Overseas Departments.[24] Admittedly, this does not directly involve the immigrants from the French Caribbean countries in mainland France who are the subject of the present study. But it is not altogether irrelevant, either, since in both situations it is the same identity—or, at least, an identity claimed to be held in common—whose glorification is in question. In consequence, the risk entailed in that glorification cannot be neatly split between the two sides of the Atlantic. This point has been made from the start of this study, by highlighting the paradox that Caribbean nationals going to live and work in other Caribbean countries (in this case, Guadeloupe and French Guiana) encounter a reception that is just as unfriendly as that accorded to migrants from those two countries into Europe or North America.

It is true that, through the immigration policies and policing of foreigners that they implement in the French Overseas Departments, the French authorities bear a heavy responsibility for the difficulties encountered by Caribbean migrants into those countries, both in entering them and during their stays there. But it cannot be maintained that this policy and policing is carried out in a social vacuum, with the local population and local authorities watching from a distance without taking part. On the contrary, it seems that they consent to it in some degree or even become active accomplices. This was the case in Guadeloupe in 1979, when some Guadeloupeans became de facto auxiliaries of the French police force in its policy of expelling Dominican immigrants.[25] It was recently confirmed in the physical attacks on people, and the destruction of their homes, suffered by Haitians and Dominicans, again in Guadeloupe.[26]

The refusal of French living in mainland France to be confused with "foreign" immigrants is often imputed, as we have mentioned, to the mark left by assimilationist ideology on their thinking and activity. In the same way, the rejection of immigrants from neighboring countries into the French Caribbean Overseas Departments is attributed to the colonial alienation that is alleged to be a powerful factor there still. More precisely, that rejection is said to be connected to a desire to escape at all costs from what Frantz Fanon called "the great black hole" of poverty and to get as close as possible to the enviable world of the dominant species, the "whites." Thus, when Dominicans and Haitians in Guadeloupe suffered discrimination and violence, culminating in the racist attacks on Dominicans on September 28–29, 1979, in which men were beaten up and women raped and then handed over to the police, who expelled them on the spot, the Haitian sociologist Laennec Hurbon saw in all this an "effect of the interminable task of assimilation to French culture" in which Guadeloupeans have been engaged since the era of slavery.[27] Although this interpretation is not to be rejected altogether, it should also be recognized that it leaves out one of the main features of the paradox. The xenophobic attitudes described earlier developed not during the heyday of colonialism or even at the apogee of assimilationism; nor did they stem solely from the assimilationists in the French Caribbean. They appeared, even among nationalists, at the time when assimilationism was being widely questioned. This development, then, must be linked to the growing awareness of identity that is the subject of this study—or, at least, with some of its manifestations.

As against the threats of cultural engulfing involved in colonialism, this awareness strengthened, or actually rigidified, the boundaries of the identity to be preserved, bringing about what Hurbon rightly described as a "passion for homogeneity."[28] The result was not only a rejection of the authority of the colonizer, but also, in a sort of ricochet effect, the exclusion of other nationalities. This is all the more noticeable in the case of immigrants. The reason for this is that the arrival of immigrants means more competition for access to the sought-after resources of the country as a French Overseas Department in terms of pay, the right to employment, social security, health care, free education, and so on, and the local population wants to keep these resources for themselves. A further reason is that migration is part of the process of transnationalization that challenges the model of the nation-state on which the new political sovereignties of the Caribbean have been set up, and others could be in the future. This process, and the migrations that are one of its vectors, help to destabilize the nationalist aim in areas where such an aim is only held by minorities and is strongly contested by large sectors of public opinion. Accordingly, they are necessarily an object of suspicion in the "patriotic camp" in these areas. In the French Caribbean and French Guiana, like everywhere else, competition for access to scarce facilities is the primary factor in xenophobia, but it is also nourished by the tension with regard to identity which very often accompanies the effort to leave colonialism behind.

In my opinion there can be no doubt that the people from former French colonies, including Martinique, Guadeloupe, and French Guiana, who migrate to mainland France, confronted with restrictive social marginalization backed up by colonial-style racism, are inspired at bottom by the desire for equal rights for everyone. This desire springs from such a longstanding ideal that I would not dare to speak of it in terms of a "new citizenship." It should be seen instead as the expression of the will to win the fight for decolonization on the very territory of the (former) colonial power, since that fight was not brought to a final conclusion with the acquisition of independence by African and Asian countries and the transformation of the "old colonies" into Overseas Departments of the French Republic. On a different field, it is the same fight being fought against the same enemy: the domination and exploitation of man by man, complicated by excuses such as differences in race, color, ethnicity, culture, or nationality. This fight is inspired by the same ideal as the revolutions of 1789 and 1848 but made dynamic and transformed by the general revolt of slaves on the whole American continent to bring about the abolition of slavery and the onset of universal justice and brotherhood.

However, this ideal is lost sight of from time to time by those waging the fight, who favor instead the rather doubtful claims of particularizing tendencies, tied up with the debatable idea of giving preferential treatment to an oppressed race, color, ethnic group, culture, or nation simply because it is or was oppressed. However, in present-day societies and, first and foremost, in the large immigration countries under discussion, it is never sufficient in my opinion to aim simply for improved status for stigmatized "races" and despised cultures, however legitimate this aim may be in itself. This is because these societies have long been far too diverse to permit the different groups they contain to hold together on an equal footing, unless they all share a system of norms and values. Such a system would have to be rooted in each of the different traditions represented but transcend them all. It would therefore prevent any one of those groups from giving its own "difference" as a valid reason for competing against the others and imposing the satisfaction of its own interests alone, even by cornering state resources that in theory belong to all, while thinking it has right on its side.

In France, the compatibility of the right to affirm one's own particular identity with the universal duty to work for equal rights for all, regardless of their identity, is well on the way to becoming a central element of "politically correct" discourse. However, I think it is urgent to recognize that such discourse stops short just where it ought to begin: with a discussion of the conditions that make that right compatible with that duty. How and at what price is such compatibility, which does not come ready-made, to be forged? To begin to answer that question, one has to bear in mind that the equal dignity in principle of all cultural traditions means that the common vision whose necessity is advocated above is the result of a constant process of negotiation between those traditions. Such negotiation would have to take reasonable and critical account of their differences to somehow overcome them by means of what Jürgen Habermas calls a "discursive ethic" in other words, by means of a permanent dialogue that cannot fail to be contradictory but in which it only makes sense for each side to engage if those sides are aware that they have something to learn from the others and convinced that nothing is a priori non-negotiable (prior to a free, reasoned examination of the reasons) and, hence, accepting in advance the possibility of major changes to their own credo. Because, as has been well said by the Jamaican-born British sociologist Harry Goulbourne, "It involves subjecting all cultures to criticism, and abandoning aspects of each one in a declared preference for the beneficial aspects from all."[29]

From that point of view, it seems to me, within the idea shared by many (including me) that the universal is necessarily to be found at the end of a *particular* path, there may be the illusion that such a particular path is sufficient in itself. Thus, if we adopt the brilliant formula, "the Universal is the Particular without walls," we also have to add that to attain it, we still need to knock down the walls—all the walls.

Notes

1. Le Bureau pour les migrations intéressant les départements d'outre-mer (Bureau for Migration from the Overseas Departments) was the government office set up in October 1961 to develop and organize such migrations. It was replaced in 1982 by the Agence nationale pour l'insertion et la promotion des travailleurs d'outre-mer (ANT; National Agency for the Integration and Advancement of Overseas Workers).

2. Translated from A. Anselin, *L'Emigration antillaise en France. La troisième île* (Paris: Editions Karthala, 1990), 126.

3. On England, see, e.g., W. W. Daniel, *Racial Discrimination in England* (Harmondsworth: Penguin, 1968); S. Patterson, *Dark Strangers: A Sociological Study of a Recent West Indian Migrant Group in Brixton, South London* (London: Tavistock, 1963); A. H. Richmond, *Migration and Race Relations in an English City: A Study in Bristol* (London: Oxford University Press, 1973). On Canada, see F. Henry and E. Ginsberg, *Who Gets the Work? A Test of Racial Discrimination in Employment* (Toronto: Urban Alliance for Race Relations, 1985); M. Labelle, S. Larose, and V. Piché, "Emigration et immigration: Les Haïtiens au Québec," *Sociologie et Société* 15 (1983); S. Ramcharan, *Racism in Canada* (Toronto: Butterworths, 1983).

4. Thus, from the beginnings of colonization in the seventeenth century, all of the inhabitants of Guadeloupe, French Guiana, and Martinique, including the slaves, were "deemed and reputed French *nationals*" (in the words of a royal edict of 1664). After slavery had been abolished in 1848, the Third French Republic, at the end of the nineteenth century, guaranteed them French citizenship, with the full exercise of democratic rights associated with it—notably, parliamentary representation. This movement toward political assimilation was completed in 1946 with the establishment of the four "*vieilles colonies* (lit., old colonies)"—Guadeloupe, French Guiana, Martinique, and Réunion—as departments of the French Republic.

5. According to the data of the General Population Census in France in 1954, 4 percent of those born in the French Caribbean were living in mainland France at the time.

6. An idea of how massive this emigration was may be gained from the fact that the number of people of Antillese (i.e., French Caribbean) extraction living in continental France in 1990 (337,000) practically equaled the whole population of one of the two Francophone Caribbean departments (387,000 in Guadeloupe; 360,000 in Martinique) during the same period: see C. V. Marie, *Les populations des Dom-Tom, nées et originaires, résidant in France métropolitaine* (Paris: Institut National de la Statistique et des Etudes Economiques, Ministère des départements et territoires d'outre-mer, 1993). Corresponding information from the last census (1999) unfortunately is not yet available. In 1990, over a quarter of the people born in the French Caribbean lived in continental France, and numerically, the Francophone Caribbeans ranked fifth among France's immigrant populations: see idem,

"Les Antillais en France. Histoire et réalités d'une migration ambiguë," *Migrants-Formation,* no. 94 (September 1993): 5–14. In Alain Anselin's phrase, the Francophone Caribbeans in France had become a "third island": Anselin, *L'Emigration antillaise en France.*
7. The reason given was that they would be likely to be noisy (celebrations, visits, etc.) and too numerous:

It is not unusual to find that the so-called 'excessive number' of people originating from the Caribbean in a particular housing estate is given as the reason for refusing accommodation even to solvent families. This is what happened to a young woman from Martinique, a civil servant, married, with a small boy, whose dossier had been submitted by the prefecture to apply for a vacant flat. The argument put forward by the lesser was that the number of Caribbean immigrants in the building was already too high, and he wished to observe the provision of the [Protocoles d'occupation du patrimoine social, or Protocols for the Occupation of Social Housing, measures that aimed to ensure sufficient geographical distribution of the different nationalities living in a given district] adopted by the town of Sainte-Geneviève-des-Bois. (Christian Renoir [head of the Essonne's ANT division], "L'insertion dans l'impasse," *Alizés,* no. 2 [January–March 1994]: 5; my translation)

For a comparison of the housing of Caribbean immigrants in France and in Britain, see S. Condon, "L'Accès au logement: Filières et blocages, le cas des Antillais en France et en Grande-Bretagne," photocopied document, Ministère de l'Equipement, Rapport au Plan Construction et Architecture, Paris, 1993; "L'accès au logement: Le cas antillais en France et en Grande-Bretagne," *Population,* no. 2 (1994): 522–530.
8. This is a striking illustration of the process of ethnicization or "racialization" of certain nationalities operated by a number of administrative bodies, a process denounced by some sociologists in the following terms:

These institutions are great purveyors of "practical" categories, constructed in and for action. They daily produce classifying categories to orient and justify their agents' practices, and these are generally summaries containing a combination of prejudices, interpretations, and abusive generalizations. The classifying activities of these authorities construct resemblances and differences—that is, boundary lines between real groups or groups invented by bureaucratic rationality or irrationality. (V. De Rudder, C. Poiret, and F. Vourc'h, *L'Inégalité raciste. L'universalité républicaine à l'épreuve* [Paris: Presses Universitaires de France, 2000], 186)

9. The study is cited in Marie, "Les Antillais en France." On racial discrimination in offers of employment (and in housing), see also certain surveys conducted by Jean Galap and the researchers at the Centre de Recherche et d'Etudes sur les Dysfonctions de l'Adaptation, e.g., J. Galap, "Phénotypes et discriminations des Noirs en France. Question de méthode," *Migrants-Formation,* no. 94 (September 1993): 39–54.
10. H. Mélin, "Le Rôle de l'identité culturelle dans le processus d'insertion sociale: Le cas des Antillais en France métropolitaine," Diplôme d'Etudes Approfondies thesis, Université de Lille III, 1996, 100.
11. Michel Lucas, "Rapport du Groupe de travail pour l'insertion des ressortissants des Départements d'Outre-mer en Métropole [Report by the Working Group for the Integration of People from the Overseas Departments in France]," 1983, 43. The working group

had been set up at the request of the secretary of state for Overseas Departments and Territories. It was headed by Michel Lucas, director of the General Inspectorate for Social Affairs at the Ministry for Social Affairs and National Solidarity. The report was handed in on May 16, 1983.

12. See M. Giraud and C. V. Marie, with J. Fredj, R. Hardy-Dessources, and P. Pastel, "Les Stratégies sociopolitiques de la communauté antillaise dans son processus d'insertion en France métropolitaine," photocopied document, Ministère de la Recherche, Paris, 1990, 14.

13. This biologizing concept is identified, for example, by Aristide Zolberg in general terms when he writes, "Given the self-division of the human species into imagined communities believed by most of their members to partake of something akin to biological existence, co-nationals take on the character of extended kin; concomitantly, non-nationals are 'others', whose alterity is forcefully evoked by the English legal term 'aliens.'" He states that, in these conditions, the "possibility that the incoming stranger might become a member of the receiving community entails a deviation from the community's 'natural' reproduction, somewhat like adoption as against biological filiation": A. Zolberg, "Immigration and Multiculturalism in the Industrial Societies," photocopied document, New School for Social Research, New York, 1995, 1.

14. Ibid., 2.

15. Galap, "Phénotypes et discriminations des Noirs en France," 53.

16. Translated from S. Hall, "Old and New Identities, Old and New Ethnicities," in *Culture, Globalization and the World-System: Contemporary Conditions for the Representation of Identity*, ed. Anthony D. King (London: Macmillan, 1991), 53.

17. Quoted in and translated from Mélin, "Le rôle de l'identité culturelle dans le processus d'insertion sociale," 100.

18. Since 1987, the ANT has listed a total of 826 associations of people from the French Overseas Departments in mainland France.

19. For an analysis of the underlying dynamics of this process and its development in the field of trade-union activity, its cultural expression, and its associations, see M. Giraud and C. V. Marie, "Insertion et gestion sociopolitique de l'identité culturelle: Le cas des Antillais en France," *Revue européenne des migrations internationales* 3, no. 3 (1987): 31–48, reprinted as "Identité culturelle de l'immigration antillaise," *Hommes et Migrations*, no. 1114 (July–September 1998): 89–102. For a picture of the socio-democratic circumstances of this development and another insight into its social, cultural, and political consequences, see C. V. Marie, "Les Antillais de l'Hexagone," in *Immigration et intégration. L'état des savoirs*, ed. Philippe Dewitte (Paris: La Découverte, 1999), 99–105.

20. Even this was only after they had spent some time considering the totally unrealistic possibility of setting up their own trade unions.

21. Translated from H. Béji, "Radicalisme culturel et laïcité," *Le Débat*, no. 58 (January–February 1990): 48.

22. That is one of the main features of what I elsewhere have called the paradox of ethnicity: see M. Giraud, "L'ethnicité comme nécessité et comme obstacle," in *Intégration, lien social et citoyenneté*, ed. Gilles Ferréol (Lille: Presses du Septentrion, 1998), 137–165.

23. This refers to the highly controversial directive of the French judiciary under which convicted criminals are returned to their original countries on completion of their sentences, even if they have had no connections with those countries for a very long time, or at all.

24. On this subject, see the short article I contributed to the journal of the Group for Immigrant Information and Support, "Les migrations intracaraïbéennes: L'autre exclusion," *Plein Droit,* no. 43 (September 1999): 7–8.

25. In this regard, the letter from the mayor of Saint-Martin to the prime minister dated May 17, 1994, makes interesting reading. In it, the mayor requests of the prime minister an immediate acceleration of the expulsion of foreigners from his domain. This and other documents relating to the same affair are all reproduced in the report of a fact-gathering mission carried out in certain DFAs by several associations for the defense of immigrant rights: "En Guyane et à Saint-Martin. Des étrangers sans droits dans une France bananière," Groupement d'Information et de Soutien des Immigrés, March 1996.

26. This affair came to be known by the name of the person mainly responsible, Ibo Simon, the radio reporter who incited Guadeloupeans to violence.

27. Translated from L. Hurbon, "Racisme et sous-produit du racisme: Les immigrés haïtiens et dominicains en Guadeloupe," *Les Temps Modernes,* nos. 441–442 (April–May 1983): 1991.

28. Ibid., 1998.

29. Translated from H. Goulbourne, "New Issues in Black British Politics," *Information sur les Sciences Sociales* 31, no. 2 (June 1992): 369.

3

From the Periphery to the Core

A Case Study on the Migration and Incorporation of
Recent Caribbean Immigrants in the Netherlands

Eric Mielants

The Case of Suriname

During the first half of the twentieth century, most emigration from Suriname was essentially intraregional[1]—that is, within the Caribbean: to Panama during the construction of the canal, to the sugar plantations of Cuba, and to the banana crops in Central America. In 1915, Shell installed a refinery in Curaçao, and Lago built one in Aruba in 1926. Since the oil industry offered higher wages, and particularly since those islands were also part of the Dutch empire, many Surinamese easily emigrated there. In 1947, 3,900 Surinamese were in Curaçao and 1,600 were in Aruba. From a total population of 170,000, this represented 3 percent of all Surinamese (Bovenkerk 1975: 9). After the automation of the oil industry in the late 1950s, however, the number of jobs began to dwindle, which in turn had an immediate effect on the migration process. Only 2,800 Surinamese remained in Curaçao in 1960, and by 1971 that number had dropped to 1,900. Many used their savings to migrate to the Netherlands (Bovenkerk 1975: 10); by 1972, about 55,000 Surinamese and 8,000 Antilleans had moved there (Schuster 1999: 133).[2]

However, it was the decolonization of Suriname that eventually transformed the steady migration flow into one of mass-migration. Indeed, the public debate in the mass media concerning the cessation of migration during the forced transition to independence was central in turning migration into a mass phenomenon during the period 1972–1975 (Leistra 1995: 35, 54).[3] It is tempting to interpret this massive migration process from the periphery to the core as the result of different push and pull factors. For instance, nearly 30 percent of the Surinamese labor force was unemployed in 1975, compared with a mere 4 percent in the Netherlands. In addition, the minimum wage in the Netherlands was three times higher than in Suriname. In Suriname, only minimal social-security and pension funds were available, whereas the Netherlands offered better social services and housing facilities, and unions were more powerful (Bovenkerk 1975: 21). Finally, since the late 1960s and early 1970s, transportation costs had decreased. One could be tempted to conclude, then, that emigration, from a materialistic point of view, was merely a rational decision, particularly since the population in Suriname had soared in the previous fifty years. The Surinamese themselves claim to have migrated for the purpose of study. Frank Bovenkerk (1975: 39), however, has stated that neither the study (a collective rationalization process) nor mere push and pull factors were the key elements to migration.

Rationalizing migration vis-à-vis the migrants and their social environment was very important, as emigration was not necessarily appreciated in Suriname; choosing the Netherlands implied a rejection of Suriname. It could also be that many immigrants to the Netherlands left their homelands for very personal reasons (something the push–pull theory does not explain)—for example, relationship problems, marriage problems, generational conflicts, personal confrontations in the framework of ethnic strife and political polarization, and so on (Bovenkerk 1975: 47–52). Another reason for discrediting the traditional "push and pull" model is that until November 1980, the Netherlands was the only country that completely opened its borders to Surinamese immigrants (Schuster 1999: 161). In this case, then, emigration is more than a rational comparison of pluses and minuses.[4]

Nevertheless, the existence of extensive information about the Netherlands was central to the migrants' decision-making process. Indeed, all of the mass media in the colony were focused on the Netherlands, as the periphery generally receives more information about the core than vice versa (Galtung 1971). Furthermore, the historical context of Suriname's education system must also be taken into account: curricula were completely geared toward the Netherlands; children were taught in the Dutch language; diplomas were valid in the Netherlands but not elsewhere; and the Surinamese, as Dutch citizens, had access to free education in the Netherlands (Bovenkerk 1975: 34–35).

Finally, the *agency* of the immigrants (i.e., the actual decision-making process) is a factor that should not be overlooked, even when it appears that the structural power relations between the "sending" and "receiving" areas are central to the migration process. In actuality, migration requires a huge investment by the migrant, such that everything is cast aside for migration to the Netherlands.

Many immigrants used all of their savings, sold their property (house, land, goods), and received financial help from family members in the Netherlands and Suriname.[5] Family networks were also an important element within the migration process. As the number of Surinamese in the Netherlands increased, many relied on friends and (distant) relatives for a "pied à terre" during the mass-immigration years of 1970–1980 (Schumacher 1987: 24–25). This is an important self-stimulating characteristic of emigration—that is, that emigration invites further emigration (Bovenkerk 1975: 65–66). The result is the appearance of so-called chain migration (Massey et al. 1993) wherein a base is formed in the metropolis (where an economic niche is carved out, allowing the ethnic minority to sustain itself socioeconomically and re-create itself culturally), which in turn attracts more immigrants. Other crucial factors for emigration are the increased flow of information and the reduced investment costs created by such functioning family networks.[6]

Thus while "objective" push and pull factors (differences in wealth and opportunity) clearly exist between sending and receiving areas in the world system, an essential mistake lies in reifying them as if they were the result of "objective market forces" operating within the world economy. The United Provinces (and later Holland) became a core power (with hegemonic status) precisely because of their domination and exploitation of colonies (Willemsen 2006). When the costs outweighed the benefits, independence was granted or forced on the colonies.[7]

Before I conclude this section, it is necessary to note a couple of other interesting factors regarding the complex process of Surinamese migration. From a geographic standpoint, migration from Suriname was primarily a staged process. Many impoverished peasants first moved to the district of Paramaribo, where wages were higher and the labor market was more differentiated. From there they migrated to de Randstad (the metropolis). Young men emigrated first, followed by women, children, and the elderly.

There was also an important racial element to the migration process from Suriname. Until World War II, most Surinamese immigrants residing in the Netherlands were light-colored Creoles, some Jews, Chinese, and dark-colored Creoles. In the early 1970s, more dark-colored Creoles and Hindustanis migrated. Later on, Javanese and Indians also migrated (Leistra 1995: 59–69). By the mid 1970s, emigration had become an option for broad layers of the Surinamese society. Up to 1974, all income groups were equally distributed among the emigrants (Oostindie 1988: 59), but eventually the Surinamese emigrants became more representative of the Surinamese population as a whole as far as ethnicity, sex, age, and income groups were concerned. When the newly independent state of Suriname immediately collapsed into socioeconomic disaster and political turmoil, resulting in a small-scale civil war in the mid-

1980s (Leistra 1995: 30), about half of the population emigrated to the Netherlands. By 2007, approximately 330,000 people of Surinamese origin were living
in the Netherlands, while about 500,000 remained in Suriname.

The Case of the Dutch Antilles

The economic development of the islands was and is determined by the world
capitalistic system that used them as (1) a trade entrepôt (slave and contraband
trade in the seventeenth and eighteenth centuries); (2) a location to refine raw
materials (e.g., oil) extracted from the periphery for consumption in the core
(1915–1980s); and (3) strategic military naval bases for major Western powers
in the period 1915–1991 (cf. Koot and Ringeling 1984).[8]

As with the Surinamese case discussed earlier, a distinction must be drawn
between intraregional and peripheral migration and migration from the (semi-)
periphery to the core. The geographic proximity of the ABC Islands to the oil
fields of Venezuela, the availability of good harbors, and the Dutch guarantee
of stability influenced Shell's and Exxon's decisions to build oil refineries on
Curaçao (1915) and Aruba (1924). The population in the Leeward Islands
increased during the period 1930–1950 due to intra-Caribbean immigration,
as well as migration from the Windward Islands. The immigrants had come to
work in the oil industry that had made the ABC Islands some of the wealthiest
in the region. Dependence on foreign capital, however, remained a structural
problem in that the industry's profits were not reinvested in the islands.

The Dutch Antilles were granted autonomy in 1954,[9] while defense and
diplomatic relations (i.e., foreign policy) remained under Dutch control (Gastmann 1968). In the 1960s, the islands were used as tax havens for multinationals
or "P.O. box companies." While state revenues from these multinationals were
considerable, the commercial services offered to the companies were minimal.
Once other islands began to compete for their business, multinationals began
"island hopping," and revenues decreased. By the 1960s, jobs in the oil industry
had also started to dry up. Tourism, however, proved to be quite profitable after
the disappearance of Cuba as a main tourist attraction for Americans. Tourism
enabled the Dutch Caribbean (with the exception of Curaçao) to thrive, especially in the hotel sector (Koot and Ringeling 1984: 38), and most notably in
St. Maarten and Aruba. Nevertheless, (casino) tourism tended to be very cyclical and seasonal, while inflation (and soaring prices) only hurt the local population. In the past few decades, the Curaçao labor market shrank, and "develop-
mental aid" was not able to construct an autonomous economic position on the
islands vis-à-vis the Netherlands, nor did it enable the local authorities to tackle
soaring unemployment. Among the least skilled of the population, unemployment remained very high and income distribution remained extremely unequal

(Koot and Ringeling 1984: 44). The islands were said to be little more than a "minuscule satellite of international capital" (van Dieten and Maduro 1978). Many inhabitants (approximately 300,000 in the Dutch Caribbean) were obliged to make ends meet in the informal sector. Compared with the surrounding islands in the Caribbean, wage levels were relatively high (Koot and Ringeling 1984: 47),[10] but when compared with the situation in the Netherlands, one can easily discern differences between the core and the semi-periphery. Since the Antillean government did not grant unemployment benefits, approximately 20 percent of the Antillean population lived below the poverty line, despite the fact that since 1969 unions had gained more influence in the political process on the larger islands (Koot and Ringeling 1984: 50; Verton 1976).

The conclusion of this brief socioeconomic overview is that the Antillean economy has been structurally dependent on foreign capital for tourism, "development aid" from the Netherlands and the European Union, oil refining (albeit in its last stages), some trade and employment in free zones and harbor facilities, and the temporary financial benefits of the aforementioned P.O. box companies. This situation, together with the structural differences between the Netherlands and the Antilles (a creation of their neocolonial power relationship within the present constraints of the capitalist world economy), is one that attracts and promotes international migration from the periphery to the core. For example, during the period 1964–1971, Dutch companies actively attracted Antillean migratory labor (Schuster 1999: 128–129);[11] after the economic downturn (the B phase of the Kondratieff cycle in the world economy) had manifested itself, however, the campaign to attract Antillean laborers came to a halt, while Mediterranean (especially Turkish and Moroccan) immigrants were invited to the Netherlands (Koot 1979: 57–58). (This new development was undoubtedly linked to the fact that the latter—labeled temporary guest workers—had considerably fewer socioeconomic and legal rights than Antilleans who were, and still are, Dutch citizens [Schuster 1999: 141].) Migration from the Antilles to the Netherlands continued to increase, from students in the 1970s to more and more Antilleans of any age seeking employment within the core.[12] While Surinamese immigration was more sudden and explosive in the "rush to beat the ban" in the mid-1970s, the number of Antillean immigrants to the Netherlands has gradually increased over the past twenty years, culminating in the presence of about 130,000 Antilleans in the Netherlands today. Like the Surinamese, the Antilleans link the migration process to educational improvement (Amesz et al. 1989: 40), but when scrutinized, their migration is in reality linked with poor economic perspectives (and economic cycles) in the Antilles. Increased migration in the mid-1980s, for instance, reflected Lago's decision to close its refinery on Aruba, while Shell contemplated closing its plant on Curaçao.[13] The Antillean immigrants of the 1980s also differed from their earlier counterparts in that they tended to be young people originating from deprived areas of Curaçao (Bovenkerk 2002: 171), having minimal education and facing serious language problems (Rutgers 1997; van Putte 1997).

The Incorporation of Surinamese and Antillean Immigrants in the Netherlands

From a long-term perspective, the increased migration flow from the semi-periphery introduces structural pressures on the core. The increasing number of immigrants from the Antilles (semi-periphery) and Suriname (periphery) opens up the question of their respective (successful) incorporation in the country of destination, the Netherlands, and, more specifically, within the world city, "de Randstad" (comprising Amsterdam, The Hague, Rotterdam, and Utrecht), as 60 percent of all Surinamese and almost a third of the Antilleans currently reside in this urban area (Martens and Verweij 1997).[14]

It is important to acknowledge that the degree of incorporation and integration of Surinamese and Antillean immigrants in the Netherlands is linked with their history. During the period of imperialism, colonization processes around the globe created an ideology of legitimacy—that is, racism. Therefore it is not surprising that only thirty years after the formal end of Suriname's status as a colony, and given the maintenance of the Dutch Antilles as a "modern" colony, both Surinamese and Antillean immigrants still have to cope with racism within the Netherlands daily (Essed 1984, 1991). While under colonialism, their countries were subjugated, their resources were exploited, and their inhabitants were used as a cheap source of labor. Perhaps not surprisingly, then, the mass-migration of "colored" immigrants from various regions in the periphery (most notably, Morocco, Turkey, and Suriname) to the Dutch "homeland" has provoked racist agitation within the core and, more specifically, within the cities where they have settled.[15] Yet mass-migration from the periphery to the core, as exemplified by the Surinamese and Antillean migration to the Netherlands, is itself the result of centuries of colonial exploitation and the colonies' subsequent weak position within the world economy (van den Bergh 1972: 36). Sociological evidence reveals that the Dutch mentality of racist legitimacy in the first half of the twentieth century is now permeated with Dutch contempt wherein racism, paternalism, and colonialism are intrinsically linked. The fact that mass-migration to the Netherlands is a relatively recent phenomenon—atypical when compared with other core countries located in Western Europe (Dieleman 1993: 119)—and the fact that the recently migrated "colored" or "others" (labeled *allochtonen*) have "not yet been assigned their place in the social hierarchy" (van Hulst 1995: 102–105), are just some of the indicators that racism within the Netherlands is still prevalent. Despite the passage of decades, this racism toward Antillean and Surinamese immigrants is still based on colonialism, while the inequality in the labor and housing markets is based on skin color (Cadat and Fennema 1996: 662–663), although the latter is obviously denied or dismissed by those who embrace the modernization theory.[16]

According to the modernization theory, immigrants moving to the Netherlands face an open society. "If some have more power than others, it is because they know the rules of the game better. Integration occurs when immigrants know the rules and participate in the system as much as the Dutch do" (Rath 1991: 180). However, if one is to acknowledge that power within society is derived from a socioeconomic mode of production in which racism and discrimination are key variables, a core country cannot be an open society; some have more access to power than others *because* of the socially constructed hierarchy in which sociocultural variables and phenotypical features are a crucial obstruction for immigrants in obtaining power and equal access to the labor and housing markets and the educational system.

In the Netherlands, there tends to be a serious lack of research regarding racism. Often the impact of racism and discrimination in schools, the labor market, and society as a whole is mentioned in one or two pages but seldom elaborated on, as it cannot be properly measured. More often than not, it is relegated to a footnote in a study about immigrants and their incorporation process (e.g., Amesz et al. 1989: 69). Some authors actually refuse to use the term "racism" altogether. The prominent sociologist Jan Rath (1991), for instance, uses the term "minorization."[17] Many authors (e.g., van Niekerk 1993) discuss the "multiple forms of lagging behind" that immigrants face and the "catching up" that these immigrants (first- and second-generation) have to do, but racism itself is seldom dealt with (e.g., Martens and Verweij 1997; van Niekerk 2000a; Vermeulen and Penninx 2000).

Xenophobia, racism and discrimination are not, however, always manifest in the same form throughout the contemporary world economy; local and temporal boundaries create a certain amount of variety. While discrimination, racism, and prejudices toward groups are constant factors, over time groups can move somewhat up or down the scale (e.g., Veenman 1995: 38–39), depending, among other variables, on which group is the main target of current racist agitation and government scrutiny.[18] For instance, in the Netherlands the main target of racist agitation has occasionally changed from Surinamese in the mid-1970s (e.g., Bovenkerk 1978; Bouw et al. 1981) to Turks and Moroccans in the 1980s (Elbers and Fennema 1993: 105), to increasing concerns about Antillean criminality in the 1990s (de Jong et al. 1997) and an obsession with Moroccan youngsters (and other Muslims) after 2001. There exists, of course, a crucial link between mass-migration, on the one hand, and the recurrent surge of racism, on the other (Mielants 2002). Recent elections in the Netherlands in which political parties with anti-migration platforms gained momentum, both in the mid-1990s (e.g., van Deelen 1996: 49; van den Brink 1994: 180–280) and in the 2002 general elections revolving around the assassinated Dutch politician Pim Fortuyn, and the subsequent emergence of xenophobic political parties under Congressman Geert Wilders, and Congresswoman Rita Verdonk would appear to confirm this hypothesis. Furthermore, racism itself is central in framing immigrants in a perpetuating form of marginalization, exemplified by a relatively high degree of poverty, social exclusion, and lack of opportunity within the Dutch labor market and, consequently, within society as a whole. Dutch research, however, rarely acknowledges the existence or impact of racism on these immigrants, let alone its centrality in their subjugation and exploitation, which only reflects the general Dutch taboo on discussing the significance of "everyday racism" in their own society (von der Dunk 1992: 55; Witte 1998).[19]

To their surprise, Willem Koot and Anco Ringeling (1984: 130) found that more than 50 percent of Antilleans interviewed spontaneously raised the issue of discrimination. On top of the daily experiences of "ordinary" racism (Essed 1991, 1992; Schouten 1994), Surinamese and Antillean immigrants find themselves concentrated in specific urban "concentration areas," which structurally lag behind those of the Dutch in terms of housing quality, education levels, household income, and labor-market possibilities. This was the case in the early 1980s (e.g., Valkenburg and ter Huurne 1983), the mid-1980s (e.g., Roelandt and Veenman 1987), and the 1990s (e.g., Dagevos et al. 1996; Veenman 1994). Using the figures in Veenman (1994: 69, 77), I will give a few examples regarding the participation of minorities in the labor force and compare these data with the SPVA-94 survey (in Martens 1995). The overall evolution of the participation of minorities in the labor market is as follows:[20]

	1991	1994	2002
Turkish	55%	44%	46%
Moroccan	43%	37%	46%
Surinamese	61%	60%	61%
Antillean	59%	55%	57%
Dutch	63%	62%	69%

One should also take a brief look at the concurrent growth of the largest *allochtone* population groups in the Netherlands (Veenman 1994: 21–22; Vermeulen and Penninx 2000: 9):

	1970	1975	1980	1985	1990	1997	2007
Turkish	30,400	76,500	119,600	155,600	205,898	280,000	368,000
Moroccan	21,600	42,200	71,800	111,300	167,810	233,000	329,000
Surinamese	29,000	79,200	145,700	181,400	236,995	287,000	333,000
Antillean	17,500	23,900	36,200	46,200	81,079	95,000	130,000

As immigration gradually increased over time, the Dutch labor market remained quite segmented, and most immigrants—if employed—had to continue to perform jobs of a very low functional level (van der Werf 1992: 27, 41). Nevertheless, for most Dutch scholars, the huge discrepancies between the figures for *autochtone* Dutch and *allochtone* immigrants are not explained in terms of structural discrimination and racism, despite the fact that discrimination and racism are structural phenomena in the Dutch labor market (e.g., Choenni 1992: 77) and society as a whole (Essed 1991). However, if one takes racism as a crucial, if not central, element to explain the extravagant differences between *autochtone* Dutch and *allochtone* immigrants in unemployment rates,[21] housing quality, education levels, and political participation, one can no longer use the phrase "catching up," since this erroneously implies that the position of immigrants can be altered provided that sufficient "objective" factors such as an economic upturn or higher schooling take place. Unfortunately, the myth of education as a crucial tool for the socioeconomic mobility of Surinamese and Antillean immigrants illustrates the impact of racism quite well: actual figures indicate that when employed, immigrants are generally employed below their functional level (e.g., Martens 1995; Martens and Verweij 1997).[22]

Most Dutch researchers, however, consider discrimination and racism as nothing more than an unfortunate variable in their attempts to explain why Surinamese and Antillean immigrants lag behind the Dutch. Instead, low education levels, language problems, lack of information and networks, cultural problems, even the structural problems of an underclass are mentioned (e.g., Martens and Verweij 1997). The general tone is that of modernization theory (e.g., Vermeulen and Penninx 1995)—that is, that it takes some time, but that after the second or third generation, it will be possible to catch up with the *autochtonen*. This in turn leads to references to recent improvements in housing quality and, especially, education (being the key to labor participation in the Netherlands; e.g., Albeda et al. 1989: 64; Martens 1995). Yet the selection process for employment (especially during economic downturns) more often than not is made by Dutch *autochtonen,* and it is a fact that they prefer to hire Dutch *autochtonen* over immigrant *allochtonen* (Roelandt and Veenman 1987: 49–53).[23]

From the period of the mass-immigration of Surinamese to the Netherlands in the 1970s, the Dutch have not regarded immigrants from distant colonies as fellow citizens (although legally they were and are), since the Dutch never considered them part of their "imagined community" (Rath 1991; Schuster 1999: 222). The Dutch government did not pay much attention to these "unwelcome" immigrants until 1983–1985 (van Hulst 1995: 87), when policymakers finally recognized that these immigrants were in the Netherlands to stay (van Niekerk 1995: 71–72). Nevertheless, cultural- and social-normative criteria continue to be used to avoid hiring minorities or to target them when people must be fired.[24] In contrast with the United States and the United Kingdom, a very small number of complaints regarding discrimination and racism ever make it to court (Roelandt and Veenman 1987: 52, 61). Victims of racism are not taken very seriously, and in the majority of racial incidents (including violent ones), no legal follow-up is undertaken (Veerman 1990; Witte 1997: 82, 92).[25] Furthermore, those who face discrimination also experience victimization (Choenni 1992: 91). It seems that immigrants who cope with discrimination in their daily activities are expected to simply deal with it and regard it as a "normal social phenomenon in the cold, harsh and reserved Dutch society" (Ford 1991: 77–78). While some modernization theorists do not deny the existence of racism or discrimination in the Netherlands (after all, there is literature about it by Dutch scholars such as Frans Bovenkerk and Justus Veenman), their central argument is that these unfortunate incidents do not interfere with or undermine the structural evolution of progress and the integration of immigrants in the Netherlands in the long run (which instead are referred to as stages of generational achievement and catching up).

Modernization theory argues that every migration process goes hand-in-hand with problems that have to be dealt with and barriers that have to be (can be and will be) overcome, just like those experienced by nineteenth-century peasants when they moved from the countryside to urban centers (Vermeulen and Penninx 1995: 207). The adaptation (and integration) of immigrants into their new community is not a smooth process and takes time, but above all, excessive pessimism is not warranted; the catching-up process in the housing and labor markets and in education is already under way, and patience is necessary (Vermeulen and Penninx 1995).[26] Not surprisingly, then, most (white) Dutch scholars trumpet the fact that, with regard to education, housing, and employment, second-generation immigrants are generally better off than the first generation, and many assume that the third generation will be better-off still (e.g., Martens 1995). Immigrants with successful careers are gratefully used to prove that not all immigrants are synonymous with socioeconomic deprivation and that catching up is not a myth but a serious possibility (e.g., Dagevos and Veenman 1992). It is undeniable that second-generation immigrants tend to be slightly better off than the first generation, but as Mies van Niekerk (1993: 91) admits in a brief footnote, "The relative lagging behind of *allochtonen* in Dutch society has on the whole not diminished. In some respects the differences between *autochtonen* and *allochtonen* have even increased." This is an understatement. The Dutch themselves have progressed tremendously in the past thirty years: in the labor market, the number of people with a low education has decreased tremendously,[27] and the expected education level for anyone functioning in Dutch society has moved upward considerably, causing many to speak of "degree inflation" (Dagevos 1995: 22–25; Roelandt and Veenman 1987: 62). All of this means that *allochtonen* have rather limited chances for employment (cf. Dagevos et al. 1997). Thus, while there has been an overall improvement for the general public in the so-called education race, access to the labor market and the functional level of jobs (Veenman 1996b), the *relative position* of *allochtonen* vis-à-vis Dutch *autochtonen* has not improved that much.[28] Even optimists have to admit that the discrepancy is quite astonishing; when minorities do have jobs, "they are generally of low status, low pay and unstable by nature" (Department of Social Affairs, quoted in Vermeulen and Penninx 1995: 218). Nevertheless modernization theory tries to sing a soothing tune by pointing out how second-generation immigrants are more attuned to the Western consumer-oriented society than their parents. Given that they tend to appreciate Western culture, film, and music, their cultural identity is said to be more "liberal" than that of their parents (Buijs and Nelissen 1995: 189). Second-generation Surinamese, especially those from mixed marriages, consider themselves "Dutch" (van Heelsum 1997). This display of ethnic-cultural identity, which confirms modernization theory's hopeful song of steady integration (or sometimes assimilation) dismisses any pessimistic point of view and even raises the question as to why it would be necessary to continue monitoring the "inevitable" progress of the third-generation immigrants who are going to feel more Dutch than the Dutch themselves.[29] Even if the second generation feels Dutch, has the same aspirations as the Dutch, and is completely oriented toward Dutch society, this does not automatically imply that the Dutch *autochtones* perceive these second-generation immigrants as Dutch. In fact, Dutch racism and discrimination can at times result in second-generation immigrants' becoming more aware of their cultural-ethnic roots (Haleber 1989: 199),[30] while some try to rid themselves of the "negative identity" associated with their Surinamese or Antillean roots, as these refer to a racial inferiority and not to a specific "nationality" with which one can identity (Cadat and Fennema 1996: 674). While some want to be seen as Dutch among the Dutch, it remains to be seen whether this is possible. Increasing far-right agitation in the Netherlands (e.g., van Donselaar 1997: 194–195) indicates that the process toward successful integration is far from complete, no matter how Dutch the second generation of immigrants considers itself. That said, an increase of interethnic marriages among second-generation immigrants with the *autochtones* is often marshaled as evidence of openness in Dutch society and the concurrent weakness of racial boundaries (e.g., Kalmijn and van Tubergen 2006).

According to the dominant modernization theory, only a small minority within the immigrant community is in danger of becoming marginalized; recent low-skilled immigrants who have many language problems are said to generally lag behind and, because of their awkward position, create a specific "subculture of welfare recipients" (e.g., van Niekerk 1993: 50). It is believed that this subculture subsequently creates an underclass (see Murray 1990), which has no financial incentive to go to work because of its access to the Dutch social-welfare system (van Niekerk 1993: 24). Thus, immigrants themselves are said to construct specific cultural reactions to the multiple setbacks they encounter during their difficult "catching-up process" (especially in a period of economic downturn). These supposed cultural reactions then create a cycle of exclusion and self-exclusion. Discrimination and stigmatization are acknowledged only as a reinforcement of this so-called cultural trend of "inward-looking alternative ethnic cultural ideology" (van Niekerk 1993: 52), which is thought to maintain their marginalization within society.[31]

In short, modernization theory states that this problematic minority within a minority has created difficulties for itself since its cultural reactions to societal problems has maintained and worsened its awkward situation. Consequently, the very slow process of integration is delayed, if not made extremely difficult, not by particular problems inherent in the recipient society, but by the cultural attitude of the recent immigrants themselves. The lack of constructing alternative role models within an underclass identifying itself with "no upward ambition, no future" is regarded as an important factor in the intergenerational continuity (Böcker 1995: 174). Thus, "internal psychological and cultural mechanisms reproduce their societal position" (Vermeulen and Penninx 1995: 217), which is, of course, a restatement of Oscar Lewis's insights into the culture of poverty. The immigrants' subculture of fatalism, helplessness, feelings of inferiority, weak family structures, escapism, and so on are said to have been "imported" into the Netherlands and reproduced with a special flavor (e.g., van Hulst 1995: 98). Pierre Bourdieu's notion of *habitus* is used to explain the behavior and psychological mechanisms that are embedded in the "subculture" of (impoverished) immigrants, inducing them to exclude themselves from mainstream society and all of its opportunities (e.g., Distelbrink and Pels 1996: 107; Sansone 1992: 9).

According to modernization theory, the immigrants' lack of motivation explains their high unemployment rate (Veenman and Martens 1995: 57) or their "hustling ethic" and "anti-labor ethic," which is said to reinforce any exclusion created by Dutch society, thus creating processes of self-exclusion (Sansone 1992: 142, 236–238). In this sense, Livio Sansone (1992) concluded that the immigrants themselves are responsible for maintaining a vicious perpetuating circle of (self-)exclusion because of their own subcultural habitus and reaction to the limited opportunities society has to offer them.[32] In the Netherlands, a recent noticeable shift has occurred in some official thinking, with an emphasis on "blaming the victim" (Wrench et al. 1996: 128); recent literature has stressed that immigrants lack the necessary cultural, social, and informational capital (e.g., Veenman 1996a: 8). The argument that was used to explain the inferior position of the first generation (especially the impact of the migration process itself and the difficult integration into Dutch society) cannot, however, be used to explain the position of second-generation immigrants. Therefore, authors have turned to "the composition of their 'peer group' (social capital), the imagined identity (cultural capital), and their ties with the country of origin" as limiting their options; the second-generation immigrants who are not oriented toward integration are said to be indulging in self-exclusion (Veenman 1996a: 96–97; Odé 2002: 44), which explains why they still "lag behind" in various ways (cf. Tillie and Slijper 2007: 222). In this explanation, the belief embedded in liberal meritocracy is maintained—that is, that individuals oriented toward Dutch society and willing to integrate themselves are capable of catching up and having a normal career (e.g., Dagevos and Veenman 1992), while those living in particular areas, creating a "wrong" cultural reaction or maintaining a "wrong" subculture with insufficient build-up of necessary cultural capital (Sansone 1992: 239) are doomed to lag behind (van Amersfoort and van Niekerk 2006).[33] However, social networks—and their ensuing possibilities for integration—are constructed not only by the immigrants themselves, but also by the dominant group in society—that is, the Dutch. It was the Dutch who organized the "white flight" from "concentration schools" in de Randstad,[34] not only affecting the educational results of (Surinamese and Antillean) immigrants (Crul and Doomernik 2003: 106; Veenman 1994: 64), but also limiting any possibility for immigrants to upgrade their social capital and to construct social networks outside their own socioeconomically deprived ethnic-cultural group (Distelbrink and Pels 1996: 120). Networks have proved to be extremely important for access to the regular Dutch labor market (e.g., Dagevos and Veenman 1996: 81–103).[35] Thus, the ethnic segmentation in schools (van Niekerk 1995: 55)—reinforcing the first- and second-generation immigrants' deprivation of social, cultural, and informational capital—coincides with segmentation in the labor market.[36] The ensuing situation forces immigrants into the informal economy (drug trafficking, prostitution), the black market (Dagevos and Veenman 1996: 94–100), and eventually into criminal behavior.

After mass-migration occurred in the early 1970s, Dutch authorities attempted an assimilation policy. By 1983, this policy had been abandoned, but an integration policy based on a truly multicultural society had also failed to take root. Many intellectuals continued to favor assimilation through a gradual process of "Hollandization" instead of defending a multicultural society wherein all groups can retain their own culture and identity while living together in harmony (Haleber 1989: 185, 192). Overall, the individual Dutch person has not gradually become more open-minded about a multicultural society; in the period 1985–1991, for example, all income groups became more ethnocentric than before (Scheepers et al. 1994: 196–198). Even the most ardent propagators of Dutch tolerance have to admit that racial violence—which always existed in the Netherlands after the post–World War II mass-migrations (e.g., Buis 1988: 129–143)—has been increasing, while "ordinary" politicians are now using language (regarding immigrants) that a generation ago was only acceptable in the circles of the far right (e.g., Zonneveld 1997: 53). The "new racism," with its cultural component of separation and segregation for everyone's sake, based on a superficial reading of authors such as Samuel P. Huntington, is replacing some previously discredited forms of racism (based on biological supremacy; Barkan 1992; Schuster 1999: 227; van Hensbroek and Koenis 1994: 56–57).[37] The mainstream media (e.g., popular weeklies such as *Elsevier* magazine) contributes greatly to the perpetuation of an "us" versus "them" atmosphere by continuously publishing articles with anti-immigrant rhetoric or by exposing people to anti-immigrant and xenophobic images (cf. Shadid 1998; Vergeer and Scheepers 1998).[38] This is, of course, not in accordance with modernization theory in which immigrants will gradually become an integral part of the community (e.g., Albeda et al. 1989: 64). Instead, the fact that racism remains such an important fact fundamentally undermines the basic myth of progress and integration that modernization theory offers to resolve the problem of increasing numbers of immigrants on Dutch soil.

This does not mean that Dutch racism is identical to French, Belgian, or German racism; specific local actions and contexts affect the nature and impact of racist phenomena within the core.[39] What I would like to emphasize is that migration and racism are intrinsically linked. Racism (initially ideological and biological) functioned as an ideology of legitimacy during the mass-migrations of Europeans as they established direct colonial rule within the colonies (e.g., Bovenkerk and Breuning-Van Leeuwen 1978: 35; Koot and Ringeling 1984: 28), while colonial rule (the exploitation of the periphery by the core powers) itself created the framework for a different kind of mass migration, this time of (ex-) colonial subjects, during and after formal (nominal) independence of the periphery. With mass-migration occurring almost without interruption in the post–World War II (nominal) independence of the periphery, neo-racism (based on cultural differences) made its way to the core, whether based on forced assimilation policies or de facto separation. It seems that in the Netherlands, both policies exist. On the one hand, immigrants are expected to assimilate (Bijlsma and Koopmans 1996a: 429–446; Çörüz 1997: 132; Eddaoudi 1998: 73–75), which explains why the absence of an *allochtone* ethnic/cultural identity is regarded as a bonus for integration (e.g., van Heelsum 1997), while on the other hand, immigrants are expected to create their own "pillar" in a segmented society in which the reallocation of public funds and services is based on institutionalized segmentation among the three traditional Dutch networks

(Lijphart 1982; Penninx et al. 1993: 210; Rath 1991: 119–120).[40] It is therefore evident that newcomers have a hard time, since they do not belong to any established pillar. The construction of a minority pillar (e.g., Islamic pillars) takes quite some time (Doomernik 1991; Shadid and van Koningsveld 1990: 11), and in a sense it is clear that a new (minor) pillar for some minorities (e.g., Muslim immigrants from Suriname, Turkey, and Morocco) will not create ample resources and network benefits for all immigrants, since immigrant communities themselves (e.g., the Surinamese) are far from homogenous (e.g., Leistra 1995: 59–75). This in turn makes it very hard for them to emancipate according to a model of "pillarization" (cf. Cross and Entzinger 1988: 16). Besides, almost all resources were partitioned among the existing pillars a long time ago. "Codified institutionalized pluralism" is therefore quite difficult to achieve (Entzinger 1988) and very problematic from the ethnic minorities' point of view (Gowricharn 1997).

Last but not least, modernization theory trumpets any statistical improvement it can find to illustrate the unimportance (or secondary importance) of racism that immigrants face and to highlight the success of steady integration. True, some social policies directed by the Dutch welfare state for the poor do benefit first- and second-generation immigrants, since they are located at the bottom rungs of society. Unfortunately, however, the Dutch welfare state has restricted its involvement in the housing market and the allocation of unemployment benefits over the past fifteen years. Furthermore, heralding statistics that highlight the helping hand of the government in its fight against poverty (financial deprivation) does not necessarily guarantee the end of social exclusion (Room 1997: 221–231). For some, it is actually the other way around. In Dutch literature on "social exclusion," minorities are proved to be four times more likely to be unemployed (over the long term) than are Dutch people (van der Werf 1992: 34). Some link this phenomenon to their "structural dependence on the government." They deplore their "consistent dependence on the state regarding income, housing, health, juridical assistance and so forth." "It seems," to quote Godfried Engbersen (1994: 126), "that the structure and execution of the social security system have contributed to the construction of an idle class of social security benefactors. . . . It is, of course, this prolonged structural dependence on the state which leads to social isolation and societal alienation, and ultimately to the creation of a permanent underclass."

Public-opinion research also indicates that since the 1990s, the Dutch— particularly people between twenty and twenty-five years of age—have become less tolerant toward immigrants (Deraeck 1994: 21).[41] On several occasions, the Dutch government has enacted legislation to promote equal treatment and to combat discrimination, but "the power of legislation should not be overestimated. . . . [C]ompliance with self-regulating agreements cannot be enforced through criminal law" (van den Braak 1996: 49–50). Despite government actions and well-intentioned legislation to integrate new immigrant groups and reduce their unfavorable position in the labor market, these plans have not been very effective. Affirmative action enacted in government organizations and institutions has helped, but there were limited spillover effects in the private sector. Not only do employers resist affirmative-action policies, which in Dutch is called "positive discrimination," but public opinion is also opposed to these measures; they have been supported by no more than 10–20 percent of the population (Gras 1996: 62–64). In many cases, job advertisements from companies emphasizing equal opportunity are mere window dressing (Leistra 1995: 87). Constant variables such as education, age, sex, occupational level, and region indicate that there is still a large discrepancy between the unemployment figures of native Dutch and those of first- and second-generation immigrants (Wrench et al. 1996: 40). Nor are prospects very bright for immigrants in the Netherlands. Most immigrants (such as the Surinamese and Antilleans) live within certain concentrated areas of de Randstad (Engbersen and Snel 1997: 293–298) and face high unemployment, poverty, and crime rates.

Low-level education likely has something to do with this problem. But the "white flight" of Dutch pupils from concentration schools reinforces the cultural isolation and educational limits of first- and second-generation immigrant children. Of 230 elementary schools in Amsterdam, 89 were white, 71 were mixed, and 70 were black (Leistra 1995: 85). Modernization theory has always assumed that first- and second-generation immigrants lag behind in education because of their socioeconomic status, which will improve in the long run (van Langen and Jungbluth 1990). Indeed, the official government line of thought was that no distinction should be made between immigrant children and *autochtone* children from a low socioeconomic background, since both groups have to overcome the problems inherent to their backgrounds (Driessen 1990; Wolbers and Driessen 1996: 349–364). Others focus predominantly on the cultural factor; the "cultural capital" of immigrants is said to be incompatible with the mainstream culture of Dutch society (Pels and Veenman 1996: 139–140; Teunissen and Matthijssen 1996: 90–91). Some want to emphasize both socioeconomic and cultural aspects (e.g., Latuheru and Hessels 1996). But what is too easily forgotten is precisely the fact that a racial phenomenon such as "white flight" from concentration schools (e.g., Tazelaar 1996: 77–78; Teunissen 1996: 25–26) actually prevents (or, at least, interferes with) "catching up" and societal integration, since "black schools" become the equivalent of bad schools, where low-class white Dutch only reluctantly study (Tazelaar 1996: 73). Even in "white" schools, the status of immigrant children is generally low, and discrimination is rampant. Isolation from Dutch society and its networks in "colored" concentration schools and the provocation of or discrimination against minority immigrants in "white" schools (Teunissen and Matthijssen 1996: 92)—both results of Dutch racism—undermine the myth of Dutch tolerance toward immigrants and the possibility of immigrants' "catching up" in the Netherlands. This racial stratification in the educational system, in which ethnic-based educational inequality remains very apparent (Tolsma et al. 2007), reflects the society they live in and the polarization they have to endure in the labor market.[42] It is not surprising, then, that many feel compelled to flee into the semi-illegal activities of the informal economy (prostitution, selling drugs, etc.), which is reflected in crime rates. Surinamese made up 12 percent of the total number of inmates in Dutch prisons while representing only 2 percent of the general population (Leistra 1995: 179). In 1996, Antilleans constituted 6 percent of the total number of inmates in Dutch prisons (Bovenkerk 2002: 178) while not representing even 1 percent of the general population (Abrahamse 1997: 63). In addition, of all Surinamese and Antillean youngsters, 12 percent have attempted suicide at least once, compared with 5 percent of Dutch youngsters (Leistra 1995: 186). Ethnic minorities also suffer worse health (Stronks et al. 2001) and disproportionate mortality rates due to their disadvantageous socioeconomic condition (Bos et al. 2004). The general trend of violent crimes committed by Antilleans—and by young Antillean immigrants in particular (de Jong et al. 1997: 65–66)—raises the question whether "(sub)cultural factors" lead immigrants to crime and depression? Or, rather, is it Dutch society that prevents these groups from "catching up" in the first place?

The impossibility of catching up because of the immigrants' position within society is publicly denied by modernization theorists. Just as any Third World "developing country" is (at least, theoretically) capable of catching up in the world economy and developing like a European nation, so every immigrant is capable of adapting and integrating himself or herself and of catching up after some time (Tinnemans 1994: 400). However, Dutch society, propagated as an open and pluralistic society (e.g., Roelandt 1997) in contrast to the United States (which represents a segmented, stratified system), is actually less tolerant than it is inclined to believe.[43]

Modernization theorists point out that surveys indicate employers claim to discriminate less towards immigrants than in the past (e.g., Veenman 1995: 43), but figures show that a substantial portion of the Dutch population does not like or accept the reality of a Dutch multicultural society (e.g., Abrahamse 1997: 9). True, there has always been less outright violence in the Netherlands toward immigrants than in France, Germany, or the United Kingdom (Ford 1991: 76). But far-right agitation against immigrants has increased (Scheepers et al. 1994: 185), as has racial violence (van Donselaar 1995: 59). More important, the Dutch "soft, compensatory welfare state" is gradually being transformed into a leaner and meaner social-security system. Government subsidies in the housing sector—particularly helpful to ethnic minorities—have also diminished (e.g., van Dugteren 1993).[44] This leads one to question the extent to which racism will increase within the core as immigration from the periphery continues to increase.

Conclusions and Afterthoughts

Reallocations of industries from the core to the semi-periphery (a world-system phenomenon) and processes of automation wherein high technology replaces blue-collar jobs (in which immigrants are over-represented) have a serious impact on the position of immigrants in the labor markets of core countries. Given the large pool of unemployed, discrimination in the selection process will remain an option for employers and job agencies. More highly educated workers will continue to replace the very low educated (an aspect of degree inflation) within the world cities of the core. New immigrants (refugees and asylum seekers) will increase competition for low-wage jobs in the labor market. Moreover, the nature of these jobs will be less appealing: temporary jobs with no long-term employment security, fewer benefits or entitlements, and less favorable working conditions. At a time when increasing numbers of immigrants are moving from the periphery or semi-periphery to core nation-states such as the Netherlands, the gap between the "haves" and the "have nots" is widening. The external socioeconomic polarization between the North and the South as a result of the division of labor among the core, semi-periphery, and periphery is now manifesting itself within the world cities of the world system and, most predominantly, among the immigrants from the periphery. De Randstad is a good example of a world city within the core coping with escalating problems, tensions, and strife between an increasing number of immigrants from the periphery and semi-periphery, on the one hand, and the *autochtone* population (in this case study, the Dutch), on the other.[45]

In de Randstad, where immigrants are over-represented, some jobs have been disappearing in the last few decades, particularly in the industrial sector where immigrants are over-represented. Instead, those jobs are mostly being replaced by low-paid, part-time work in the service industry (known as "junk jobs")—that is, flexible, part-time, seasonal jobs that demand no investment from employers and are easily done away with at the next economic downturn. At the same time, the educational requirements for those low-quality jobs steadily increase due to degree inflation. Add to all this indirect and direct methods of discrimination, and the future does not look very bright for first- and second-generation immigrants in the labor market of a core country like the Netherlands. Unfortunately, voluntary "codes of practice" against racism and discrimination, or the favoring of affirmative action, are seldom observed, and their effects have been "relatively insignificant" in the Netherlands (e.g., Wrench 1996: 137).

An indication of the enormous pressures of mass-migration on core nation-states is the general tightening of immigration laws and controls and the continuing experiments with various return migration policies since the 1970s.[46] This is also the case in the Netherlands, where during the 1990s more than $1 million was spent in the Dutch Antilles, not on investments or "developmental aid," but on information campaigns with the explicit purpose of dissuading Antilleans from immigrating to the Netherlands (van Hulst 1995: 109). Several job-related educational projects have also been organized by the Netherlands in major emigration countries such as Morocco and Turkey, and even in the Dutch Antilles, to lure immigrants back to their places of origin, but with very limited results. Repatriation by force of illegal immigrants has also been on the increase in most core countries, and the Netherlands is no exception in this matter, either.

After the economic profitability of the Dutch Antilles disappeared, it had been the position of multiple successive Dutch governments that the Antilles must be "prepared" for independence. Nevertheless, important plebiscites in the Antilles in 1993 overwhelmingly rejected independence (Oostindie 1998: 339), leaving the Dutch authorities with two major fears: one of potential military intervention, as in 1969; the other of massive migration to the Netherlands.[47] Indeed, the twin burden of increased Caribbean immigration to the Netherlands and continuing financial aid to the Dutch semi-peripheral islands are the main reasons the Dutch have continually attempted to push the islands toward independence (van Hulst 2000: 117). It is important to acknowledge, however, that this curbing of financial aid to the periphery is linked with the curbing of the welfare state within core states throughout the entire world system, which in turn is linked to globalization and worldwide socioeconomic polarization undermining interstate stability and civil society alike (Kentor and Mielants 2007).

It is true that in the past, the Dutch government crafted legislation to protect immigrants, although against the will of the majority of employees and employers alike (Veenman 1995: 66). Therefore, it is questionable whether any future legislation will have a serious effect on employment figures for first- and second-generation immigrants. Nor is there evidence that the much praised Dutch "racial tolerance" is increasing toward immigrants; rather, the opposite is true, and during the past two decades a clear racial/ethnic hierarchy has been in the making, with the Dutch currently on top, followed by Surinamese and Turkish immigrants, and Antilleans and Moroccans at the bottom (cf. Hagendoorn and Hraba 1989; Essed and Trienekens 2008: 56).

As of 2000, more and more scholars, journalists and politicians alike started to question the Dutch version of multiculturalism and its variants based on modernization theory (e.g., Scheffer 2000; Koopmans 2002). In the context of the terrorist attacks of September 11, 2001, and the assassination of the prominent Dutch artist Theo van Gogh by a Dutch Muslim in 2004 (see Buruma 2006), a remarkable turn towards Islamophobia can be noted (Tayob 2006). Dutch society has hardened considerably over the past few years in terms of migration policies, as well as in its perception of ethnic minorities, particularly those who embrace Islam (Coenders et al. 2008). A challenge to the long-lasting modernization-theory paradigm unfortunately did not result in a genuine critical reevaluation of postcolonial relations and interethnic policies (Essed and Nimako 2006). Instead, the continuation of a long-lasting tradition of problematizing the "other" while minimizing the effects of pervasive institutional discrimination and the persistence of racism remains in vogue (Vasta 2007), some notable scholarly exceptions notwithstanding. Unfortunately, more racism and hostility toward immigrants loom on the horizon. Pretending otherwise and naively believing in modernization theory is simply a theoretical fallacy.

Notes

1. One must commence by acknowledging that the Surinamese are themselves a product of historical migration within the Dutch colonial empire; together with the original Indians who lived there, the Dutch "imported" nearly 300,000 African slaves and, after 1863, nearly 65,000 Javanese of Chinese origin (Leistra 1995: 18–19).

2. There was a long tradition of migration from colonies to the colonizing countries, and the Dutch empire was no exception to this phenomenon. In the eighteenth century, hundreds of house slaves and concubines were "imported" to the United Provinces, and some children born of Surinamese concubines were also sent there for their education. Jews in Suriname often emigrated to the Netherlands to study, many returning to Suriname to form part of the upper class as lawyers and doctors. Since 1882, when the medical school in Paramaribo was founded, a continuous flow of students specializing as doctors and teachers has studied in the Netherlands (Vogel 1992). Thus, until the Great Depression, emigration to the Netherlands was mostly an elitist phenomenon (Bovenkerk 1975: 6–8). From the 1930s on, more impoverished Surinamese moved to the Netherlands (Openneer 1995: 8), but the overall number of Surinamese immigrants living in the Netherlands remained small—for example, about 3,000 in 1946 (Oostindie 1998: 253).

3. In November 1971, the Dutch Parliament approved in principle the independence of Suriname and the Dutch Antilles. Throughout the 1960s, the enormous fear of an overflow of immigrants from Suriname spread from the tabloids to respected newspapers, creating a mentality of criminalization of the Surinamese migrants (Schuster 1999: 129–131). Surinamese reluctance to work, the impact of crime, and the depiction of Surinamese as parasites of the Dutch social-security system made headlines in 1972. In December 1972, some members of Parliament (MPs) claimed that the constitution had to be amended to stop the inflow of these immigrants. In the summer of 1973, the Dutch Parliament debated putting a halt to immigration. In October 1974, some MPs proposed sending unemployed Surinamese back, while headlines about a possible stop in immigration were reprinted in Suriname. This created exactly the opposite result from what the Netherlands had wanted

to achieve, as more Surinamese became determined to move to beat the deadline (van Amersfoort 1987: 475–490). The same phenomenon occurred in England during the parliamentary debates on the Commonwealth Act (between November 1961 and July 1, 1962): immigration from the West Indies, Pakistan, and India soared due to a "rush to beat the ban" (Bovenkerk 1975). Ironically, it was the Dutch government's desire to stop Surinamese immigration to the Netherlands that caused it to push Suriname toward independence (Buddingh' 2000: 298–299). During the mid-1970s, the Dutch government also attempted to exclude many Surinamese who were already residing in the Netherlands from obtaining Dutch citizenship the moment Suriname became independent (Schuster 1999: 157–158; van Amersfoort and Penninx 1998: 49).

    4. Mass-migration is thus not so much a question of geographic distance or the desire of an ideal-typical "homo economicus" to migrate from a region in the periphery to any wealthy region in the core. Ultimately, the migration process has to be analyzed in the historical context of the postcolonial world system, on the one hand, and the existing immigrant networks within it, on the other, since these are crucially important variables in defining the parameters in which most households make decisions regarding their strategies for international mobility (Rex 1999: 154–155).

    5. Some used a savings system known as *kasmoni* to finance their passage. A form of collective capital formation that is used by its participants to finance huge costs, *kasmoni* involves a kind of rotating credit association (Bovenkerk 1975).

    6. As Alejandro Portes and Ruben Rumbaut (1996: 276) indicate, "The migration process may become self-sustaining through the construction of increasingly dense social ties across space."

    7. In the case of Suriname, it succeeded, whereas in the case of the Antilles, it failed.

    8. The Dutch Antilles consist of Aruba (pop. 103,000), Bonaire (pop. 11,500), and Curaçao (also known as the Leeward or ABC Islands; pop. 137,000) close to the coast of Venezuela, and St. Eustatius (pop. 2,700), Saba (pop. 1,500), and St. Maarten (the Windward Islands; pop. 39,000) to the east of Puerto Rico. These population figures are only estimates for 2007 provided by the Dutch Bureau of the Census (available online at www.cbs.an/population). When discussing "Antilleans," I am referring to Dutch Antilleans, unless specified otherwise.

    9. In the statute of 1954, which granted autonomy, both parts of the kingdom (i.e., the Dutch Antilles and the Netherlands) are obliged to offer each other financial aid. In this sense, the Dutch Antilles are somewhat like a Dutch province overseas (Koot and Ringeling 1984: 43), though in the spring of 2007, a new agreement was in the making between the Netherlands and its Caribbean islands: see www.minbzk.nl/aspx/download.aspx?file=/contents/pages/86296/akkoord.pdf.

    10. The implementation of a minimum wage in 1972, legislation to protect employees from being randomly sacked by large companies in 1974, and a minimal social-security system (without unemployment benefits) are still better than what can be found on several of the other islands in the region.

    11. This does not imply that the Antilleans did not face any discrimination, as is pointed out by Koot (1979: 139). "In the Netherlands there is strong discrimination against people of color, and the majority of unemployed Antilleans would only be candidates for work that Dutch do not find attractive."

    12. After 1973, there was an important change in the socioeconomic status of the migrants in that more Antilleans came to the Netherlands without jobs: in 1973, only one in three Antillean immigrants had a job; in 1981, this group had decreased to one in six. From

1972 on, the number of blue-collar laborers increased compared with the number of white-collar laborers and small businessmen. In 1973, the ratio of white-collar to blue-collar laborers was three to one, while in 1980 it was almost one to one (Koot and Ringeling 1984: 95).

13. The closure of the Lago refinery in 1985 caused a harsh socioeconomic crisis; aside from the loss of jobs, small suppliers also went out of business. There appears to be a direct relationship between the closure of the refinery, which led to diminished government income and purchasing power for the population near the site, and increased emigration (Nicolaas 1990: 106–107; Oostindie 1988: 63).

14. Thus, 8 percent of all people living in de Randstad are Surinamese, while Surinamese represent only 2.5 percent of the general population in the Netherlands. Of course, special areas within those cities are highly concentrated (from 10 percent to 30 percent; Martens and Verweij 1997). Yet the Dutch (e.g., Quispel 1997; van Gemert 1995: 76; van Niekerk 2000b: 77) insist that, unlike in the United States, ghettos are nonexistent in the Netherlands because they constitute not "mono-ethnic districts" but, rather, a mix of heterogeneous neighborhoods (Surinamese, Antillean, Moroccan, Turkish immigrants, etc.). Similarly, racism is a phenomenon that exists in Anglo-Saxon societies, and therefore the word clearly is not applicable to the situation in the Netherlands (which is a recurrent theme in Aalberts 1996; Bovenkerk et al. 1985: 313–314, 322; Entzinger 1980; Polhuis 1994: 126–127, 142–143; van den Berg 1992; Vuijsje 1986). Dutch scholars who study "ethnic concentrations" in the Netherlands also often conclude that these are not problematic in themselves (Bolt et al. 2002).

15. This was particularly the case in de Randstad in the period 1971–1976, during the first wave of mass-migration from the periphery (de Bokx 1997; Elbers and Fennema 1993: 101). The mass-migration of almost 300,000 Dutch Indonesian refugees during the 1950s did not provoke similar riots, since the government and the public regarded the Dutch Indonesians not as immigrants but as fellow Dutchmen who were part of their collective imagined identity and were only "returning home" during a period of national reconstruction (Schuster 1999: 112–116).

16. In Dutch, the dictionary defines *allochtonen* as referring to those immigrants who have a different *cultural* background from that of the Dutch. According to Dutch government authorities, the first generation of *allochtonen* refers to non-Western immigrants who were born abroad, whereas the second generation of *allochtonen* refers to those who were born in the Netherlands but have at least one parent who was born abroad.

17. Influential scholars such as Rinus Penninx, Jeanette Schoorl, and Carlo van Praag (1993: 191) also do not like to use the concepts of racism and discrimination. Instead, they use the concept "negative position allocation" in the labor and housing markets. The Dutch like to see themselves as tolerant toward strangers and immigrants: geographers mention the "openness of land and sea routes"; psychologists interpret tolerance as part of the Dutch character; historians herald the tolerant profitmaking spirit of the United Provinces as welcoming all traders (developing a cosmopolitan attitude of tolerance); and political scientists regard the Dutch "pillarization" as a model of consensus, accepting different points of view (Schuster 1999: 250–252). Accusations of racism and discrimination toward immigrants are not appreciated (Bovenkerk 1978: 9). On the contrary, the Netherlands is proudly pointed to as a tolerant country that has always welcomed the arrival (and subsequent integration) of new immigrants (e.g., Lucassen and Penninx 1994). One of my goals, then, is to deconstruct "the illusion of exemplary tolerance" in the Netherlands (Oostindie 1988: 55), as if the Netherlands was different from other core countries in the capitalist world economy.

18. As Cadat and Fennema (1996: 676) put it, "All human beings who are discriminated against are equal, but some victims are more equal than others."

19. Of course, it is not taboo to state publicly all kinds of "truths" about refugees or minorities, as this is said to "clarify the discussion," but discussing racism simply is not done, as Teun van Dijk (1998: 119) points out. At best, the Dutch talk about prejudices, discrimination, minorization, or ethnic hierarchies (e.g., Hagendoorn 1986). But actually using the word "racism" is unjustifiable (Witte 1997: 82), as it undermines the collective myth and self-image of Dutch tolerance (van Dijk 1998: 128). Preferences for terms such as "pluralism" and "ethnicism" rather than "racism," as Blakely (1993: 288) points out, could provide possible "new shields for racism." Is it coincidental that before the twenty-first century, not a single monument in the Netherlands was dedicated to the existence of slavery (cf. Oostindie 1999; Willemsen 2006)?

20. SPVA stands for Social Position and Use of Provisions by Ethnic Minorities. Some clarifications are necessary. The general overhaul of the Dutch welfare system in the 1980s created many part-time jobs (Dagevos 1995: 39–41) and deliberately pushed many from unemployment figures to the "disabled"/"unfit to work" category, which increased from fewer than 200,000 people in 1970 to more than 900,000 in 1994 (Dagevos 1995: 11). The longtime unemployed and those unemployed of a certain age (over fifty), as well as people who interrupt their careers and stop working (for a year or so) without pay, including those who are looking for work but who are not officially registered as such, and the "blackballed unemployed" are not included in these figures (Wolff and Penninx 1994). The "blackballed" are those who were caught working while receiving unemployment benefits (thus avoiding taxes); they are often financially penalized by not receiving any unemployment benefits for a period of several months (or even longer, depending on the infraction). During this period, they also "disappear" from the official unemployment figures, which are used to attract foreign businesses. Also, the frequent changes in the definition of "unemployment" (e.g., in 1981 and 1991) left a lot of people out of the unemployment statistics (van der Werf 1992: 32–34). A good statistical overview in English can be found online at www2 .fmg.uva.nl/imes/stats.htm.

21. After the first mass-migration of Surinamese immigrants to the Netherlands, Bovenkerk (1978) clearly demonstrated that there was discrimination in the Dutch labor market; people with darker skin had fewer opportunities to find jobs than did Dutch with the same education and experience. In 28 percent of the investigated cases, there were clear forms of discrimination against people with darker skin. More recently, Bovenkerk—one of the few Dutch social scientists who bothered to study the phenomenon of discrimination in the Netherlands—stated that discrimination had increased significantly over the past fifteen years and that it is probably the main cause of unemployment among *allochtonen* (quoted in Wolff and Penninx 1993: 25–26). Qualitative research such as that conducted by Bovenkerk has indicated many prejudices against foreign employees; in a 1993 survey, 80 percent of personnel managers interviewed preferred applicants with a Dutch background in the case of equally qualified applicants, while 20 percent of the interviewees found a person from an ethnic minority to be completely unacceptable (Wrench et al. 1996: 43). Unemployment among the Surinamese and Antilleans remained very high during the 1980s and early 1990s: 26 percent and 31 percent, respectively, were unemployed in 1991, whereas the unemployment rate among Dutch *autochtonen* did not exceed 7 percent. Even though the unemployment rate of Surinamese and Antilleans had declined to 10 percent and 13 percent, respectively, by 1998, after the economic upturn of the late 1990s set in, their unemployment rate was still about three times higher than that of Dutch *autochtonen*

(4 percent). Registered unemployment among Moroccan and Turkish immigrants was even higher, at 18 percent and 20 percent, respectively (Vermeulen and Penninx 2000: 13).

22. Thus, for immigrants higher education does not necessarily lead to a job with a higher functional level. Higher-educated Surinamese and Antilleans often end up in lower functions (Martens and Verweij 1997: 42–44; Wolff and Penninx 1993: 91), which is related to pre-entry and post-entry discrimination (Dagevos 1995: 86–87). In addition, both low-educated and highly educated minorities are three times more likely to be unemployed than their Dutch counterparts, revealing that ethnic background perhaps has more to do with "employability" than does education.

23. Job agencies that mediate between employers and employees have pre-selections that correspond to the basic demands of the employer. These can be ethnocentric and therefore explain why minorities with equal education and work experience still have fewer opportunities in the Dutch labor market. Ethnocentrism and discrimination are also apparent when selecting employees (Bovenkerk and Breuning-Van Leeuwen 1978: 52–56; Koot and Ringeling 1984: 132–133). People in charge of selecting employees are motivated by various factors, including the fear of extra costs such as child care, separate holidays, and extra attention for minorities. Minorities are also considered "risk groups" as they are perceived as being less motivated, unreliable, and more often sick and as taking longer holidays. There is also a fear of negative reactions within the existing team of employees and the "unpleasant surprise" for clients and customers when they are faced with minorities (Choenni 1992: 85–86; Wolff and Penninx 1993: 24, 65–68; Wrench et al. 1996; cf. also Meertens 1997: 45; Veenman 1995: 58). Job agencies discriminate because employers stimulate them to do so. Thus, prejudices such as the following are maintained: immigrants are lazy because they do not want to work; immigrants are four times more often unemployed than the Dutch, confirming that they are lazy. For an overview of studies related to discrimination from job agencies, see Choenni (1992: 83–84). The question is the extent to which this attitude will induce minorities to behave in ways that the Dutch expect of them (Bovenkerk 1978: 27; Veenman 1995: 60).

24. In the Netherlands, 40 percent of those questioned in a survey preferred firing an *allochtone* to an *autochtone* employee (Fennema 1997: 156). A commonplace prejudice is that Antilleans "wander around" without employment before they are thirty, because this is a part of their "cultural way of life" (e.g., Koot and Ringeling 1984: 126–127; Schumacher 1987: 123). Of course, such "common knowledge" reinforces the tendency not to hire Antilleans, which in turn is regarded as evidence that they are culturally lazy.

25. "A policy of active prosecution is lacking, and only in a small amount of cases, a complaint will lead to actual criminal prosecution. In principle, the onus of proof is with the plaintiff, and demonstrating the occurrence of discrimination is very difficult. Litigation is often a lengthy and costly matter, and sanctions are often too light. Complaints are not often dealt with seriously enough by the Police or the Public Prosecutor, and furthermore, most cases do not lead to conviction of the perpetrators. Even when they do, the penalties imposed are insignificant" (Wrench et al. 1996: 135).

26. Not surprisingly, most Dutch studies on migration and immigrants present themselves just as a-theoretically as International Monetary Fund recommendations for developing countries. But the complicity of bureaucrats who transform themselves into academics (and subsequently legitimize the public policies of politicians who will later order the next series of technical studies from them) should not be underestimated, as they enable American modernization theory and its structural-functionalist variants to colonize the entire field (Martiniello 1993). Not coincidentally, critical voices emanating from ethnic minorities

themselves (e.g., Philomena Essed, Ruben Gowricharn) are often suppressed when they do not conform to the prevailing orthodoxy (cf. El-Fers and Nibbering 1998: 92–99) and therefore are frequently relegated to minor and obscure alternative presses (e.g., Eddaoudi 1998; Helder and Gravenberch 1998), effectively de-legitimizing dissenting voices (cf. Essed 1999).

27. If one compares the average monthly income (after taxes) of ethnic minorities with those of the Dutch, the gap actually increased in the period 1988–1991 (Veenman 1994: 86).

28. Veenman (1996b: 164) and other scholars have repeatedly claimed that second-generation Antilleans have almost "caught up" with the Dutch. It remains to be seen to what extent this is actually so. Most Antilleans who arrived before the mid-1970s were part of a relatively small "elite" migration (Koot 1979) and were able to profit from the economic upturn of the 1960s. Those who arrived after the mid-1970s were from a lower social class and had to deal with an economic downturn. Furthermore, not all Antilleans are black, so some may escape discrimination (e.g., Koot and Ringeling 1984: 157–167; van Hulst 1995: 100). From the 1990s onward, more socioeconomically deprived Antilleans arrived in de Randstad, where some were responsible for committing crimes (cf. de Jong et al. 1997). Since there is a correlation between unemployment among Antilleans and their housing with other (recently arrived) Antilleans in the same area (e.g., Tesser et al. 1995), it remains to be seen whether the Antillean community of immigrants will be able to achieve significant upward social mobility in the years to come.

29. It is clear that some second-generation Surinamese still identify themselves as Hindustani, Creoles, Javans, and so on (Veenman and Martens 1995: 8–9).

30. Although the electoral breakthrough of the far right continues to be more difficult in the Netherlands than in France or Belgium because of different political-juridical structures (e.g., van Donselaar 1997: 189–206), the Dutch communal and general elections in the spring of 2002 gave a tremendous boost to Islamophobic and anti-immigrant politicians within the party of the assassinated politician Pim Fortuyn. At the same time, the "respectable" ruling right-wing conservative party, the Volkspartij Voor Democratie (People's Party for Democracy), took over some of the far-right rhetoric, promoting a more restrictive policy toward political refugees and asylum seekers, as well as taking an outright assimilationist position (van den Brink 1994: 238; Vermeulen and Penninx 1995: 12; Schmeets et al. 1996: 131–141). Interestingly, the leftist Socialist Party (SP) embraced a similar assimilationist position earlier (Tinnemans 1994: 258).

31. The studies by Mies van Niekerk (1993, 2000) are a good example of the way mainstream Dutch social scientists embrace modernization theory. In her magnum opus on the presence of the Surinamese in the Netherlands, van Niekerk (2000a: 209) concludes that it is the "perception of discrimination and stigmatization that initiates a reaction which in turn has an impact on one's attitude towards social development. . . . [E]ven more obvious is the oppositional attitude amongst low educated Surinamese males who prefer non-regular forms of survival over the traditional path of social success." And when Surinamese with Hindustani backgrounds appear to be more successful in Dutch society than the Creoles who left Suriname at the same time, this is due to "the strong cohesion of kinship networks prevalent in this ethnic community that functions as a moral community," as opposed to the more "ghetto-specific behavior" among the Creoles (van Niekerk 2000: 215). It should therefore come as no surprise that both John Ogbu's (1987) "folk theory of success" and Alejandro Portes's (1995) emphasis on "ethnic networks" form the theoretical backbone of her study, which was subsequently translated into English with special funds from the Dutch government (van Niekerk 2002). For a condensed English version of her arguments about

the "optimism" of the Indo-Surinamese versus the "attitudes" of the Afro-Surinamese, see van Niekerk 2004.

32. For Hans van Hulst (1997), the main problem with Antillean migrants is their "cultural luggage" and their socialization in the Antilles: they left a segregated society and look on the Dutch with ambivalence and resistance caused by their lifestyle and experiences in the Antilles. Their negative self-image, low-profile attitude, and lack of self-esteem are also said to be part of their subculture (van Hulst 1997: 127). Yet aggressiveness and a lack of insight into their real opportunities are due to their dismal education in the Antilles by their (lower-class) families. Their subculture is described as one of no future, drug use, criminal behavior, and so on. A large part of the Antillean immigrants were already marginalized in the Antilles (van Hulst 1997: 148), and this situation merely continues (van Hulst 1997: 180) in the Netherlands. According to van Hulst, a re-socialization process in the Netherlands is necessary, as is re-education from zero (van Hulst 1997: 233), together with redefining the Antilleans' mental attitudes and cultural assertiveness (van Hulst 1997: 235, 249), which of course reinforces the negative self-perception of Antilleans (maintaining a self-fulfilling prophecy of negativism and failure; van Hulst 1997: 274). It is the mentality of the Antilleans, passed on from generation to generation through education and socialization and embedded in their psyches, that is the problem (van Hulst 1997: 280). The negative self-image of Antilleans on an individual and collective level, caused by centuries of segregation and anti-cohesive sentiments, has left its subjective mark upon the lower class (van Hulst 1997: 295), causing extreme forms of apathy, inertia, and lethargy (van Hulst 1997: 306). These psychological factors do not exist in a cultural vacuum. Therefore, the lower-class subculture of negativism, rejection, and resistance are the main problems that have to be dealt with (van Hulst 1997: 307). See also van San (1998). A similar treatment of Moroccan youngsters can be found in the study by Frank van Gemert (1998).

33. From here it is only a small step to advocate the reconstruction of social-control mechanisms within immigrant families and communities (as advocated by Daniel P. Moynihan in 1969), since it is primarily their (ethnic-cultural) behavior and attitudes that have to change (Veenman 1996a: 113).

34. As of 1996, approximately 30 percent of all Antilleans and more than 50 percent of all Surinamese immigrants lived in de Randstad (Abrahamse 1997: 67). In Amsterdam and Rotterdam, respectively, 48 percent and 45 percent of all elementary schools had more than 60 percent *allochtone* pupils (Abrahamse 1997: 79). Jan Rath (1991: 177–232) provides fascinating accounts of organized white flight (thus creating these concentration schools) and of the futile attempts by *allochtone* parents to register their children in "non-concentration schools."

35. Many immigrants are constrained within their own networks. Since second-generation immigrants remain in de Randstad; a third of them do not participate in any social-cultural activity (Huls 1997: 25–29, 43–50); and many are claimed to face an "ethnic mobility trap" (Dagevos and Veenman 1992: 180).

36. Even leisure time is segmented. Peer groups are quite homogenous by ethnicity (e.g., Veenman 1996a: 105, 1996b: 163).

37. As Ron Haleber (1989: 201–215) pointed out, one can implement racist policies from a relativistic point of view, resulting in apartheid (i.e., every culture has its own values and cannot coexist with the other one, as is often propagated by the extreme right), but also from a universalistic point of view, forcing immigrants to assimilate and adapt to the dominant culture of the nation-state (propagated at times by the extreme left and mainstream liberal reformism).

38. The European Monitoring Center on Racism and Xenophobia's report on racism in the Dutch media concludes that, "in the Dutch press, Muslims were viewed as a fifth column in international conflicts and their problems were explained in terms of a homogeneous Islamic culture. Distinctions between religion and nationality were blurred. Muslims were represented as a depersonalised collectivity, images of Islam and Muslims were distorted and Islamic societies were represented as violent and backward" (ter Wal 2002: 48). An example of the latter is the publication of an interview with Professor Henk Wesseling, president of the Center for the Study of European Expansion, adviser to the queen of the Netherlands, and tutor to the crown prince, who stated in the magazine HP/De Tijd on March 8, 1991, "I believe that one may argue that Arabic countries are medieval societies. For the time being, people there do nothing more than shoot each other to death" (quoted in van der Valk 2002: 293). In addition, "Denial of the racist nature of violent attacks against immigrants was found to occur quite commonly" in the Netherlands (ter Wal 2002: 58).

39. In Surinamese circles, one often hears, "Dutch are hypocritical, at least in the [United States] you know that discrimination exists" (Bovenkerk 1975: 12–13). In contrast to the United States, in the Netherlands "discrimination [against] people of color occurs in a secretive, subtle way" (Buchner 1972: 40; Choenni 1992: 122). However, the Dutch welfare state provides legal immigrants with access to social-security benefits, medical care, and housing allowances (Dieleman 1993: 132). This does not mean, however, that the majority of Dutch voters agree with this policy. Moreover, the Dutch welfare state has been trimmed considerably over the past fifteen years (cf. Engbersen and Snel 1997; Salverda et al. 2008; van Luijk 1994: 227–237).

40. It is my intention to focus not on the process of pillarization (known in Dutch as verzuiling) within the Netherlands but on the consequences of this political structure for newly arrived immigrants.

41. More eighteen- to thirty-four-year-old Dutch people (40 percent) have a negative attitude toward minorities than do thirty-five- to fifty-four-year-olds (38.9 percent), while only 8.4 percent and 10.2 percent, respectively, have a positive attitude toward them. The others claim to be neutral toward minorities (Huls and van der Laan 1995: 83). For a more recent discussion in English of why Surinamese and Antillean minorities are currently better off in the Dutch labor market than their Turkish and Moroccan counterparts see Snel et al. (2007).

42. A transition from Dutch mono-cultural toward multicultural education clearly has not taken place (Shadid and van Koningsveld 1990: 117–118). Furthermore, immigrants are looked on negatively within the educational vestiges themselves. Thorough analysis of racism in Dutch schoolbooks illustrates this quite well (e.g., van den Berg and Reinsch 1983; van Dijk 1987). It is no wonder that the educational results of, for instance, Surinamese immigrant children are disappointing when the materials used in schools are "not adapted to the ethnic and cultural backgrounds of the children" (Koot and Venema 1988: 201–203). For instance, Surinamese children are often confronted with "the mono-cultural character of the education, the stereotypical images about Surinamese pupils, low expectations of teachers and discrimination" (van Niekerk 1995: 55).

43. According to the 1994 SPVA survey, 18 percent of Dutch adults would object to their children dating a person who belonged to an ethnic minority, while 31 percent answered "Don't know very well," and 52 percent stated they had no objection. More eighteen- to twenty-five-year-old Dutch people objected to this idea (15 percent) than did twenty-five- to thirty-five-year-olds (12 percent) or thirty-five- to forty-five-year-olds (13 percent; Martens 1995: 106). That political parties that embrace xenophobia were generally not success-

ful does not mean that many people do not have racist ideas or attitudes (Leiprecht 1997; Verkuyten 1997). Dutch society is essentially as racist as most other Western European countries (Vogel 1992: 149).

44. Differences in income between minorities and the Dutch increased in the 1980s; the average income of ethnic minorities decreased about 5–10 percent. Taking into account inflation, one has to add another 10 percent. Minorities experienced a decrease in purchasing power of 15–20 percent in 1982–1990, and the average income of those living in de Randstad has decreased more than anywhere else in the Netherlands (van Dugteren 1993: 50–51). In the "social rent sector," the government has considerably raised rent (van Dugteren 1993: 104); newly constructed subsidized residences are unaffordable to the lowest-income groups. The welfare state is considering even more budget cuts, including to the housing sector, so that gaining access to a single-family residence will become even harder for many minorities. The near future does not look bright, either: more budget cuts in the welfare state tend to hit low-income groups hardest, in which immigrants are over-represented (van Dugteren 1993: 105).

45. Tiede Bijlsma and Frits Koopmans (1996b) demonstrate the statistical significance between immigrant concentrations in areas of de Randstad, where one in three inhabitants is an *allochtone,* and the electoral success of the far right in those same areas (varying from 2 percent to 15 percent).

46. Since the early 1990s, immigration on the basis of family reunification was made more difficult (Sprangers 1995: 30). Implementing more restrictions on immigration control (an inevitable outcome of immigration policies by core countries) can be interpreted as an official condoning of the "insider–outsider" and "us–them" mentality, which does not help to soften tensions between already established immigrants and *autochtones* (Brochmann 1996: 147–148). The creation of ever more demarcation lines offers little hope that core countries will achieve the kind of multicultural society that its proponents usually have in mind (Collinson 1993: 34). For examples of experiments with return-migration policies, see van Amersfoort and Penninx 1998.

47. Thousands of illegal immigrants from the periphery manage to move to the Dutch Caribbean semi-periphery, and from there it is quite likely that many will be able to move to the Netherlands (e.g., by marrying or presenting themselves as Dutch-Caribbean citizens; Bovenkerk 2002: 172).

References

Aalberts, M. M. J. 1996. "Rassenrellen. Waardevolle beschouwingen, valse vergelijkingen." *Justitiële Verkenningen* 22, no. 3: 37–50.
Abrahamse, A. P. J., ed. 1997. "Allochtonen in Nederland." Centraal Bureau voor de Statistiek, Voorburg/Heerlen, July.
Albeda, W., et al. (Wetenschappelijke Raad voor het Regeringsbeleid). 1989. "Allochtonen-beleid." 's-Gravenhage: SDU.
Amesz, I., F. Steijlen, and H. Vermeulen. 1989. "Andere Antillianen. Carrieres van laagge-schoolde Antilliaanse jongeren in een grote stad." Amsterdam: Het Spinhuis.
Barkan, E. 1992. *The Retreat of Scientific Racism.* Cambridge: Cambridge University Press.
Bijlsma, T., and F. Koopmans. 1996a. "Allochtonen in Nederland, verontrusting en beleid." *Tijdschrift voor Sociologie* 17, no. 4: 429–446.
Bijlsma, T., and F. Koopmans. 1996b. "Stemmen op extreem-rechts in de Amsterdamse buurten." *Sociologische Gids* 43, no. 3: 171–182.

Blakely, A. 1993. *Blacks in the Dutch World.* Bloomington: Indiana University Press.

Böcker, A. 1995. "Op weg naar een beter bestaan." Pp. 145–176 in *Het democratisch onge-duld,* ed. H. Vermeulen and R. Penninx. Amsterdam: Het Spinhuis.

Bolt, Gideon, P. Hooimeijer, and R. van Kempen. 2002. "Ethnic Segregation in the Nether-lands: New Patterns, New Policies?" *Tijdschrift voor economische en sociale geografie* 93, no. 2: 214–220.

Boomkens, R. 1994. "Vreemd over het belang van zwakke grenzen." Pp. 17–27 in *Burgers en Vreemdelingen. Opstellen over filosofie en politiek,* ed. D. Pels and G. de Vries. Amster-dam: Van Gennep.

Bos, Vivian, et al. 2004. "Ethnic Inequalities in Age- and Cause-Specific Mortality in the Netherlands." *International Journal of Epidemiology* 33, no. 5: 1112–1119.

Bouw, C., J. van Donselaar, and C. Nelissen. 1981. *De Nederlandse Volks-Unie. Portret van een racistische splinterpartij.* Bussum: Het Wereldvenster.

Bovenkerk, F. 1975. "Emigratie uit Suriname." Anthropologisch Sociologisch Centrum, pub-lication no. 2, report no. 4, Amsterdam.

Bovenkerk, F., ed. 1978. *Omdat zij anders zijn. Patronen van rasdiscriminatie in Nederland.* Amsterdam: Meppel/Boom.

Bovenkerk, F. 2002. *Misdaadprofielen.* Amsterdam: Meulenhoff.

Bovenkerk, F., and E. Breuning-Van Leeuwen. 1978. "Rasdiscriminatie en rasvooroordeel op de Amsterdamse arbeidsmarkt." Pp. 31–77 in *Omdat zij anders zijn. Patronen van rasdiscriminatie in Nederland,* ed. F. Bovenkerk. Amsterdam: Meppel/Boom.

Bovenkerk, F., et al. 1985. *Vreemd volk, gemengde gevoelens.* Amsterdam: Boom.

Brochmann, G. 1996. *European Integration and Immigration from Third Countries.* Oslo: Scandinavian University Press.

Buchner, G. 1972. "Gesprek met socioloog Mual over Zuidmolukkers in Nederland." Pp. 38–41 in *Racisme in Nederland,* ed. G. de Bruijn. 's-Gravenhage: NVSH.

Buddingh', H. 2000. *Geschiedenis van Suriname.* Utrecht: Het Spectrum.

Buijs, F., and C. Nelissen. 1995. "Tussen continuiteit en verandering." Pp. 177–206 in *Het Democratisch ongeduld,* ed. H. Vermeulen and R. Penninx. Amsterdam: Het Spinhuis.

Buis, H. 1988. *Beter een verre buur. Racistische voorvallen in buurt en straat.* Amsterdam: Socialistische Uitgeverij Amsterdam.

Buruma, Ian. 2006. *Murder in Amsterdam: The Death of Theo van Gogh and the Limits of Tolerance.* New York: Penguin Press.

Cadat, B. Y., and M. Fennema. 1996. "Het zelfbeeld van Amsterdamse migrantenpolitici in de jaren negentig." *Amsterdams Sociologisch Tijdschrift* 22, no. 4 (March): 655–681.

Choenni, C. 1992. "Rassendiscriminatie op de arbeidsmarkt." Pp. 77–92 in *Allochtonen aan het werk,* ed. S. van der Werf. Muiderberg: Dick Coutinho.

Coenders, M., et al. 2008. "More than Two Decades of Changing Ethnic Attitudes in the Netherlands." *Journal of Social Issues* 64, no. 2: 269–285.

Collinson, S. 1993. *Beyond Borders.* London: Royal Institute of International Affairs.

Çörüz, C. 1997. "De Nederlandse imam-opleiding." *Justitiële Verkenningen* 23, no. 6 (August): 130–141.

Croes, R., and L. M. Alam. 1990. "Decolonization of Aruba within the Netherlands Antilles." Pp. 81–102 in *The Dutch Caribbean: Prospects for Democracy,* ed. B. Sedoc-Dahlberg. Amsterdam: Gordon and Breach Science Publishers.

Cross, M., and H. Entzinger. 1988. "Caribbean Minorities in Britain and the Netherlands: Comparative Questions." Pp. 1–33 in *Lost Illusions: Caribbean Minorities in Britain and the Netherlands,* ed. M. Cross and H. Entzinger. London: Routledge.

Crul, M., and J. Doomernik. 2003. "The Turkish and Moroccan Second Generation in the Netherlands." *International Migration Review* 37, no. 4: 1039–1064.

Dagevos, J. M. 1995. *De rafelrand van de arbeidsmarkt.* Assen: Van Gorcum.

Dagevos, J. M., L. van der Laan, and J. Veenman. 1997. *Verdringing op de arbeidsmarkt.* Assen: Van Gorcum.

Dagevos, J. M., and J. Veenman. 1992. *Succesvolle allochtonen.* Amsterdam: Meppel.

Dagevos, J. M., and J. Veenman. 1996. "Werkloosheid en het voortduren van achterstand" and "Sociale netwerken en hun functionaliteit." Pp. 39–62 in *Keren de kansen? De tweede generatie allochtonen in Nederland,* ed. J. Veenman. Assen: Van Gorcum.

Dagevos, J. M., J. Veenman, and E. P. Martens. 1996. *Scheef Verdeeld.* Assen: Van Gorcum.

de Bokx, M. 1997. "Van rassenrel tot allochtonenbeleid. De rellen in de Afrikaanderwijk van augustus 1972." *Weena:* 20–34.

de Jong, W., T. Steijlen, and K. Masson. 1997. *Hoe doe je je ding.* Delft: Eburon Publishers.

Deraeck, G. 1994. *Vreemd volk? Over integratie en uitsluiting van migranten en vluchtelingen.* Leuven/Amersfoort: Acco.

Dieleman, F. 1993. "Multicultural Holland: Myth or Reality?" Pp. 118–135 in *Mass Migrations in Europe: The Legacy and the Future,* ed. R. King. London: Belhaven Press.

Distelbrink, M., and T. Pels. 1996. "Ontwikkelingen in de etnisch-culturele positie." Pp. 105–131 in *Keren de kansen? De tweede generatie allochtonen in Nederland,* ed. J. Veenman. Assen: Van Gorcum.

Doomernik, J. 1991. *Turkse moskeeën en maatschappelijke participatie: de institutionalisering van de Turkse Islam in Nederland en de Duitse Bondsrepubliek.* Amsterdam: Koninklijk Nederlands Aardrijkskundig Genootschap.

Driessen, G. W. J. 1990. *De onderwijspositie van allochtone leerlingen.* Nijmegen: ITS.

Eddaoudi, A. 1998. *Marokkaanse jongeren: Daders of slachtoffers?* Rotterdam: Ad. Donker.

Elbers, F., and M. Fennema. 1993. *Racistische partijen in West-Europa.* Leiden: Stichting Burgerschapskunde.

El-Fers, M., and C. Nibbering. 1998. *Hoe gevaarlijk zijn de Turken?* Amsterdam: Turkevi Amsterdam.

Engbersen, G. 1994. "De weg naar Anomia? Armoederegimes en levenskansen." Pp. 113–141 in *Zorgen in het Europese huis,* ed. G. Engbersen, A. Hemerijck, and W. Bakker. Amsterdam: Boom.

Engbersen, G., and E. Snel. 1997. "Arm Nederland: Schaduwen over de polder." Pp. 287–301 in *Armoede en Sociale Uitsluiting. Jaarboek 1997,* ed. J. Vranken, D. Geldof, and G. Van Menxel. Leuven: Acco.

Entzinger, H. B. 1980. "The Non-Usage of Race in the Netherlands." *New Community* 8: 1–2.

Entzinger, H. B. 1988. "Migranten na de verzorgingsstaat." Pp. 67–73 in *Sociale problemen in Belgie en Nederland,* ed. M. Borghardt, C. Corver, and E. Lissenberg. Vlaams-Nederlandse studiedagen voor sociologen en antropologen, SISWO publication no. 326, April 7–8. Amsterdam: Netherlands Institute for the Social Sciences.

Essed, P. 1984. *Alledaags racisme.* Baarn/The Hague: Ambo.

Essed, P. 1991. *Inzicht in alledaags racisme.* Utrecht: Het Spectrum.

Essed, P. 1992. "Cultuurverschil, racisme en het Nederlandse tolerantievertoog." Pp. 125–136 in *Gezichten van hedendaags racisme,* ed. E. Desle and A. Martens. Brussels: Vrije Universiteit Brussel Press.

Essed, P. 1999. "Ethnicity and Diversity in Dutch Academia." *Social Identities* 5, no. 2: 211–225.

Essed, P., and K. Nimako 2006. "Designs and (Co)Incidents: Cultures of Scholarship and Public Policy on Immigrants/Minorities in the Netherlands." *International Journal of Comparative Sociology* 47, nos. 3–4: 281–312.

Essed, P., and S. Trienekens. 2008. "Who Wants to Feel White?" *Ethnic and Racial Studies* 31, no. 1: 52–72.

Fennema, M. 1997. "Het recht op vrije meningsuiting tegenover het recht op bescherming tegen rassendiscriminatie." Pp. 155–170 in *Bestrijding van racisme en rechts-extremisme,* ed. H. De Witte. Leuven: Acco.

Ford, G., ed. 1991. "Verslag namens de Onderzoekscommissie racisme en vreemdelingenhaat." Government report, European Parliament, Brussels.

Galtung, J. 1971. "A Structural Theory of Imperialism." *Journal of Peace Research* 8: 81–117.

Gastmann, A. 1968. "The Politics of Surinam and the Netherlands Antilles." University of Puerto Rico.

Gowricharn, R. 1997. "Integratiekolder?" *Justitiële Verkenningen* 23, no. 6 (August): 73–82.

Gras, M. 1996. "Positive Action Programs in the Netherlands." Pp. 62–64 in *European Conference on Preventing Racism at the Workplace: Proceedings.* Dublin: European Foundation for the Improvement of Living and Working Conditions.

Hagendoorn, Louk. 1986. *Cultuurconflict en vooroordeel.* Alphen aan den Rijn: Samsom.

Hagendoorn, L., and J. Hraba. 1989. "Foreign, Different, Deviant, Seclusive, and Working Class: Anchors to an Ethnic Hierarchy in the Netherlands." *Ethnic and Racial Studies* 12, no. 4: 441–468.

Haleber, R. 1989. "Etniciteit, antiracisme en moslim-identiteit." Pp. 183–220 in *Rushdie-effecten. Afwijzing van moslim-identiteit in Nederland?* ed. R. Haleber. Amsterdam: Socialistische Uitgeverij Amsterdam.

Helder, L., and S. Gravenberch, eds. 1998. *Sinterklaasje, kom maar binnen zonder knecht.* Berchem: EPO.

Huls, F. 1997. "De tweede generatie allochtonen neemt flink toe." In *Allochtonen in Nederland 1997,* ed. A. Abrahamse. Voorburg/Heerlen: Centraal Bureau voor de Statistiek.

Huls, F., and P. van der Laan, eds. 1995. *Allochtonen in Nederland 1995.* Voorburg/Heerlen: Centraal Bureau voor de Statistiek.

Kalmijn, M., and F. Van Tubergen. 2006. "Ethnic Intermarriage in the Netherlands." *European Journal of Population* 22, no. 4: 371–397.

Kentor, J., and E. Mielants. 2007. "Connecting the Global and Local: The Impact of Globalization on Civil Society, 1990–2000." Pp. 27–52 in *Civil Society: Local and Regional Responses to Global Challenges,* ed. M. Herkenrath. Berlin: LIT Verlag.

Koopmans, R. 2002. "Zachte heelmeesters." *Migrantenstudies* 18, no. 2: 87–92.

Koot, W. 1979. "Emigratie op de Nederlandse Antillen." Unpublished Ph.D. diss., University of Leiden.

Koot, W., and A. Ringeling. 1984. *De Antillianen.* Amsterdam: D. Coutinho.

Koot, W., and P. Venema. 1988. "Education: The Way up for Surinamese in the Netherlands?" Pp. 185–203 in *Lost Illusions: Caribbean Minorities in Britain and the Netherlands,* ed. M. Cross and H. Entzinger. London: Routledge.

Latuheru, E., and M. Hessels. 1996. "Schoolprestaties en etnische en sociaal-economische herkomst." *Sociologische Gids* 43, no. 2: 100–113.

Leiprecht, R. 1997. "De goede pool versterken." Pp. 101–104 in *De multiculturele samenleving,* ed. R. Aspeslagh and S. Raven. The Hague: Instituut Clingendael.

Leistra, G. 1995. *Parbo aan de Amstel. Surinamers in Nederland.* Amsterdam: de Arbeiderspers.

Lijphart, A. 1982. *Verzuiling, pacificatie en kentering in de Nederlandse politiek*. Amsterdam: De Bussy.

Lucassen, J., and R. Penninx. 1994. *Nieuwkomers, nakomelingen, Nederlanders. Immigranten in Nederland 1550–1993*. Amsterdam: Het Spinhuis.

Martens, E. P. 1995. *Minderheden in beeld. Kerncijfers uit de SPVA-94*. Rotterdam: Instituut voor Sociologisch-Economisch Onderzoek/EUR.

Martens, E. P., and A. O. Verweij. 1997. "Antillianen en Arubanen in Nederland. Kerncijfers 1996," "Surinamers in Nederland," and "Turken in Nederland." Reports, Instituut voor Sociologisch-Economisch Onderzoek, Rotterdam.

Martiniello, M. 1993. "De sociologie van migratieprocessen en de etnische relaties." Pp. 83–98 in *Denken over migranten in Europa*, ed. E. Deslé, R. Lesthaeghe, and E. Witte. Brussels: Vrije Universiteit Brussel Press.

Massey, D., et al. 1993. "Theories of International Migration: A Review and Appraisal." *Population and Development Review* 19, no. 3: 431–466.

Meertens, R. 1997. "Verminderen van vooroordeel en discriminatie." Pp. 43–63 in *Bestrijding van racisme en rechts-extremisme*, ed. H. De Witte. Leuven: Acco.

Mielants, E. 2002. "Mass Migration in the World System: An Anti-systemic Movement in the Long Run?" Pp. 79–102 in *The Modern/Colonial/Capitalist World-System in the Twentieth Century: Global Processes, Antisystemic Movements, and the Geopolitics of Knowledge*, ed. A. M. Cervantes-Rodríguez and R. Grosfoguel. Westport, Conn.: Greenwood Press.

Murray, C. 1990. *The Emerging British Underclass*. London: Institute for Economic Affairs.

Nicolaas, J. R. 1990. "Ontwikkelingen in de arbeidsmarktpositie van vrouwen in Aruba." Pp. 95–112 in *Op de bres voor Eigenheid*, ed. R. Allen, P. van Gelder, M. Jacobs, and I. Witteveen. Amsterdam: University of Amsterdam.

Odé, A. 2002. *Ethnic-Cultural and Socio-Economic Integration in the Netherlands: A Comparative Study of Mediterranean and Caribbean Minority Groups*. Assen: Van Gorcum.

Ogbu, J. 1987. "Variability in Minority School Performance." *Anthropology and Education Quarterly* 18: 312–334.

Oostindie, G. 1988. "Caribbean Migration to the Netherlands: A Journey to Disappointment?" Pp. 54–72 in *Lost Illusions: Caribbean Minorities in Britain and the Netherlands*, ed. M. Cross and H. Entzinger. London: Routledge.

Oostindie, G. 1998. *Het paradijs overzee*. Amsterdam: Bert Bakker.

Oostindie, G., ed. 1999. *Het verleden onder ogen*. The Hague: Arena and Het Prins Claus Fonds.

Openneer, H. 1995. *Kid Dynamite*. Amsterdam: Jan Mets.

Pels, T., and J. Veenman. 1996. "Onderwijsachterstanden bij allochtone kinderen. Het ontbrekende onderzoek." *Sociologische Gids* 43, no. 2: 131–145.

Penninx, R., J. Schoorl, and C. van Praag. 1993. *The Impact of International Migration on Receiving Countries: The Case of the Netherlands*. Amsterdam/Lisse: Swets and Zeitlinger.

Polhuis, A. 1994. *Lotgenoten bondgenoten?* Zoetermeer: Boekencentrum.

Portes, A. 1995. "Children of Immigrants: Segmented Assimilation and Its Determinants." Pp. 248–280 in *The Economic Sociology of Immigration*, ed. A. Portes. New York: Russell Sage Foundation.

Portes, A., and R. Rumbaut. 1996. *Immigrant America*, 2nd rev. ed. Berkeley: University of California Press.

Quispel, G. C. 1997. "Getto's en concentratiewijken." *Justitiële Verkenningen* 23, no. 6 (August): 150–160.

Rath, J. 1991. *Minorisering: De sociale constructie van "etnische minderheden."* Amsterdam: Socialistische Uitgeverij Amsterdam.

Rex, J. 1999. "Multiculturalism and Political Integration in European Cities." Pp. 149–162 in *European Societies: Fusion or Fission?* ed. T. Boje, B. van Steenbergen, and S. Walby. London: Routledge.

Roelandt, T. 1997. "Ethnic Stratification: The Emergence of a New Social and Economic Issue?" *Netherlands Journal of Social Sciences* 32, no. 1: 39–50.

Roelandt, T., and J. Veenman. 1987. "Minderheden in Nederland. Achtergrondstudie 1987." Report, Instituut voor Sociologisch-Economisch Onderzoek, Rotterdam, July.

Room, P. 1997. "Sociale uitsluiting en sociale rechten." Pp. 221–231 in *Armoede en sociale uitsluiting. Jaarboek 1997,* ed. J. Vranken, D. Geldof, and G. Van Menxel. Leuven: Acco.

Rutgers, W. 1997. "De postkoloniale taalsituatie op de Nederlandse Antillen en Aruba." Pp. 275–291 in *Koloniale taalpolitiek in Oost en West,* ed. G. Kees. Amsterdam: Amsterdam University Press.

Salverda, W., et al. 2008. *Low-Wage Work in the Netherlands.* New York: Russell Sage Foundation.

Sansone, L. 1992. *Schitteren in de schaduw.* Amsterdam: Het Spinhuis.

Scheepers, P., R. Eisinga, and E. Linssen. 1994. "Etnocentrisme in Nederland: Veranderingen bij kansarme en/of gepriviligeerde groepen?" *Sociologische Gids* 41, no. 3: 185–201.

Scheffer, P. 2000. "Het multiculturele drama." *NRC Handelsblad,* January 29.

Schmeets, J., P. Scheepers, and A. Felling. 1996. "Het minderhedenvraag-stuk en de partijkeuze in 1994." *Mens en Maatschappij* 71, no. 2: 131–141.

Schouten, M. 1994. *Kleur.* Amsterdam: De bezige bij.

Schumacher, P. 1987. *De minderheden: 700000 immigranten minder gelijk.* Amsterdam: Van Gennep.

Schuster, J. 1999. *Poortwachters over immigranten.* Amsterdam: Het Spinhuis.

Sedoc-Dahlberg, B., ed. 1990. *The Dutch Caribbean: Prospects for Democracy.* Amsterdam: Gordon and Breach Science Publishers.

Shadid, W. 1998. *Grondslagen van interculturele communicatie.* Houten/Diegem: Bohn Stafleu Van Loghum.

Shadid, W., and P. van Koningsveld. 1990. *Moslims in Nederland. Minderheden en religie in een multiculturele samenleving.* Alphen aan den Rijn: Samsom Stafleu.

Snel, E., J. Burgers, and A. Leerkes. 2007. "Class Position of Immigrant Workers in a Post-Industrial Economy: The Dutch Case." *Journal of Ethnic and Migration Studies* 33, no. 8: 1323–1342.

Sociaal-Economische Raad. 1991. "Advies inzake beleidsnota Remigratie 91–92." Publication no. 22, The Hague, October 30.

Sprangers, A. 1995. "Gezinsherenigende en gezinsvormende immigratie." Pp. 29–35 in *Allochtonen in Nederland 1995,* ed. F. Huls and P. van der Laan. Voorburg/Heerlen: Centraal Bureau voor de Statistiek.

Stronks, K., A. Ravelli, and S. Reijneveld. 2001. "Immigrants in the Netherlands: Equal Access for Equal Needs." *Journal of Epidemiology and Community Health* 55, no. 10: 701–707.

Tazelaar, C. A. 1996. "De school in de wijk." Pp. 73–100 in *Kleur van de school,* ed. C. Tazelaar, A. Joachim-Ruijs, J. Rutten, and J. Teunissen. Lelystad: Koninklijke Vermande.

Tayob, A. 2006. "Muslim Responses to Integration: Demands in the Netherlands since 9/11." *Human Architecture: Journal of the Sociology of Self-Knowledge* 5, no. 1: 73–90.

ter Wal, J., ed. 2002. *Racism and Cultural Diversity in the Mass Media.* Vienna: European Monitoring Center on Racism and Xenophobia/European Research Centre on Migration and Ethnic Relations.

Tesser, P., et al. 1995. *Rapportage Minderheden 1995. Concentratie en segregatie.* Rijswijk/ The Hague: Sociaal en Cultureel Planbureau/Vuga.

Teunissen, J. 1996. "Ethnische segregatie in het basisonderwijs: Een onderwijskundige benadering." Pp. 23–43 in *Kleur van de school,* ed. C. Tazelaar, A. Joachim-Ruis, J. Rutten, and J. Teunissen. Lelystad: Koninklijke Vermande.

Teunissen, J., and M. Matthijssen. 1996. "Stagnatie in onderwijsonderzoek naar de etnische factor bij allochtone leerlingen." *Sociologische Gids* 43, no. 2: 87–99.

Tillie, J., and B. Slijper 2007. "Immigrant Political Integration and Ethnic Civic Communities in Amsterdam." Pp. 206–225 in *Identities, Affiliations and Allegiances,* ed. S. Benhabib, I. Shapiro, and D. Petranovich. Cambridge: Cambridge University Press.

Tinnemans, W. 1994. *Een gouden armband.* Utrecht: Nederlands Centrum Buitenlanders.

Tolsma, J., M. Coenders, and M. Lubbers. 2007. "Trends in Ethnic Educational Inequalities in the Netherlands: A Cohort Design." *European Sociological Review* 23, no. 3: 325–339.

Valkenburg, F., and A. ter Huurne. 1983. *Werkloosheid in oude stadswijken. Een studie naar de arbeidsmarktpositie en het arbeidsmarktgedrag van werklozen.* Tilburg: Instituut voor Sociaal-Wetenschappelijk Onderzoek.

van Amersfoort, H. 1987. "Van William Kegge tot Ruud Gullit. De Surinaamse migratie naar Nederland." *Tijdschrift voor Geschiedenis* 100, no. 3: 475–490.

van Amersfoort, H., and R. Penninx. 1998. "Western Europe as an Immigration Area." Pp. 42–68 in *International migration,* ed. H. van Amersfoort and J. Doomernik. Amsterdam: Institute for Migration and Ethnic Studies/Het Spinhuis.

van Amersfoort, H., and M. van Niekerk. 2006. "Immigration as a Colonial Inheritance: Post-Colonial Immigrants in the Netherlands, 1945–2002." *Journal of Ethnic and Migration Studies* 32, no. 3: 323–346

van Deelen, B. 1996. "The Benelux." In *The 1994 Elections to the European Parliament,* ed. J. Lodge. London: Pinter.

van den Berg, H. 1992. "Racismeonderzoek en discoursanalyse." *Migrantenstudies,* no. 1: 38–64.

van den Berg, H., and P. Reinsch. 1983. *Racisme in schoolboeken. Het gladde ijs van het westerse gelijk.* Amsterdam: Socialistische Uitgeverij Amsterdam.

van den Bergh, L. 1972. "Gesprek met 'Ons Suriname,'" Pp. 31–37 in *Racisme in Nederland,* ed. G. de Bruijn. 's-Gravenhage: Dutch Society for Sexual Reform (NVSH).

van den Braak, J. W. 1996. "Codes of Good Practice in the Netherlands." Pp. 49–51 in *European Conference on Preventing Racism at the Workplace: Proceedings.* Dublin: European Foundation for the Improvement of Living and Working Conditions.

van den Brink, R. 1994. *De internationale van de haat. Extreem-rechts in West-Europa.* Amsterdam: Socialistische Uitgeverij Amsterdam.

van der Valk, I. 2002. "The Netherlands." Pp. 287–309 in *Racism and Cultural Diversity in the Mass Media,* ed. J. ter Wal. Vienna: European Monitoring Center on Racism and Xenophobia/European Research Centre on Migration and Ethnic Relations.

van der Werf, S. 1992. "Allochtonen op de arbeidsmarkt." Pp. 18–35 in *Allochtonen aan het werk,* ed. S. van der Werf. Muiderberg: Dick Coutinho.

van Dieten, M., and L. Maduro. 1978. *De Nederlandse Antillen: Een analyse van hun afhankelijkheid.* Tilburg: Instituut voor Ontwikkelingsvraagstukken.

van Dijk, A. T. 1987. *Schoolvoorbeelden van racisme. De reproduktie van racisme in schoolboeken voor maatschappijleer.* Amsterdam: Socialistische Uitgeverij Amsterdam.

van Dijk, A. T. 1998. "Sinterklaas en Zwarte Piet." Pp. 118–135 in *Sinterklaasje, kom maar binnen zonder knecht,* ed. L. Helder and S. Gravenberch. Berchem: EPO.

van Donselaar, J. 1995. *De Staat paraat? De bestrijding van extreem-rechts in West-Europa.* Amsterdam: Uitgeverij Babylon-De Geus.

van Donselaar, J. 1997. "Reageren op extreem-rechts." Pp. 189–206 in *Bestrijding van racisme en rechts-extremisme,* ed. H. De Witte. Leuven: Acco.

van Dugteren, F. 1993. *Woonsituatie minderheden.* Rijswijk: Sociaal en Cultureel Planbureau.

van Gemert, F. H. M. 1995. "Gangs in Amerika en Nederland." *Justitiële Verkenningen* 21, no. 9: 68–83.

van Gemert, F. H. M. 1998. *Ieder voor zich.* Amsterdam: Het Spinhuis.

van Heelsum, A. J. 1997. *De ethnisch-culturele positie van de tweede generatie Surinamers.* Amsterdam: Het Spinhuis.

van Hensbroek, P. B., and S. Koenis. 1994. "Het Westen bestaat niet. Over de implicaties van culturalisme." Pp. 51–62 in *Burgers en Vreemdelingen,* ed. D. Pels and G. de Vries. Amsterdam: Van Gennep.

van Hulst, H. 1995. "Op advies van de minister van Kolonien." Pp. 81–115 in *Het Democratisch Ongeduld,* ed. H. Vermeulen and R. Penninx. Amsterdam: Het Spinhuis.

van Hulst, H. 1997. *Morgen bloeit het diabaas. De Antilliaanse volksklasse in de Nederlandse samenleving.* Amsterdam: Het Spinhuis.

van Hulst, H. 2000. "A Continuing Construction of Crisis: Antilleans, Especially Curaçaoans, in the Netherlands." Pp. 93–122 in *Immigrant Integration: The Dutch Case,* ed. H. Vermeulen and R. Penninx. Amsterdam: Het Spinhuis.

van Langen, A., and P. Jungbluth. 1990. *Onderwijskansen van migranten: De rol van sociaal-economische en culturele factoren.* Amsterdam/Lisse: Swets and Zeitliger.

van Luijk, H. 1994. "De solidaire burger." Pp. 227–237 in *Burgers en Vreemdelingen,* ed. D. Pels and G. de Vries. Amsterdam: Van Gennep.

van Niekerk, M. 1993. *Kansarmoede. Reacties van allochtonen op achterstand.* Amsterdam: Het Spinhuis.

van Niekerk, M. 1995. "Zorg en hoop. Surinamers in Nederland." Pp. 45–79 in *Het Democratisch Ongeduld,* ed. H. Vermeulen and R. Penninx. Amsterdam: Het Spinhuis.

van Niekerk, M. 2000a. *De krekel en de mier.* Amsterdam: Het Spinhuis.

van Niekerk, M. 2000b. "Paradoxes in Paradise: Integration and Social Mobility of the Surinamese in the Netherlands." Pp. 64–92 in *Immigrant Integration: The Dutch Case,* ed. H. Vermeulen and R. Penninx. Amsterdam: Het Spinhuis.

Van Niekerk, M. 2002. *Premigration Legacies and Immigrant Social Mobility: The Afro-Surinamese and Indo-Surinamese in the Netherlands.* Lanham, Md.: Lexington Books.

Van Niekerk, M. 2004. "Afro-Caribbeans and Indo-Caribbeans in the Netherlands: Premigration Legacies and Social Mobility." *International Migration Review* 38, no. 1: 158–183.

van Putte, F. 1997. "De Nederlandse koloniale taalpolitiek op de Benedenwindse Antillen." Pp. 251–273 in *Koloniale taalpolitiek in Oost en West,* ed. G. Kees. Amsterdam: Amsterdam University Press.

van San, M. 1998. *Delinquent gedrag van Curaçaose jongens in Nederland.* Amsterdam: Het Spinhuis.

Vasta, E. 2007. "From Ethnic Minorities to Ethnic Majority Policy: Multiculturalism and the Shift to Assimilationism in the Netherlands." *Ethnic and Racial Studies* 30, no. 5: 713–740.

Veenman, J. 1994. *Participatie in Perspectief.* Lelystad: Koninklijke Vermande.

Veenman, J. 1995. *Onbekend maakt onbemind. Over selectie van allochtonen op de arbeids-markt.* Assen: Van Gorcum.

Veenman, J., ed. 1996a. *Heb je niets, dan ben je niets. Tweede generatie allochtone jongeren in Amsterdam.* Assen: Van Gorcum.

Veenman, J., ed. 1996b. *Keren de kansen? De tweede generatie allochtonen in Nederland.* Assen: Van Gorcum.

Veenman, J., and E. Martens. 1995. "Op de toekomst gericht: tweede generatie allochtonen in Nederland." 's-Gravenhage: Vuga.

Veerman, G. 1990. "Strafrechtelijke bestrijding van rasdiscriminatie." *Justitiële Verkenningen* 16, no. 5: 54–74.

Vergeer, M., and P. Scheepers. 1998. "Publieke versus commerciele programmering." Pp. 271–292 in *De rol van de media in de multiculturele samenleving,* ed. E. Schelfhout and H. Verstraeten. Brussels: Vrije Universiteit Brussel Press.

Verkuyten, M. 1997. *Redelijk Racisme.* Amsterdam: Amsterdam University Press.

Vermeulen, H., and R. Penninx, eds. 1995. *Het Democratisch Ongeduld.* Amsterdam: Het Spinhuis.

Vermeulen, H., and R. Penninx. 2000. "Introduction." Pp. 1–35 in *Immigrant Integration: The Dutch Case,* ed. H. Vermeulen and R. Penninx. Amsterdam: Het Spinhuis.

Verton, P. 1976. "Emancipation and Decolonization: The May Revolt and Its Aftermath in Curaçao." *Revista/Review Interamericana* 7: 88–101.

Vogel, H. P. 1992. "Nederland en Latijns-Amerika." Pp. 81–177 in *Nederland en de Nieuwe Wereld,* ed. H. W. van den Doel, P. C. Emmer, and H. P. Vogel. Utrecht: Het Spectrum.

von der Dunk, H. W. 1992. *Sprekend over identiteit en geschiedenis.* Amsterdam: Prometheus.

Vuijsje, H. 1986. *Vermoorde onschuld.* Amsterdam: Bert Bakker.

Willemsen, G. 2006. *Dagen van gejuich en gejubel.* Amsterdam: Amrit.

Witte, R. 1997. "Reacties op racistisch geweld. Ervaringen en aanbevelingen." Pp. 79–94 in *Bestrijding van racisme en rechts-extremisme,* ed. H. De Witte. Leuven: Acco.

Witte, R. 1998. "Een kwestie van gewenning?" Pp. 127–142 in *Extreem-rechts in Nederland,* ed. J. van Holsteyn and C. Mudde. The Hague: SDU.

Wolbers, M., and G. Driessen. 1996. "Milieu of migratie?" *Sociologische Gids* 43, no. 5: 349–366.

Wolff, R., and R. Penninx. 1993. "De ontwikkelingen van de positie van minderheden op de Nederlands arbeidsmarkt 1979–92." Tijdelijke Wetenschappelijk Commissie Minderhedenbeleid study, Amsterdam.

Wolff, R., and R. Penninx. 1994. "Donkere wolken boven de arbeidsmarkt." *Migrantenstudies* 10, no. 1: 1–18.

Wrench, J., et al. 1996. "Preventing Racism at the Workplace: A Report on Fourteen European Countries." European Foundation for the Improvement of Living and Working Conditions, Dublin.

Zonneveld, M. 1997. *Het platte land. Het succes van de Nederlandse democratie.* Amsterdam: Prometheus.

4

Puerto Ricans in the United States and French West Indian Immigrants in France

Monique Milia-Marie-Luce

Introduction

A study of the Caribbean region reveals not only the differences between countries, but also the similarities that have resulted from a shared colonial past. However, while many fields of study benefit from comparative approaches, relatively few attempts have been made to write a comparative history of the Caribbean.[1] One could opt, for example, as does the historian Marc Bloch, to choose "in one or more different social environments, the two or more phenomena that seem, at first sight, to be similar, to describe the restraints on their development, observe the similarities and the differences, and as far as possible account for these" (Bloch 1995: 95). In terms of writing a history of the Caribbean migrations, the comparative approach is useful for analyzing the post–World War II period. Not only do these migrations constitute an unprecedented historical event but, despite the fact that they took place in different societies, they present a number of similarities.

The postwar period saw huge migratory movements not only between Caribbean territories, but also, most significantly, from the Caribbean to the United States and Europe. These movements mainly were from the American, British, French, and Dutch territories. While migration to the United States and Europe is not a new historical phenomenon, the migrations that followed World War II mark a turning point in the history of these territories. On the one hand, these migrations define themselves by movement almost exclusively

to the colonial countries; on the other hand, they are characterized by significant flows of people who in many cases are leaving their islands for good
(although, of course, a significant number do return). The similarities between
the Caribbean migratory experiences, either at the level of departure or in terms
of integration into host societies, have been underlined by such scholars as
Alain Anselin (1979), Barry Levine (1987), and Ramón Grosfoguel (1997),
among others. What do they reveal concerning the contemporary history of the
Caribbean area? What can an analysis of Caribbean migrations brings to the
broader study of migration?

This chapter proposes an examination of the cases of Puerto Rico and the
French West Indies from the end of the war to the 1960s to show the importance
of analyzing Caribbean migrations within a comparative framework. The first
part will highlight the reasons for choosing to compare the Puerto Rican and
the French West Indian cases and the difficulties presented by this choice. The
second part will examine the main issues emerging from the comparative study
of the Puerto Rican and the French West Indian migrations.

Particular Characteristics of Puerto Rico and
the French West Indies

The Puerto Rican and French West Indian migrations lend themselves more
readily to comparison than those from elsewhere in the Caribbean because,
over time, they present three aspects that have not yet been found in a con-
comitant way for other Caribbean migrations. First, both Puerto Rico and the
French West Indies are non-independent territories still legally linked to their
former colonial metropolises. Puerto Rico, a Spanish colony until 1898, became
an American territory following the Spanish–American War.[2] Since 1952, the
status of the island has been that of Free Associated State (*Estado Libre Aso-
ciado*). There is a local government that has a good deal of autonomy, but
decisions concerning international relations, defense, the monetary system, and
external trade are taken by the U.S. Congress. In addition, Puerto Rico has a
resident commissioner in Washington, D.C., who may attend all debates but is
not allowed to vote. On March 1946, the colonies of the French West Indies—
Martinique and Guadeloupe (as well as French Guiana and the island of
Réunion)—became departments integrated into the French Republic. These
Overseas Departments (DOMs), as they are called, are similar in administrative
and legislative terms to the departments of mainland France.

Second, the Puerto Rican and French West Indian migrations involve people who are citizens of the host society. Puerto Ricans became U.S. citizens following the Jones Act of 1917. French West Indians have been French citizens
since the abolition of slavery in 1848. In each case, individuals can enter, live,

and work in the United States or France without a visa. This was not the case for migrants from the English and Dutch territories in the Caribbean that became independent. Legislation relating to Caribbean migration in Great Britain and the Netherlands also drew distinctions between the different categories of British and Dutch citizenship—that is, resident versus non-resident or subject versus citizens.

Third, the Puerto Rican and French West Indian migrations are composed of two distinct flows: on the one hand, there were and are "spontaneous" migrations whereby Puerto Ricans and French West Indians use their personal contacts to leave, generally through family networks; on the other hand, there also until recently were organized migrations. Migrants left Puerto Rico and the French West Indies with the support of agencies created by the Puerto Rican government and the French government, respectively.[3] In Puerto Rico, the agency was called the Migration Division of the Department of Labor for Puerto Rico; in Guadeloupe and Martinique, the agency was the Bureau for Migration from the Overseas Departments (Le Bureau des migrations intéressant les départements d'outre-mer, better known as BUMIDOM). Barbados and Jamaica also had agencies of this type, but their activities ceased after these countries became independent. The Migration Division and BUMIDOM operated until the 1980s.[4]

The characteristics and, in particular, the similarities of the migrations guided the choice to compare the Puerto Rican and French West Indian situations. Nevertheless, construction of the comparison presented some difficulties, mostly related to the context of analysis in the United States and France and the general representation of immigration in these countries.

Terminology

Constructing a reading grid plan for a comparative study is both demanding and intellectually stimulating for the researcher. It requires searching for a common and intelligible language to describe situations and concepts and an awareness that similar terms do not necessarily refer to the same things in the societies studied. A comparative study of the Puerto Rican and French West Indian migrations highlights the difficulties in discussing the same subject in relation to countries with different histories and traditions. This is demonstrated by differences in terminology. Take, for example, the term "race." American society is based on racial and ethnic distinctions that are institutionalized in statistical tools. Its usage by legislators and in research suggests that the word "race" does not refer solely to biological features; rather, it identifies social and cultural features determined both by the people concerned and by government agencies and researchers. In the United States, the words "race" and "ethnicity" are basic concepts in analyzing immigration. In contrast, in France, classifications rest not on ethnicity or race but on nationality. Unlike the U.S. federal state, the French state does not officially recognize the existence of minorities; ethnicity thus remains in the private sphere in France. Moreover, the word "race" does not have a sociocultural connotation in France, as it does in the United States. It has retained its biological meaning, which originally included assumptions about the superiority of one "race" over others.

"Citizenship" is also a contentious term, for similar reasons. The history of immigration in the United States and the idea of the melting pot is dominated by white, Anglo-Saxon Protestant (WASP) ethnicity. From the formation of the United States, being an American citizen meant being white with European origins. Ethnicity and race, in fact, became very important features of exclusion and inclusion in relation to American citizenship, as seen in the exclusion of blacks and Indians from full citizenship rights. In France, by contrast, the French Revolution made all people living in the country French citizens, with no ethnic distinctions.[5] It was not immigrants but *citizens* who built the French nation.

American citizenship also has a national dimension: it conveys a unity in American society that is synonymous with nationality in France. In other words, the English word "citizenship" describes an experience in the United States that is covered by two distinct words in France: "citizenship" and "nationality." Following the universalist meaning of "citizenship" given at the time of the French Revolution, the concept became confused with the fact of being a member of the French nation. A foreigner was a person who was born outside France, not someone who lived in France.[6] However, this concept of citizenship did not express legal membership in the nation following new legislation at the end of the nineteenth century relating to the acquisition of French nationality and the stay of foreigners. The words for "citizenship" and "nationality" are still separate in French law, and, as Danièle Lochak (1991) has noted, the clear concept of citizenship of the French Revolution has disappeared from the French legal vocabulary.[7]

Another word that has almost disappeared from the French vocabulary is "assimilation." This highlights an important conceptual difference between France and the United States. In France, "assimilation" is rarely used in the social sciences because of its pejorative meaning: it recalls the colonial period, the disappearance of original cultures, and total absorption of the migrant in the host society.

It is clear that comparative reading raises questions about the use of words, and the researcher must be careful to take into consideration the political and institutional histories of countries studied. This makes a study of the history of immigration and the representation of migrants in the United States and France an important starting point for research into the Puerto Rican and French West Indian migrations. As Nancy Green (1991: 68) points out, "A comparison between the history of immigration in France and in the United States is fruitful not only because it reveals historical similarities and differences, but also because it underlines the gap between history and memory." This is illustrated by the treatment of the Puerto Rican and French West Indian migrations in American and French historiography. Indeed, there are clear differences in the importance given to these migrations, reflected in the fact that considerably more studies are available on Puerto Rican migration than on French West Indian migration. Also, while works on Puerto Rican migration were available well before World War II, those on the French West Indian migrations date only from the 1970s (Chenault 1938). This reflects not only the chronology of the Puerto Rican and French West Indian migrations,[8] but also interest in the issue of immigration in the United States and France. Immigration has always been valued in the United States; it has not in France. As Gérard Noiriel (1998: 20) rightly said, immigration "is an 'internal' problem to the American society and its past," whereas in France, "immigration is an 'external' question (momentary, new, marginal) that has nothing to do with the construction of France." The Puerto Rican migrations hold a particular place in American immigration history, and for this reason their situation is similar to that of the French West Indian migrations.

There are very few, if any, references to Puerto Ricans and French West Indians in general works on immigration to the United States and France. This reflects an important point: immigration is generally represented as concerning foreign people, but because of their peculiar legal status, Puerto Ricans migrating to the United States and Martinicans and Guadeloupeans migrating to France largely have been perceived as merely changing their place of residence. However, Puerto Ricans and French West Indians, as American citizens and French citizens, respectively, experienced and experience conditions similar to those described by "foreign" migrants. Moreover, they do not feel included in representations of what are called "typically French stock" and "Middle American." In fact, as Abdelmalek Sayad (1997: 268) has said, "If 'foreign' is the definition of a status, 'immigrant' is above all a social condition."

This is an important point for the study of immigration. The possession of citizenship does not constitute a guarantee of acceptance or inclusion for migrants. The migrations of the Puerto Ricans and French West Indians have challenged the usual frontier between nationals and foreigners. As de facto citizens, they are "special migrants," as demonstrated by the migratory policies created for them.

Government Agencies: A Political Response
to the Issue of Migration

These are some reasons for undertaking a comparative study. Another important issue concerns the organization of Puerto Rican and French West Indian migration. The aim is to show how these migrations were perceived by the French and Puerto Rican governments and how they served as exchange links on migration policies between different governments in Europe and the United States.

World War II was a turning point in the twentieth century that had multiple consequences in the Caribbean, as elsewhere. The period from the end of the war to the 1960s brought about important economic and social changes in Puerto Rico, Martinique, and Guadeloupe. They took place within a new political framework, with a change of status that is still at the heart of numerous debates today. In Puerto Rico, the advent of the Popular Democratic Party (PPD) and its charismatic leader, Luis Muñoz Marín, marked a turning point in the history of the country. The PPD remained in power until 1968 and had a significant effect on Puerto Rican society; indeed, it was under Marín's various mandates that important political and economic changes took place. In 1947, the U.S. Congress approved the passage of the Elective Governorship Act, which allowed the Puerto Ricans to elect their own governor. One year later, Marín became the first Puerto Rican-born governor elected by the Puerto Rican people. On July 25, 1952, the island of Puerto Rico changed its status to that of ELA.

In the French West Indies, the political changes were different in nature. The colonies of Martinique and Guadeloupe became Overseas Departments after a law known as law of assimilation passed in France on March 19, 1946. The law, regarded as following from French colonial policy that had prevailed in these territories for three centuries, ratified that Martinique and Guadeloupe formed part of the French Republic and, above all, confirmed the doctrine of incorporation into the French nation. However, some legislative measures limited the scope of this change, imposing a narrow application of French law in the Overseas Departments—especially that concerning social legislation. Since the end of the 1940s, there has been a gap between the promise of total incorporation into France and the economic, politic and social reality of the DOMs.

Nevertheless, the economic and social changes have been considerable. The period from the end of the war to the 1960s saw modernization of West Indian societies. Since 1946, the French government has made several arrangements to bring the Overseas Departments up to the same economic and social level as the departments of continental France. Various plans have been devised to develop and modernize the French West Indies, which is characterized by overpopulation (Martinique and Guadeloupe had an estimated 468,250 inhabitants in 1954; by 1970, this had risen to around 738,000 inhabitants[9]) and an economy based on the quasi-monoculture of sugar. These plans were aimed at improving economic production (developing other industrial sectors such as tourism and fishing and farming of crops other than sugar cane, banana, and pineapple); improving the infrastructure (building and renovating roads, hospitals, and airports); and improving sanitary conditions (supply of drinking water; preventive measures for hygiene). Yet despite considerable financial investment and some clear improvement at all levels of society, the French West Indies experienced a relatively low level of modernization.

This contrasts with Puerto Rico, where the industrial program that began after the war radically transformed society. The island was propelled onto the world stage at the end the 1940s, when its economic reforms were presented as a model of economic development for the countries of the Third World. As in the French West Indies, the Puerto Rican economic system depended on the production and exportation of sugar. Puerto Rico is also considered an over-populated territory. (The rate of natural growth was 21 people per thousand for the period 1935–1940, against 15.2 people per thousand between 1899 and 1910. In comparison, the rate of natural growth was 8.6 people per thousand in the United States between 1935 and 1940). Economically, World War II brought many advantage to the island, which the PPD used and made a clear choice to adopt an industrial model of development based on a privileged relationship with North American capital. This model, known as "Operation Bootstrap," was intended to act as an incentive to foreign enterprises and investment in Puerto Rico. Its basis was exemption from income tax for enterprises located on the island and the free circulation of goods. Exports became the main source of income for Puerto Rico, and "Operation Bootstrap started to show amazing results" (Morales Carrión 1983: 286). The rural and agrarian society was radically transformed into an urban and industrial society. But the increase in the standard of living did not benefit the whole Puerto Rican population. In fact, the new economic and social situation provoked huge movements of the population from countryside to towns and off the island toward the big American cities.

For Puerto Rico, the latter migrations were a consequence of the spectacular postwar economic expansion. Indeed, the PPD's choice to intensify industrialization led to the decline of the agricultural sector. Many agricultural workers went to work in the new factories in towns; others, as we shall see, went to work on U.S. farms with the help of the Migration Division. Furthermore, the federally mandated minimum wage did not apply in Puerto Rico. This attracted investment, but for the Puerto Ricans it created a situation in which they could hope for better social conditions in the United States than in their own country.[10] Although Operation Bootstrap resulted in the creation of a large number of jobs (55,000 in 1950; 81,000 ten years later[11]), the rate of unemployment remained high, permanently fluctuating between 11 percent and 13 percent.[12] Even as the standard of living on the whole improved, it was limited by the high population growth. One way to guarantee success of this development strategy lay in bringing about equilibrium between economic resources and the number of inhabitants. For this reason, the Puerto Rican government adopted two measures to reduce the size of the population. The first was a policy to lower the birth rate (Puerto Rico became an experimental laboratory for U.S. research in the field of contraception following the legalization of birth control in 1937[13]), along with a sterilization campaign known as "*la operación* (the operation)."[14] The second involved encouraging and assisting migration by means of a governmental agency. These measures are reflected in the sudden increase in Puerto Rican migrants to the United States from 13,573 in 1945 to 38,811 in the following year.[15]

The arrival of the Puerto Ricans, especially in New York City, caused violent reactions among the American public. The issue of migration itself—and, to some extent, the actions of Puerto Rican nationalist militants[16]—led to new public policies in Puerto Rico. Faced with growing hostility toward Puerto Ricans in the United States, the Puerto Rican governor called for an investigation into Puerto Rican migration to be conducted at Columbia University and headed by Puerto Rico's secretary of labor and the American sociologist Clarence Senior.[17] Public Law No. 25, enacted on December 5, 1947, defined the public policy of the government of Puerto Rico on migration: "the government neither encourages nor discourages migration but considers that it is the responsibility of the government to properly orient all those who wish to migrate so as to reduce their adjustment problems to a minimum."[18] The law also created the Migration Division (at that time named the Bureau of Employment and Migration). According to Secretary of Labor Fernando Sierra Berdecia, the government of Puerto Rico was the first to commit itself to helping the government of the host society in which Puerto Ricans decided to live.

Others countries, such as France, also opted to set up legal arrangements for migration, for similar demographic reasons. In 1946, expectations regarding the incorporation of Martinique and Guadeloupe into France began to appear with the law of assimilation. It became the basis for the provisions made by the government in all the different plans for the Overseas Departments. But ten years later, without turning back on the principle of departmentalization, Planning Department officials in France suggested taking into account the specificities, and an adaptation of the French legislation for the Overseas Departments was included in the new Constitution of October 4, 1958. Since the end of the World War II, the French West Indies had been considered overpopulated islands, and the steady population-growth rate and high unemployment rate provided the rationale for government intervention during the Third Plan

(1958–1962). Two measures similar to those taken in Puerto Rico were instituted. One was to reduce population growth by controlling the number of births. The French government, unlike Puerto Rico, chose to run a sensitization campaign rather than to publicly support a policy of birth control and sterilization.[19] Contraception was officially proscribed in France until 1967, and abortion (other than for health reasons) was illegal.

Birth control provided the government with a means of reducing the size of the population in the long term. For a short-term solution, a second choice was outlined: migration of French West Indians. The massive migrations that took place in the 1960s were seen by the government as an important element in the islands' development. From the end of the 1940s, the French government organized the migration of French West Indians (above all, Martinicans) to French Guiana,[20] whose proximity and lack of manpower provided an attractive solution to the population surplus of the West Indies.[21] But lack of resources and infrastructure in French Guiana limited these efforts. Only continental France could welcome large-scale migrations from the French West Indies.

At the same time, these geographic changes were occurring in a very precise historical context: since the mid-1950s, French West Indians had been mounting strong protests against their status as a French department. The economic and social equality promised in 1946 between the DOMs and the departments of continental France was far from being realized. Moreover, the fight for independence in the French colonies (especially Algeria) and in the British territories of the Caribbean contributed to the building opposition to France. As Alain-Philippe Blérald (1988: 123–124) has said, "If there is a subject that dominates the contemporary period, it is precisely the upheaval of the Guadeloupean and Martinican national question that stands as the antithesis of the 'assimilationist' path."

In the 1960s and 1970s, these local claims were expressed in violent social conflicts and, particularly, in the birth of movements in favor of autonomy, in which West Indian youth are especially implicated.[22] The French government tried to calm the situation with a new economic and social development plan (the law program of July 1960) and, above all, by setting up a migratory policy toward France. It was a political answer to the crucial situation of the French West Indies. This policy was partly a way to control West Indian youth; indeed, the establishment of the Adapted Military Service in the French West Indies in 1961 authorized the assignment of 60 percent of the contingent to France.[23] The migratory policy was also envisaged as a response to the demographic and unemployment problems in the French West Indies. On October 21, 1961, the Inter-Ministerial Committee officially approved the principle of a migratory policy, which was defined by the minister of the Overseas Departments as "calling on volunteers only, the social improvement of the migrants whose applications are accepted, progressive movement to success whereby the achievement of a former migrant would attract new applicants."[24] There is no policy of this kind in France for departments other than the DOMs. Thus, one can see that, socioeconomic and politic reasons aside, similarities at the institutional level exist in Puerto Rico and the French West Indies.

Exchanges around Migration

A study of BUMIDOM and the Migration Division enables us to see the importance of the postwar migrations. Because these agencies indicate important exchanges between the Caribbean territories, the exchanges take place within the Caribbean Commission. This body, as its name suggests, was created for the Caribbean region and is in itself evidence of close collaboration among the United States, Great Britain, France, and the Netherlands in relation to the territories led by each state.

The Caribbean Commission was the prolongation of a collaboration begun in the area between the United States and Great Britain during World War II. On March 9, 1942, an agreement between these two countries established the Anglo-American Caribbean Commission to facilitate constant exchanges in the Caribbean and ensure economic and social development in their colonies. The commission had a temporary Caribbean Research Council and the Conference of the West Indies (CIO), which carried out technical studies on the American and British colonies. The first CIO took place in Barbados in 1944; some representatives of France and the Netherlands were invited to participate in the August 1946 session held in Saint-Thomas. The Caribbean Commission was born out of this meeting. Under the patronage of the English, American, French, and Dutch governments, the "main goal of the Caribbean Commission [was] the economic and social well-being of the non self-governing territories of the Caribbean area."[25] The Caribbean Commission brought together its members two or three times a year.[26] Convened every two years, the CIO constituted a regular forum of exchange and discussions among the delegates of each territory. In addition to political questions, any subject could be dealt with in the Caribbean Commission—notably, questions about migration.

Indeed, the theme of migration was often at the top of the agenda in the CIO sessions. Demographics and the movement of populations in the non–self-governing Caribbean territories had been the subjects of studies since the creation of the Caribbean Commission.[27] Because of its status, the commission could not take measures to address the problems, but the studies did reveal that demographic growth was seen as an obstacle to the territories' economic and social development. Puerto Rican migration was the most debated case in the Caribbean session because of its volume, plentiful data, and model of organization through the Migration Division. The Puerto Rican Migration Division, in different ways, served as a model for other governments. In 1955, Clarence Senior was asked by Jamaican Prime Minister Norman Manley to study Jamaican migration and provide technical assistance in creating a program similar to that of Puerto Rico. Between 1948 and 1956, the government of Barbados set up the Barbados Liaison Service. And in 1963, the French government created BUMIDOM. All of these agencies, while different in their operations, had similar goals.

Life and Work in France and the United States

The Puerto Rican Migration Division and BUMIDOM had two main goals. The first was to provided manpower for American and French industry. The second was to facilitate the settlement of Puerto Rican migrants in the United States and French West Indians in France.

To achieve the first goal, both agencies created sections charged with coordinating supply and demand. Originally, the Puerto Rican Migration Division was called the Bureau of Employment and Migration. In 1951, the Wagner-Peyser Act, which created a state employment service in the United States, was extended to Puerto Rico, and the Bureau of Employment and Migration became affiliated with the U.S. Employment Service. It acquired a new name, the Bureau of Employment Security, and a new division—the Migration Division—was created within the bureau. The Migration Division had a central office in New York City, several regional offices in the United States, and offices in Puerto Rico. It ran a program that provided orientation for jobs at all levels, from industry to the civil service, and assistance with interviewing and job placement for Puerto Rican migrants. The farm-labor program, however, was the agency's main service. The program oversaw the placement of Puerto Rican seasonal agricultural workers during the inactive season (July to October) in Puerto Rico. Puerto Rican farm workers went to the United States with contracts that guaranteed a minimum wages, free housing, and good living conditions.[28] Between 1948 and 1969, 300,195 agricultural workers went to work on American farms, where they replaced American labor that had turned to industry after World War II.

BUMIDOM also tried to address the shortage of labor in some sectors of the French economy. The agency was officially created on March 26, 1963, under the secretariat in charge of the Overseas Departments and Territories and the Ministry of the Treasury and Economic Affairs. Like the Migration Division had in the United States, BUMIDOM had a central office in Paris, regional offices in France, and one office in each Overseas Department (Martinique, Guadeloupe, French Guiana, and Réunion). Its employment program consisted of placing French West Indians migrants in jobs (mainly in domestic work for women and the building trades for men without a high education level), preparing them for the competitive civil-service examinations, putting them in touch with contractors, and, above all, offering them training. BUMIDOM placed the migrants in existing training program in France and set up its own centers, four of which were opened between 1965 and 1978.[29] This employment program, like that of the Migration Division, aimed to disperse the migrants around the territories and thus keep French West Indian migrants from concentrating in Paris.

The Migration Division and BUMIDOM addressed the second goal—to facilitate the settlement of Puerto Rican migrants in the United States and French West Indians in France—by giving the migrants assistance. The Migration Division had six programs to assist the Puerto Rican migrants, including education, research, identification, documentation, community organization, and public relations. BUMIDOM guided migrants toward relevant social services, took care of family regrouping, provided financial help, and provided assistance with housing and travel back to the West Indies for holidays. It also maintained links with West Indian associations. Yet despite all these services, the French West Indian and Puerto Rican migrants became integrated in varying degrees in the host societies. Despite their shared citizenship, they were confronted by racial discrimination in job, housing, and so on. Because they focused on citizenship, the migration policies implemented through BUMIDOM and the Migration Division underestimated these difficulties.

Conclusion

The postwar migrations have an important place in the history of Puerto Rican and French West Indian migration. Indeed, they show a transition from movements that involved relatively few people, generally from the upper classes of society, to a collective movement that touches entire populations. The postwar migrations helped to reinforce the small Puerto Rican and French West Indian communities that had already been established in the United States and France. The result is that there are nearly as many Puerto Ricans in the United States and French West Indians in France today as there are in the Caribbean. The 2000 Census shows that 2.65 million Puerto Ricans live in the United States, while 3.55 million live on the island of Puerto Rico. And according to the census taken in 1999, one-quarter of French West Indians born in Martinique and Guadeloupe reside in France.

The French and Puerto Rican governments played an important part in bringing about this change by asserting institutional control over a portion of the migrations through BUMIDOM and the Migration Division. These agencies created a continual circulation of people between the islands and the mainland and by directing and promoting "spontaneous" migrations. But the settlement of Puerto Ricans and French West Indians did not occur without problems. This reflects the ambiguity of their legal situations and social conditions— a highlight of the specificity of the Puerto Rican and the French West Indian migrations. Their migration history also reflects questions of identity and issues related to the links between host societies and home islands, especially in terms of the political status of Puerto Rico, Martinique, and Guadeloupe—hence, the value of a comparative study.

Notes

1. The most significant is Williams 1975.

2. The Treaty of Paris also granted Guam, Cuba, and the Philippines to the United States. Puerto Rico became an American territory but is not included in the union of American states. During the last referendum, in 1998, concerning a possible change of this status, 50.2 percent of the Puerto Ricans who cast votes rejected the island's becoming the fifty-first state of the United States (see Cohen 1999).

3. The U.S. federal government financially supports the running of the Puerto Rican agency. Moreover, the Migration Division is similar to an agency for Puerto Rican migrants created under the U.S. governorship in the 1930s.

4. BUMIDOM was replaced by another government agency in 1982. The Migration Division partly ceased its activities in 1989 and was renamed the Department of Community Affairs in the United States.

5. This does not means that in the collective mentality, the representation of being a French citizen is not linked with whiteness. But officially, the separation is not based on race or ethnicity, as it officially is in the United States.

6. Citizenship is a feature of belonging as a member of the French nation. It does not give the "quality of Frenchness" in the way that being born in France or being French through one of your parents does. But the universalism of the Revolutionary period provided foreigners with some of the prerogatives of nationals.

7. She underlines that today, "except by mistake, the words 'citizen' and 'citizenship' are not used in any text of the French positive law" (Lochak 1991: 180).

8. The massive migration of French West Indians to France (1960s–1970s) took place later than the migration of Puerto Ricans to the United States (1950s–1960s). Nevertheless, there was a Puerto Rican community in the United States and a French West Indian community in France before World War II.

9. The numbers are from the Institut National de la Statistique et des Études Économiques census of 1954 and the previsions formulated in the report "Opération pour le Ve Plan des DOM," available at the National Archives.

10. In 1950, for example, the minimum hourly wage was 42 cents in Puerto Rico and 50 cents in the United States.

11. The numbers are from Daniel 1996: 194.

12. The numbers are from Baggs 1962.

13. The pill was tested on the island at the end of the war, before its commercialization in the United States in 1960. Dr. Clarence J. Gamble, an eminent member of the American Birth Control League, opened several clinics in Puerto Rico in the mid-1930s.

14. "By 1968, 35% of the women between twenty and forty-nine years of age had been sterilized—a proportion several times larger than the closest comparable figure for any other country": quoted in History Task Force 1979: 132.

15. The emergence of air traffic between San Juan and New York City favored these departures.

16. As in the French West Indies, there was a strong movement of contestation against the political status of the island. The most striking incident is undoubtedly the one that took place on March 1, 1954, when three nationalist militants shot to death members of the U.S. Congress in Washington, D.C.

17. Clarence Senior, who was born in Missouri in 1903, played an influential part in defining Puerto Rican migration policy. He worked in the Social Sciences Research Department at the University of Puerto Rico before joining Columbia University.

18. *The Puerto Rican Agricultural Migrant Workers Program*, 6. Box "Administration of the Migration Division, New York," Archives of the Center for Puerto Rican Studies, Hunter College, New York.

19. This consisted of "making householders aware of the necessity to not have more children than they can afford to educate": Note sur le IIIe Plan, July 1957.

20. Martinicans have had a strong presence in French Guiana since the nineteenth century; thus, the organized migration to French Guiana after World War II was not the first. After the eruption of Mount Pelée in 1902, the government proposed that some victims of the disaster go to French Guiana to reclaim the town of Rémire-Montjoly.

21. As underlined elsewhere, a government agency created in 1950 named the Bureau for People Immigrating to Guiana (BIPIG) aimed to settle West Indians in the town of Saint-Laurent-du-Maroni. BIPIG was originally created for the displaced people (Milia 1998).

22. Many associations were created, including the Organization of Anticolonialist Martinican Youth and the Group of National Organizations of Guadeloupe in the French West Indies, and the General Association of Guadeloupean Students in France.

23. The numbers are from General Nemo in an annual report. Since the end of the war, the regime of budgetary leave has been applied in the French West Indies, which means that only part of the contingent is performing military service.

24. Activity Report of the Bureau pour le Développement Agricole, 1962, 2.

25. Monthly Report of the Caribbean Commission, October 1948, National Library, Paris, 79.

26. Four commissioners, some of whom came from the non–self-governing territories, represent each government. Each member country had greater representation in the two auxiliary bodies of the Caribbean Commission, the Council of Caribbean Research and the CIO.

27. In 1948, for example, the Caribbean Commission asked Michael Proudfoot, a geography professor at Northwestern University in Illinois, to carry out a six-month study of population movements in the Caribbean.

28. A contract covering wages, living and working conditions, and health insurance was negotiated between the Puerto Rican Department of Labor and the growers' associations.

29. Crouy-sur-Ourcq, opened in 1965, is exclusively for women. Simandres, near Lyon, opened in 1968; Marseille opened in 1973; and Cassan, near Béziers, opened in 1978.

References

Anselin Alain. 1979. *L'émigration antillaise en France, du Bantoustan au ghetto.* Paris: Anthropos.

Anselin, Alain. 1990. *L'émigration antillaise en France, la 3e île.* Paris: L'Harmattan.

Baggs, W. 1962. "Puerto Rico, Showcase of Development." In *Britannica Book of the Year 1962: Events of 1961.* Chicago: Encyclopedia Britannica, Inc. [Box "The Historical Archives of the Puerto Rican Migration to the United States," Archives of the Center for Puerto Rican Studies, Hunter College, New York.]

Blérald, A-P. 1988. *La question nationale en Guadeloupe et en Martinique.* Paris: L'Harmattan.

Bloch, E. 1995. *Histoire et historiens.* Paris: Armand Colin.

Chenault, L. 1938. *The Puerto Rican Migrant in New York City.* New York: Columbia University Press.

Cohen, J. 1999. "Consensus introuvable à Puerto Rico." *Le monde diplomatique,* April.

Daniel, Justin. 1996. "Développement et compétition politique: Vers une mutation du modèle portoricain?" Pp. 185–225 in *Les îles Caraïbes, modèles politiques et stratégies de développement,* ed. Justin Daniel. Paris: Karthala.

Green, Nancy. 1991. "L'immigration en France et aux Etats-Unis, historiographie comparée." *Vingtième siècle,* no. 29 (January–March): 68.

Grosfoguel, Ramón. 1997. "Colonial Caribbean Migrations to France, the Netherlands, Great Britain and the United States." *Ethnic and Racial Studies* 20, no. 3: 31–33.

History Task Force, Center for Puerto Rican Studies, City University of New York. 1979. *Labor Migration under Capitalism: The Puerto Rican Experience.* New York: Monthly Review Press.

Levine, Barry. 1987. *The Caribbean Exodus.* New York: Praeger.

Lochak, Danièle. 1991. "La citoyenneté: Un concept juridique flou." In *Citoyenneté et nationalité: Perspectives en France et au Quebec,* ed. Dominique Colas, Claude Emeri, and Jacques Zylberberg. Paris: PUF.

Morales Carrión, A. 1983. *Puerto Rico: A Political and Cultural History.* New York: W. W. Norton.

Noiriel, Gérard. 1998. *Le creuset français, histoire de l'immigration 19e–20e siècles.* Paris: Seuil.

Sayad, Abdelmalek. 1997. "Immigration et conventions internationales." In *L'immigration ou les paradoxes de l'altérité.* Brussels: De Boeck Université.

Williams, Eric. 1975. *De Christophe Colomb à Fidel Castro: L'histoire des Caraïbes 1492–1969.* Paris: Présence Africaine.

II

Identities, Countercultures, and Ethnic Resilience

5

Puerto Rican Migration and Settlement in South Florida

Ethnic Identities and Transnational Spaces

Elizabeth Aranda

Migration has long been a central component of Puerto Rican life. For the first time, more than half of all persons of Puerto Rican origin currently live in the mainland United States (U.S. Census Bureau 2006). For many years, New York City and other Northeastern cities were the most popular destinations for Puerto Ricans looking to escape island poverty and joblessness. In recent decades, Puerto Ricans have dispersed throughout the country, making their homes in emerging communities in the South and West. Florida, California, and Texas are increasingly the states of preference for Puerto Rican settlement (Acosta-Belén and Santiago 2006; Baker 2002).

While new communities in the Southern United States might offer Puerto Ricans greater economic opportunities, there is a gap in the literature regarding the full range of factors that play into the formation of communities in, and increasing mobility to, the South on the part of both island-born and U.S.-born (second-generation) Puerto Ricans. Florida in particular has seen the emergence of vibrant communities in Orlando, Tampa, Miami, and Fort Lauderdale (Acosta Belén and Santiago 2006). As Puerto Ricans from diverse migration and class backgrounds come together in these communities, what it means to be Puerto Rican has emerged as the subject of much discussion (Acosta Belén and Santiago 2006). What is unclear is under what conditions Puerto Ricans converge on Southern communities as opposed to their traditional areas of settlement.

Using data from a study of South Florida immigrants, I examine island-born and U.S.-born Puerto Ricans in Miami by focusing on their migration experiences and the conditions under which they have made their homes in Miami. I am interested in what factors led Puerto Ricans to choose Miami as their destination, particularly those related to their status as a U.S. racial minority. This chapter also examines the role of Miami as an emerging transnational hub in structuring Puerto Ricans' settlement options. I discuss the theoretical implications of settlement choices for the research on transnational communities, particularly the role of a larger Latino culture in Miami in shaping settlement decisions.

Puerto Rican Migration

Since U.S. colonization of the island in 1898, Puerto Rico has been under U.S. economic, political, and cultural influences. U.S. imperialism, agrarian capitalism and the practices of U.S. agribusiness, and subsequently the displacement of urban workers due to the weak labor-absorption capacity of Puerto Rico's industrialized economy have all resulted in massive migration. For example, in the late 1940s and 1950s, migration from the island grew dramatically due to active Puerto Rican government sponsorship of emigration and the recruitment of Puerto Rican laborers to work abroad to ease the pressures of overpopulation and poverty on the island (Hernández Cruz 1985; Pérez 2004).

Evidence of return flows to the island emerged in the late 1960s. Three-fourths of the Great Migration (1945–1965) remained on the mainland, while one-quarter returned to Puerto Rico (Bonilla and Colón Jordan 1979). More recently, statistics from the Puerto Rican Planning Board (cited in Duany 2004) reveal that migration in the 1980s surpassed 1950s figures. Since the 1970s, the Puerto Rican population on the mainland has grown by an average rate of 41 percent each decade, a total growth of 138 percent as of 2000 (Acosta Belén and Santiago 2006: 219). Moreover, in the 1990s alone, almost 8 percent of islanders relocated to the mainland (Duany 2007). Recent figures also illustrate that circular migration persists (Duany 2007). The percentage of the island's population in 2000 that was living outside Puerto Rico in 1995 is 3.2 percent. In addition, 6.1 percent of Puerto Ricans on the island were born in the United States (U.S. Census Bureau 2000b). Puerto Rican patterns of migration and the establishment of communities throughout the mainland have led some to view the case of Puerto Ricans as transnational in nature (Duany 2002; Pérez 2004).

Puerto Rican Transnational Communities

Recent research has focused on how emigrants and immigrants construct transnational lives and maintain their linkages across borders, anchored in sending and receiving communities. In his study of Mexicans in New York, Robert C.

Smith defines transnationalization and transnational life as "that sphere of life that flows out of the regular contact between sending and receiving societies, a social field of relations that, in the second generation especially, has a character akin to associational life and is particularly strong in particular phases of life" (Smith 2002: 148). While Puerto Rican communities on the mainland are not traditionally considered immigrant communities, research suggests that their linkages to island ones resemble the transnational connections studied in other immigrant groups.

In a study of Puerto Rican communities in Puerto Rico and Chicago, Gina Pérez examines how Puerto Ricans use migration to contend with the struggles of everyday life, including raising children and pursuing opportunities to increase their socioeconomic standing. She argues that while Puerto Ricans live their lives locally, their social horizons transcend the bounds of their communities in either Puerto Rico or Chicago, embarking on migration as necessary. In short, high rates of back-and-forth mobility continue to link island and mainland communities; emerging communities on the mainland are increasingly composed of both island migrants and U.S.-born Puerto Ricans, and island communities are witnessing the arrival of mainland emigrants and return migrants. Unclear in these patterns, however, is the full range of factors that have led not just to circular migration between the island and mainland, but also to Puerto Rican patterns of dispersion throughout the mainland itself and whether these trends could also be interpreted with a transnational perspective.

Puerto Rican Dispersion and Emerging Communities in the South

As circular migration between the island and mainland continues, other trends regarding mainland Puerto Rican settlement have concurrently emerged. Francisco Rivera-Batiz and Carlos Santiago, for example, identified internal migration trends on the mainland during the 1980s and 1990s in which Puerto Rican dispersion to other states increased (Rivera-Batiz and Santiago 1994, 1996). While states such as New York, New Jersey, and Illinois were among those with the largest number of Puerto Ricans, this period saw declines in the rate of growth of these states' Puerto Rican populations (Rivera-Batiz and Santiago 1994). In New York—the center of Puerto Rican mainland society—the 1990s for the first time saw a decrease in the number of Puerto Ricans residing there (Duany 2004).[1] At the same time, states such as Florida, Massachusetts, Pennsylvania, Connecticut, Texas, and California saw increases in their concentrations of Puerto Ricans, signs of their growing dispersion. In particular, Sunbelt states with large concentrations of Latinos have become increasingly popular among Puerto Ricans (Acosta-Belén and Santiago 2006; Rivera-Batiz and Santiago 1994).

TABLE 5.1   RESIDENCE FIVE YEARS PRIOR TO U.S. CENSUS (1985, 1995)
FOR THE POPULATION FIVE YEARS AND OVER

Residence five years prior was in Puerto Rico	1990 Census	2000 Census
Northeast	120,082	113,589
Midwest	19,334	21,835
South	64,115	96,195
West	10,355	11,354

Sources: U.S. Census Bureau 1990; U.S. Census Bureau 2000.

Census data from 1990 and 2000 indicate that, while most regions of the
United States have increased their numbers of island migrants, these numbers
have decreased in the Northeast (see Table 5.1). Furthermore, the South experienced the largest gain in island migrants. Although these numbers include all
who migrated from the island (including non-Puerto Ricans), they nevertheless
contribute to the pattern of Puerto Rican dispersion on the mainland. Moreover, the 1980s and 1990s saw increases in the migration of island professionals
(Grosfoguel 2003; Santiago and Rivera-Batiz 1996) with higher levels of education. Of island professionals moving to the mainland in the period 1985–1990,
about one-third moved to Florida and Texas (Rivera-Batiz and Santiago 1994,
20). Moreover, five of the ten most popular destinations for recent island
migrants are in Florida (Duany 2007).

As the dispersion of the Puerto Rican population to the South and West has
increased, Susan Baker (2002) has found, U.S.-born Puerto Ricans in particular
are more likely to head to the South. In her analysis of Puerto Rican patterns
of internal migration, Baker argues that the popularity of Southern states, especially for Northeasterners, is due to a greater ability to advance economically
(Baker 2002). She argues that U.S. Puerto Ricans leaving New York "are not as
dependent on established communities to maintain strong ethnic ties because
they are generally more 'Americanized'" than their island-born counterparts
(Baker 2002: 96). Even though wages are lower and family median incomes
seem to drop when New York Puerto Ricans relocate to the South, Puerto
Ricans who undertake this move are more likely to escape extreme poverty as
their lower wages go further (Baker 2002: 87).

As suggested earlier, of the Southern states that have been receiving increasing numbers of Puerto Ricans, Florida has emerged as the state with the second-
largest population (U.S. Census Bureau 2000a; Duany 2007). The 2000 Census
showed that Florida had almost half a million Puerto Ricans, half the number
of New York's Puerto Rican population, which stood at one million (U.S. Census Bureau 2000a). Unclear in these trends, however, is the full range of factors
that has made Florida such a popular state for Puerto Rican settlement.

As of 2005, Florida was home to 17 percent of the mainland Puerto Rican population (Duany 2007). The movement of both island-born and mainland-born Puerto Ricans to this state has led one scholar to refer to them as "Florirricans," a "new hybrid species in search of the American and Puerto Rican dream of a better quality of life" (Duany 2005). The greatest concentrations of Puerto Ricans in the state are in central and South Florida. Orange County (Orlando) has over 86,000, and Miami-Dade County (Miami) has a little over 80,000 (followed by Broward County [Fort Lauderdale] and Hillsborough County [Tampa], with 55,000 and 52,000, respectively; U.S. Census Bureau 2000a). While Orlando has the largest Puerto Rican community in the state, the numbers indicate that Miami does not lag far behind. Moreover, cities such as Fort Lauderdale and Tampa are also home to emerging communities of Puerto Ricans. This chapter focuses on Miami as the second-most-popular Florida destination for island- and U.S.-born Puerto Ricans.

Puerto Ricans in the Global City: A Look at Miami

In 1993, Alejandro Portes and Alex Stepick described the city of Miami as at "the edge of a future marked by uncertainty, but also by the promise of path-breaking innovations in urban life" (Portes and Stepick 1993: xiv). The suggested innovations relied not only on increasing immigration of Cubans and other Latin Americans into the city, but also how these groups would blend into the white and black communities in South Florida. Fifteen years after their well-known work on Miami's ethnic and race relations, the city has undergone even more changes.

Miami-Dade County has the highest immigration rate of any U.S. metropolitan area (Henderson 2003); the growing Latino population in South Florida is largely a result of immigrants coming from Caribbean and Latin American countries. However, most studies on South Florida immigrants and communities focus almost exclusively on Cuban and Cuban Americans (García 2003; Levine and Asís 2000; McHugh et al. 1997; Pérez-Lopez 1991; Portes and Stepick 1993; Stepick et al. 2003) and, to a lesser extent, Nicaraguans and Haitians. While the Latino population in Miami-Dade County rose in the 1990s (49.2 percent of the population in 1990 to 57.3 percent in 2000), the Cuban population decreased from 59.2 percent of Latinos in Miami-Dade in 1990 to 50.4 percent in 2000 (U.S. Census 1990, 2000a). Even though Cubans continue to be the majority group of Latinos, Puerto Ricans make up the next largest Latino presence in this county (U.S. Census Bureau 2000a). In Broward County, Puerto Ricans are the largest Latino group. These trends highlight the importance of studying the Puerto Rican populations in Miami specifically, and in Florida generally.

The dispersion of Puerto Ricans on the mainland suggests that it is important to understand how Puerto Rican settlement in South Florida is affected by Miami's position as a global hub for capital and people. Moreover, the shifting demography of the city suggests that more work is needed to understand the role of Miami as a place of settlement for the non-Cuban Latino communities that have grown over the past few decades. In the case of Puerto Ricans specifically, I explore the range of factors that lead to their (both U.S.-born and island-born) relocation to Miami.

Methodology

The data used in this chapter come from an ongoing study of Latin American immigrants in South Florida (Aranda et al. 2003). This study explores patterns of adaptation among immigrants settled in Miami, interethnic relations, and transnational patterns of living, among other issues. In-depth, open-ended interviews were conducted with immigrants from Peru, Colombia, Cuba, the Dominican Republic, Haiti, Puerto Rico, and Mexico, for a total of about 115 interviews. This chapter will focus on the data compiled from the subsample of Puerto Ricans. This subsample consists of fifteen in-depth interviews with island-born migrants to the mainland. In addition, five interviews were conducted with Puerto Ricans who were born and raised on the mainland but who had migrated to Miami as either children or adults. The total number of interviews analyzed for this chapter is twenty.

All interviews were conducted in participants' language of choice. Most interviews with island migrants were conducted in Spanish, while most interviews with U.S.-born Puerto Ricans were conducted in English. All interviews were transcribed verbatim and analyzed for recurring themes. All names used in this chapter have been changed to protect the identities of respondents.

Among the Puerto Ricans residing in Miami who were interviewed, thirteen were born in Puerto Rico and moved to the United States as children or adults; two were born on the mainland but were raised on the island, later moving back to the mainland; four were born on the mainland and moved to Miami from the Northeast as children or adults (some of these had lived on the island for a year or two), and one was born and raised in Miami.

Of the fifteen island-born (and raised) migrants, four migrated to the mainland and returned to live in Puerto Rico at least once before settling in Miami. Three migrated to the Mid-Atlantic and Northeastern regions before relocating in Florida, and eight came straight from the island to Miami.

Given the small sample size, generalizations cannot be drawn from these data. However, they do provide insight into some of the reasons behind the trends in Puerto Rican migration and dispersion discussed thus far. They also illustrate the conditions under which place factors into emerging transnational connections binding mainland and island communities.

The Global City and the Creation of Transnational Social Space

In his analysis of Puerto Rico's position in the global coloniality, Ramón Grosfoguel (2003) makes the case that Miami is an example of a recently formed world city. He argues that while peripheral regions in the Caribbean Basin grew to be the sites of intensification for global capital, the need for more direct supervision over capital investments grew, rendering cities such as New York obsolete in terms of their ability to closely manage Caribbean investments. In this context, Miami "became known as the capital of the Caribbean" (Grosfoguel 2003: 87)

Miami's status as a global city has led to what Michael P. Smith and Luis Guarnizo (1998) have called "transnationalism from above." The concentration of multinational corporations in Miami has further bound the United States to other countries by reinforcing the existence of transnational institutions that then pave the way for "transnationalism from below," which involves, among other things, flows of people. For example, a 2008 study by *WorldCity Business* magazine, backed by the Beacon Council (Miami-Dade's economic development agency), shows that South Florida is home to 1,183 multinational corporations from fifty-six countries, with combined revenue of $203 billion (Wyss 2008). This institutional infrastructure has led to the growth of a multinational professional workforce in Miami and the transformation of South Florida into transnational social space for those who move there.

Thomas Faist (2000: 190) has argued that transnational social spaces are characterized by "a high density of interstitial ties on informal or formal, that is to say, institutional levels." In his analysis of transnational social spaces, Peter Kivisto (2003) has called for a reconsideration of the role of space in defining transnational immigrant communities. He argues that immigrants' social horizons affect the social construction of their community as one existing in a border-crossing space. He adds, however, that place still matters in that it exists with space in a dialectical relationship (Kivisto 2003). Miami's placement as a hub for international trade and finance has led to the city's status as home to populations from various countries, creating a space in which multinational populations come into contact with one another and in which cultural diversity is more the norm than the exception. Multiple languages are spoken in Miami, and ethnic businesses abound. Moreover, the social space in Miami is configured in such a way that patterns of social relations transcend the boundaries of any one country, making it into a transnational, or multinational, place that in many ways meets the needs of global populations, given the easy access to travel and cultural diversity that eases the process of immigrant incorporation. This is especially the case for Puerto Ricans, who find themselves two hours away from the island by plane and who can successfully navigate the Spanish–English code-switching that linguistically defines Miami.

Miami's location in the international division of labor as the headquarters for corporations with subsidiaries in Latin America pulled many of the Puerto Ricans in our sample and their families toward settlement in South Florida. Zaida, for example, moved to Miami with her parents due to her father's job relocation. "Dad was working at this research company, and an opportunity opened up for director of technology for the Latin American region," she said. "It would be a promotion, so he moved." While both push and pull factors at the individual level affect Miami's settlement patterns, the location of the city as a global economic hub structures these pathways. The father of one U.S.-born Puerto Rican, María, worked for an American company and was transferred several times between New York and San Juan before he finally settled in Miami. Zaida's and María's fathers both make up part of the transnational professional workforce that has settled in Miami. In these cases, settlement decisions were structured by corporate decisions.

The data in this study indicate, however, that for many Puerto Ricans, resettlement decisions are also related to the dynamics of incorporation experienced in other parts of the United States and the role of place in shaping integration experiences. As I will illustrate in the following sections, there are aspects of Puerto Ricans' resettlement decisions that represent a search for cultural citizenship that a place such as Miami can provide. These findings illuminate the context in which Puerto Rican dispersion in the South has occurred.

Island-Born Migrants and Settlement in the South

Some of the island migrants who had moved to other parts of the United States from Puerto Rico ultimately reconsidered their choice of destination and relocated to the South. The reasons for these changes in settlement decisions are multifaceted. Previous research on Puerto Ricans' motivations for migration reveals that there are both instrumental and underlying factors that lead to migration (Aranda 2001, 2006). For example, if resettlement is undertaken to pursue a job opportunity, there are often underlying reasons that resulted in the job search to begin with. The remainder of this chapter aims to capture these underlying motivations for resettlement with the goal of exposing the social dynamics at the roots of Puerto Rican dispersion.

Among the Puerto Ricans in this study, many resettlement decisions were rooted in the racial configurations of the cities in which they had previously lived. Depending on the level of diversity of an area and experiences with racism that might have emerged, Puerto Ricans reassessed their settlement decisions. Teresa is one such example.

Teresa moved to Boston from Puerto Rico and lived there for thirteen years. She then moved to Miami in search of a different environment for her children:

> I have two kids, and I lived in Boston for thirteen years. . . . [I]t was very cold; there were few Hispanics from varying social classes and different opportunities for Hispanics and I wanted my children to grow up bilingual. The warmth [of Miami] is similar to Puerto Rico's. . . . There are more opportunities than in Puerto Rico.

Several issues in this quote shaped the context for Teresa's move. Teresa's experiences with marginalization shaped her views regarding the kind of environment she wanted for her children. She tied the socioeconomically diverse Latino community in Miami to greater opportunities for her children. It was also important to her to nurture bilingualism and biculturalism in her family, and Miami proved to be the location in which she could achieve this. She also made a comparison regarding having more opportunities in Miami than in Puerto Rico, suggesting that the only other alternative in her mind to attain what she wanted for her family was to return to the island. Faced with these options, Miami emerged as a better choice, given the greater economic opportunities available in comparison with the island, as her quote suggests. Finally, Teresa's reference to the harshness of the cold weather up north was a factor in that Miami's warmer climate better approximates Puerto Rico's climate. While seemingly insignificant, climate relates to how one feels in one's surroundings, and the discomfort that one develops in a climate that is not familiar can erode the desire to remain in such a place. Coupled with the other motivations for resettlement, the outcome was that Teresa relocated to Miami with her family.

The issues raised in Teresa's interview reveal that she was in search of a kind of belonging that Miami could offer. This was particularly the case with regard to the racial hierarchy of the Northeast compared with that in Miami, as the earlier quote suggested. This is seen in Teresa's answer to a question about whether she had ever felt rejected (in the United States or Puerto Rico):

> The curious thing was that when I went to Boston, being black. . . . Blacks there did not accept me at first because they would say that I was not really black because I was Hispanic. And my best friend was white. And the whites obviously did not accept me very much, because they did not know . . . how to make sense of me since I was black. But my best friend

was white, and either way, she was Hispanic, so they did not know how to classify me. . . . The worst experience that I've had here in the United States was when a group of neo-Nazis threw a bottle at me in Cambridge. I was in Harvard Square, and they threw a bottle that hit my heel.

Teresa's feelings of not fitting into either racial group appeared to fracture her ability to develop relationships and bonds with others. At the same time, despite being "in-between," she was subjected to racial prejudice, seen in the incident she recounted in Harvard Square. These experiences suggest that there were barriers to feeling fully integrated into her reference group in Boston.

In previous work on Puerto Ricans' experiences of incorporation into a low-immigrant-receiving city (Aranda 2006), Puerto Ricans experienced varying levels of emotional embeddedness, or feelings of belonging to a certain place. These subjective assessments of integration were defined by life experiences rooted in class, gender, and racial hierarchies. These feelings varied over the life course, as levels of emotional embeddedness were linked to states of well-being that emerged from positive and negative experiences of incorporation. While a dominant theme in this research was that Puerto Ricans often felt incompatible with their surroundings in predominantly white communities (largely due to racial discrimination and feelings of marginalization), many of the return migrants interviewed in Puerto Rico discussed how these feelings led them to renegotiate previous settlement decisions.

These processes are also found among Miami Puerto Ricans. However, rather than return migration, resettlement elsewhere in the United States was the outcome. Teresa mentioned that she liked that Miami was home to Latinos from different class backgrounds and that she perceived that there were more opportunities, as well as "warmth." She was attracted to Miami and formed an image of Miami as a city in which she could find more diversity and, thus, acceptance:

> I've always liked big cities with life, and Miami is like the model Hispanic city here. Not like Chicago or New York. . . . [They] are Hispanic, but there is . . . not so much diversity within the Hispanic community, and that is why I wanted to come here.

The diversity Teresa is alluding to is socioeconomic diversity among Latinos. In this quote, she draws comparisons to other large cities that have significant Latino populations; however, these groups are over-represented among the lower rungs of the local social-class hierarchies. One can infer from her allusion to Miami as the "model Hispanic city" that Miami represents to Teresa a place in which Latinos have more opportunities to transcend stereotypes.

Others, too, were attracted to the city and notion of being culturally aligned with the dominant group of an area. For example, before moving to Miami, Beatriz had an impression of Miami as a predominantly Cuban city. She said:

I thought Miami was a city for Cubans (laughs); that only Cubans lived here and people only spoke Spanish and that things were like another American country, but that people mainly spoke Spanish. And to a certain point it is true, but I discovered there were not only Cubans, but that there are people here from all parts of the world and that, thank God, there are many of us Puerto Ricans.

Beatriz found the Latino environment in Miami appealing, especially the notion that in addition to the Cuban community there was a community of Puerto Ricans. This was of particular importance because she had experienced the opposite when she initially settled in Washington, D.C.:

It was even difficult to open a bank account. When I brought my check from Puerto Rico's Medical School to open my bank account in Washington, they asked me whether those were American dollars or if they were another kind of currency and that they would not be able to accept them. . . . I told them that we were not Indians that cover up with our tails or anything along those lines. (laughs)

Although Beatriz laughed off this and other experiences in which she felt marginalized, they did have an effect on her. Her quote reveals that she interpreted a question about currency to be a statement about Puerto Rico's level of development and civilization. Her retort, in which she emphatically stated that Puerto Rico is not inhabited by Indians and therefore that she was not an Indian who covered up "with our tails" illustrates her attempts to fight off negative stereotypes associated with the island and Puerto Ricans in general. In short, Beatriz and her husband were seeking an environment free of prejudice and marginality. Moreover, the following quote suggests that this led them to settle in Miami:

One of the reasons why we decided to come to Miami, aside from the environment being so horrible there [in Washington, D.C.] and much better here, is because we had a son, and we did not want to raise him in an area in which. . . there is so much racism, much more than what I would have ever encountered in the South. We did not want our son to grow up in that environment. We wanted him to be accepted as if he were any other child.

Beatriz did not want her child to grow up as "the other" or to experience the marginalization she had felt. In this way, moving to Miami reflected a desire for greater cultural citizenship on the mainland. William Flores, Rena Benmayor, and Renato Resaldo discuss the theme of "Latino cultural citizenship," which they define as "the right to feel at home in claiming space or rights despite one's ethnic or racial difference from others in the community (Smith 2006: 10). The desire to move away from stigmas applied to Latinos and to be able to raise one's children in an environment in which they would not be "othered" embodies a search for cultural citizenship in the United States.

Another indicator of this search is found in comparisons that Puerto Ricans made about the experience of being Latino in various parts of the mainland United States. Luz, an island-born migrant, said that it was easier to be Latina in Miami than the rest of the country. Luz grew up in Puerto Rico and moved to Miami for the first time to attend college. Having an older brother living in the city made it easier for her parents to let her go. She returned to the island after two years because of a relationship. Two years after that, in the early 1990s, she moved to Miami again, this time with her new husband. In the late 1990s, she moved to Texas for three years, then returned once again to Miami. Discussing her adjustment to Texas, she stated:

> A Latino in Texas is not considered the same as a Latino in Miami; you have to prove yourself a lot. For example, my kids talked with their hands a lot, and that was considered a lack of respect. . . . One time they asked me where my dark skin came from—my skin, the skin complexion is a bit dark—and if I was Latina because it looked like my skin complexion was different. I mean I would hear comments . . . that were . . . sometimes annoying, and later it made me laugh, but at the beginning it was a bit shocking.

Luz indicates that her children stood out in Texas because of their mannerisms, which she associates with Latino culture, implying that these cultural forms of expression did not racially mark them in Miami. Interestingly, her observation regarding reactions to her complexion reveal that it is in fact aspects of culture—and, perhaps, even her Spanish accent—that designated her as belonging at the bottom of the racial hierarchy in Texas, since her complexion was not in fact dark. Like those of other island-born Puerto Ricans, Luz's interactions with whites and her experiences with this kind of treatment were alienating, which did not appear to be the case in Miami. As she indicated, a Latino in Texas had to prove himself or herself a lot more.

The other issue that comes up in Luz's example, as it does in others, is the likely future of the Puerto Rican second generation. Settlement decisions are made by parents trying to shield their children from future experiences with being on the fringes. This is, in fact, corroborated by some of the U.S.-born Puerto Ricans in this sample who discussed their families' moves to Miami.

U.S.-Born Secondary Migrations

Among those who were born and raised on the mainland, one woman relocated to Miami from Massachusetts to take a professional job, and the other three came from New York with their families (two of the three had also engaged in circular migration between New York and Puerto Rico before settling in Miami). Among those moving from the Northeast, some cited drugs and crime as responsible for their exodus from New York. Their parents were concerned for their children's well-being, fearing that they would be influenced by drugs. María, for example, was born and partly raised in New York; her family moved to Puerto Rico when María was twelve and returned to New York when she was sixteen. She resided in New York until she turned twenty-three, when she moved with her family to Miami. She explains that both moves—the one to the island and the one to Miami—were to improve the family's quality of life:

> My mother and father [were] trying to make sure that we had a good life, trying to protect us, because in New York there were certain times that it got a little rough. You know, always trying to get my brother and myself out of that kind of life. . . . Our neighbors would sometimes get into trouble. . . . [T]he neighborhood boys, they were . . . you know how they try to show how tough they are; they break things. It was starting to become a trend, and I think my mother saw that with a good eye. And she was like, "Let's go there [Puerto Rico]." And she wanted us to know Puerto Rico, as well. My mother had family and my father had family, and they just thought it would be a good idea.

As a Puerto Rican from New York, María felt marginalized when she and her family resettled on the island at when she was twelve. She attributed the suspicion cast on her ethnic authenticity to the way she spoke Spanish (which, she explained, was different from how islanders spoke), her accent, and even cultural differences (e.g., dress) resulting from living and having been raised in New York. Thus, while her family tried to move away from the everyday manifestations of racial segregation and poverty, María found that relocating to her parents' "home," Puerto Rico, did not necessarily shield her from the stigma of being a Nuyorican in Puerto Rico.

Desires to resettle on the island are often romanticized, as return migrants potentially face being ostracized for their histories of migration, patterns of acculturation, and where they fit into the island's many social hierarchies. There are indeed stigmas attached to Puerto Ricans who return to the island (Lorenzo-Hernández 1999; Pérez 2004), as they are viewed as "inauthentic" and "Americanized." María explained:

> I remember pretty much being isolated in Puerto Rico because of that. I was young and I didn't know that many . . . I had my family from my father's side but it was . . . they were at a different town so it wasn't that they were nearby. Luckily, we met a few friends that were also from New York, New Jersey. You know, you cling to those people.

María's father had a managerial job with an American company that facilitated his transfer to Puerto Rico and his transfer four years later back to New York. The reasons that drove them from New York the first time resurfaced once again when they returned; therefore, they decided to settle in Miami, where María's uncle lived. Important to note is that the company that employed Maria's father allowed his movement to various cities.

María explained that, in addition to the family she already had in Miami, the bicultural nature of the city was what attracted her parents to it, particularly the fact that they could be English speakers in a Latino environment:

> It's tropical, it's nice, the weather, the clean [environment], everybody spoke English. My parents thought we would feel comfortable here, and it was very Latin because of the Cubans. They thought it was a good mix. It was *in-between* [emphasis added].

This "in-betweenness" mirrors the hybridity of Maria's identity. On the margins of both American and Puerto Rican societies, it appears that Miami represented the space where both cultures came together. It was in this social space in which María claimed to feel most at home, an expression that can be tied to attaining cultural citizenship in transnational social space.

This is also found in Arthur's family's decision to settle in Miami over the island. Arthur, a U.S.-born Puerto Rican, spoke of similar reasons for his family's move to Miami when he was fourteen. Arthur's parents wanted their children to have a better education, which they perceived they could not find in Brooklyn. They also sought a safer environment. Arthur said that, on the way up the stairs to his apartment, it was not uncommon to bump into neighborhood drug dealers. This was the context in which his family decided to leave the city.

One note of caution is that these "push" factors should be seen in light of economic restructuring that heavily affected manufacturing in New York. In the 1990s, only 14 percent of Puerto Ricans were in manufacturing jobs, their traditional industrial niche, and over 50 percent were either unemployed or out of the labor force (Grasmuck and Grosfoguel 1997, cited in Grosfoguel 2003: 140). These economic changes are at the core of the social environment that Arthur and his family wanted to leave. The irony is that during this time, Miami's environment was also plagued by drugs and high crime rates. The image of Miami as more closely resembling Puerto Rico perhaps offset these negative factors.

As I have illustrated, many alluded to the bicultural environment of South Florida as more compatible with Puerto Rico than the rest of the United States. This made Miami appear to be hospitable to Latinos. As Arthur recounted:

> It was between Puerto Rico or Miami. I had an aunt that was living here [Miami]. She was married to a Cuban. She said, "Before you go to Puerto Rico, come here and check [this] out; this is tropical just like Puerto Rico, no snow." So I took a vacation and, yeah, it was like Puerto Rico. It was Spanish, too. In fact, by that time there was more Spanish in Miami than Puerto Rico because in Puerto Rico you practice Spanish and English.

Like those of others in this study, Arthur's discussion of the factors that tipped the balance toward settlement in Miami involved similarities between Miami and Puerto Rico. Although Arthur was born on the mainland, he was raised by Puerto Rican parents, and his family perceived Miami to be culturally compatible with island society to the point of suggesting that Miami was more Latino than Puerto Rico, given the forces of Americanization on the island. Both the climate and the cultural compatibility made the receiving cultural context in Miami appear to be friendlier, even though it was still a mainland destination. This is important in understanding how Miami factors into the conceptual map of Puerto Rican transnationalism.

In his work on Mexicans in New York and the transnational lives that linked them to their home village of Ticuani, Mexico, Robert C. Smith uses Oliver Sacks's work on physical self-perception to explain the emotional ties that the second generation in particular had to their parents' homeland and how they engaged in activities that embodied these emotional connections. Social proprioception represents an emerging awareness of your body in space, and Smith uses the concept to describe how Mexican teens jointly experienced their own bodies and emotions in relation to other people and places. In other words, Smith sees migrants' interpretations of how they fit into their social environments as cues regarding how well they felt they belonged in both New York and in Ticuani. The social spaces encapsulating the contexts of binational integration for Mexicans in New York and Ticuani contribute to shaping experiences of social proprioception, which hinge on the physical and emotional formulation of space and place.

What this means for both Arthur and María is that there is an emotional component to the notion of cultural citizenship that can be conceptualized spatially. When both of these participants said that their parents thought they would feel more comfortable in Miami, they were invoking the issue of membership in transnational social space. Neither anchoring community in this transnational social field (New York and Puerto Rico) allowed for complete feelings of integration for families in between each "pole." To achieve this level of belonging, a place "in between" the poles of the Puerto Rican transnational social field was chosen. It is in this social space that they have raised their own families, as María is currently doing with her Cuban husband and two children and Arthur is doing with his African American wife and their two children. In short, the hybridity and diversity of transnational social spaces allows for more positive experiences of integration, given greater access to cultural citizenship.

In sum, Miami was the destination of choice for Puerto Ricans from different backgrounds seeking to feel more integrated into their surroundings. While perhaps not the primary motivation for resettlement, the findings from this chapter show that seeking cultural citizenship is a significant factor that is weighed in settlement decisions. When determining the full range of factors responsible for the dispersion of the Puerto Rican population on the mainland, this study suggests that the receiving cultural context and racial and cultural diversity of an area matter. If island Puerto Ricans were attracted to Miami because it eased the linguistic transitions migration invoked and represented an environment in which they would be less likely to be exposed to racism, bilingual, U.S.-born migrants were attracted to it because it offered a cultural context that allowed them to continue to be English-dominant but also to embrace Latino culture and thus nurture their ethnic identities without having to return to their country of origin (and risk marginalization) to partake in this ethnic revival.

María's and Arthur's families are not unlike other Puerto Ricans who moved out of Rust Belt cities in efforts to achieve upward mobility by integrating into mainland suburban communities or communities back in Puerto Rico (Dávila 2004). This is a pattern also found in Gina Pérez's (2004) research on Puerto Ricans in Chicago and Peggy Levitt's (2001) research on Dominicans in Jamaica Plains, Massachusetts. When migrants perceived that the social environment surrounding them was detrimental to their efforts to raise their children in the ways they envisioned, they often returned to the home country. This study suggests, however, that the assumption that return migration alleviates all issues is misleading, as we saw in María's case. Moreover, this study highlights the importance of transnational social spaces as alternatives to return migration, particularly for "in-between" immigrants searching to fit better into their surroundings. Thus, Puerto Ricans who want to remain embedded in the social horizon of island society, yet at the same time continue with their mainland lives, have Miami as a "settlement compromise."

In sum, Miami is considered to be a place that is geographically and culturally compatible with Puerto Rican society. As Miami increasingly illustrates the configuration of the global city (Grosfoguel 2003), the area has emerged as a transnational social space connecting the island and other countries of origin with the mainland, thereby facilitating the flourishing of hybrid ethnic identities. At the same time, this space also facilitates cultural citizenship for Latinos, given that they are not disenfranchised in Miami. In other words, given that Miami is a space where Latinos can attain cultural power—and, as such, cultural citizenship—in the United States, it allows them to deflect the stigmas attached to being Latino in general, and Puerto Rican specifically.

Conclusion

This chapter has mapped the recent migration and dispersion patterns of the Puerto Rican population on the U.S. mainland. It has focused on the factors that have made migration to Miami a particularly attractive option for both island-born and U.S.-born Puerto Ricans. Mapping the role of Miami as a global city and how "transnationalism from above" has led to "transnationalism from below," I have argued that South Florida generally should be considered a transnational social space for immigrants generally, and for Puerto Ricans specifically. Moreover, the data presented here suggest that, as a transnational social space, the multiculturalism, diversity, and international dimensions of the city make it an appealing settlement option, given that it is more likely to facilitate cultural citizenship for Latinos than other places in the United States.

Puerto Ricans see Miami as a place that is culturally compatible with island society, yet a space in which they garner the benefits of living in mainland society. The combination of place-based characteristics in Miami suggests that it represents a settlement compromise, or a space in which Puerto Ricans can live in sync with their bicultural identities. Moreover, experiences with racism in other parts of the country emerge as important determinants of seeking out a Latino cultural environment, illustrating that barriers to integration in other parts of the country are contributing to an increasing concentration of Puerto Ricans in non-traditional areas of destination.

At a theoretical level, Kivisto (2003: 20) argues that the transnational nature of communities is interrelated to the patterns of assimilation or incorporation that members of these communities show. Rather than competing theoretical models, transnationalism encompasses those "social processes occurring in space," while assimilation captures the "processes transpiring over time." Moreover, transnational communities may result from approaches toward assimilation or incorporation that are mediated by the state. For example, multicultural societies could lead to the formation of open transnational communities, whereas exclusionary societies may result in closed or more parochial transnational communities. While the United States encompasses an example of a multicultural society with exclusionary social practices, those subjects who experience these contradicting forms of incorporation seek out spaces in which they can even out the disjunctures of their experiences. The importance, therefore, of transnational social spaces for positive experiences of incorporation play a part in the making of long-term settlement decisions. In short, for those who have the option to structure their settlement decisions based on the desire to "fit in," moving to Sunbelt communities such as the Latino community in Miami represents a concerted effort toward cultural decolonization, or a move away from experiences that reinforce Puerto Ricans' structural subordination to the U.S. state.

Note

1. This is also a pattern with immigrants to the United States in general (Larsen 2004).

References

Acosta Belén, Edna, and Carlos Santiago. 2006. *Puerto Ricans in the United Status: A Contemporary Portrait.* Boulder, Colo.: Lynne Rienner.

Aranda, Elizabeth. 2001. "Weighing Hearts and Minds: Emotional Transnationalism and Puerto Rican Migration." Ph.D. diss., Temple University, Philadelphia.

Aranda, Elizabeth. 2006. *Emotional Bridges to Puerto Rico: Migration, Return Migration, and the Struggles of Incorporation.* Lanham, Md.: Rowman and Littlefield.

Aranda, Elizabeth, Elena Sabogal, and Sallie Hughes. 2003. "The 'Other' Latin Americans: Identity, Assimilation, and Well-Being among Transnational Immigrants." Proposal submitted to the National Science Foundation for funding consideration.

Baker, Susan S. 2002. *Understanding Mainland Puerto Rican Poverty.* Philadelphia: Temple University Press.

Bonilla, Frank, and Héctor Colón Jordan. 1979. "'Mamá, Borinquen Me Llama!' Puerto Rican Return Migration in the 70s." *Migration Today* 7, no. 2: 1–6.

Dávila, Arlene. 2004. *Barrio Dreams: Puerto Ricans, Latinos, and the Neoliberal City.* Berkeley: University of California Press.

Duany, Jorge. 2002. *The Puerto Rican Nation on the Move: Identities on the Island and in the United States.* Chapel Hill: University of North Carolina Press.

Duany, Jorge. 2004. "Puerto Rico: Between the Nation and the Diaspora—Migration to and from Puerto Rico." Pp. 177–196 in *Migration and Immigration: A Global View,* ed. Maura Toro-Morn and Marixsa Alicea. Westport, Conn.: Greenwood Press.

Duany, Jorge. 2005. "Los 'Florirricans.'" *El Nuevo Día*, March 9.

Duany, Jorge. 2007. "La Nación en la diáspora: Las multiples repercusiones de la emigración puertorriqueña a Estados Unidos." *Revista de Ciencias Sociales* (nueva epoca) 17: 118–153.

Faist, Thomas. 2000. "Transnationalization in International Migration: Implications for the Study of Citizenship and Culture." *Ethnic and Racial Studies* 23, no. 2 (March): 189–222.

García, María Cristina. 2003. "Havana USA." Pp. 293–315 in *Latino/a Thought: Culture, Politics, and Society*, ed. Francisco H. Vázquez and Rodolfo D. Torres. Lanham, Md.: Rowman and Littlefield.

González, Juan. 2000. *Harvest of Empire: A History of Latinos in America*. New York: Penguin Group.

Grosfoguel, Ramón. 2003. *Colonial Subjects: Puerto Ricans in a Global Perspective*. Berkeley: University of California Press.

Henderson, Tim. 2003. "Highest Immigration Rate Belongs to Dade." *Miami Herald*. May 21.

Hernández Cruz, Juan. 1985. "Migración de retorno o circulación de obreros boricuas?" *Revista de Ciencias Sociales* 24, nos. 1–2: 81–112.

Kivisto, Peter. 2003. "Social Spaces, Transnational Immigrant Communities, and the Politics of Incorporation." *Ethnicities* 3, no. 1: 5–28.

Larsen, Luke J. 2004. "The Foreign Born Population in the United States: 2003." Current Population Reports, U.S. Department of Commerce and U.S. Census Bureau.

Levine, Robert M., and Moisés Asís. 2000. *Cuban Miami*. New Brunswick, N.J.: Rutgers University Press.

Levitt, Peggy. 2001. *Transnational Villagers*. Berkeley: University of California Press.

Lorenzo-Hernandez, José. 1999. "The Nuyorican's Dilemma: Categorization of Returning Migrants in Puerto Rico." *International Migration Review* 33, no. 4: 988–1013.

McHugh, Kevin, Ines Miyares, and Emily Skop. 1997. "The Magnetism of Miami: Segmented Paths in Cuban Migration." *Geographical Review* 87, no. 4: 504–519.

Pérez, Gina. 2004. *The Near Northwest Side Story*. Berkeley: University of California Press.

Pérez-López, Jorge F. 1991. "Bringing the Cuban Economy into Focus: Conceptual and Empirical Challenges." *Latin American Research Review* 26, no. 1: 75–110.

Portes, Alejandro, and Alex Stepick. 1993. *City on the Edge: The Transformation of Miami*. Berkeley: University of California Press.

Rivera-Batiz, Francisco, and Carlos E. Santiago. 1994. *Puerto Ricans in the United States: A Changing Reality*. Washington, D.C.: National Puerto Rican Coalition.

Rivera-Batiz, Francisco, and Carlos E. Santiago. 1996. *Island Paradox: Puerto Rico in the 1990s*. New York: Russell Sage Foundation.

Santiago, Carlos, and Francisco Rivera-Batiz. 1996. "La Migración de los Puertorriqueños durante la década de 1980." *Revista de Ciencias Sociales* (June): 178–207.

Smith, Michael Peter, and Luis Guarnizo. 1998. *Transnationalism from Below*. New Brunswick, N.J.: Transaction Publishers.

Smith, Robert C. 2002. "Life Course, Generation, and Social Location as Factors Shaping Second-Generation Transnational Life." Pp. 145–167 in *The Changing Face of Home: The Transnational Lives of the Second Generation*, ed. Peggy Levitt and Mary Waters. New York: Russell Sage Foundation.

Smith, Robert Courtney. 2006. *Mexican New York: Transnational Lives of New Immigrants*. Berkeley: University of California Press.

Stepick, Alex, Guillermo Grenier, Max Castro, and Marvin Dunn. 2003. *This Land Is Our Land: Immigrants and Power in Miami.* Berkeley: University of California Press.

U.S. Census Bureau. 1990. Summary Tape File 3 (STF3)—Sample Data. American Fact Finder, available online at www.census.gov.

U.S. Census Bureau. 2000a. Summary File 2(SF 2)—100-Percent Data. American Fact Finder, available online at www.census.gov.

U.S. Census Bureau. 2000b. Summary File 3 (SF3)—Sample Data. American Fact Finder, available online at www.census.gov.

U.S. Census Bureau. 2006. American Community Survey and U.S. Census Bureau, Population Estimates Program.

Vásquez, Michael. 2004. "Miami's Middle Class Shrinking." *Miami Herald,* June 6, 1B.

Wyss, Jim. 2008. "Study Shows 'Power' of South Florida Multinationals." *Miami Herald,* January 17.

6
Racialized Culture and
Translocal Counter-Publics

Rumba and Social Disorder in New York and Havana

LISA MAYA KNAUER

Introduction

This chapter analyzes the social spaces of the racially marked practices of
"traditional" Afro-Cuban music and religion—rumba and Santería—in the
New York area and Havana. I analyze these cultural practices as shaping a translocal counter-public constituted by multidirectional flows of money, goods,
practices, and people, and where varied social actors in both places craft identities through intra- and intercultural negotiation and contestation. This paper
highlights two nodes within this translocal counter-public sphere of Afro-
Cubanness: weekly rumba performances in the New York area that have become
flashpoints for competing claims of authenticity and ownership and racialized,
gendered, and class-based conflicts over public space and public culture in
Havana. The paper briefly sketches rumba's evolution in the predominantly
poor and black neighborhoods of the port cities of Havana and Matanzas in
the nineteenth century. Popular and official attitudes in Cuba toward rumba
are shown to reflect heavily gendered racial and class anxieties: like many black
urban popular cultures, rumba is associated with rowdiness, civil disorder, and
unbridled sexuality while simultaneously celebrated as an icon of national
identity. The Cuban Revolution did not erase these ambiguities, which form
part of the legacy of the "indigenized" New York rumba culture.

Rumba was not simply transplanted to New York, I argue, but actively
remade in a new environment over several decades with new social actors:

successive waves of Cuban migrants with divergent engagements with, and views of, Afro-Cuban culture "back home" and other cultural communities, particularly Puerto Ricans, other Latinos, and African Americans. The New York rumba "scene" comprises both informal open-air gatherings and staged "shows," and its history has been marked by encounters and negotiations that are aesthetic, racial, and national: among Cubans who emigrated at different times, ranging from the 1950s to last month; between Cubans and non-Cubans; and between rumba participants and the combined forces of city government, private nonprofits, and property owners. As gentrification and privatization transform public culture in New York, police and park authorities have attempted to restrict the Central Park rumba, which throughout its forty-year history has had a free-for-all and unpredictable character. Simultaneously, the "rumba Sunday" at a Cuban restaurant in Union City, New Jersey, came under fire from some neighbors and local authorities and eventually ceased in 2005. This chapter locates these sites and controversies as part of the same "cultural geography" as the rumba landscape of contemporary Havana; in both places, Afro-Cuban culture is discursively constructed as both heritage and a threat to the social order. My narrative foregrounds the voices of the predominantly black and working-class Cuban participants in the New York rumba scene, many of whom maintain contact with or even travel "back home" and who offer a counter-narrative to hegemonic views of U.S. Cubans.

I begin with a set of vignettes that outline the contours and suggest some of the dynamics of the rumba "scene" in New York. To provide a historical context, I examine the ambiguities surrounding the development of Afro-Cuban cultural practices in Cuba. Drawing on public-sphere analysis and, particularly, work on the black public sphere (Black Public Sphere Collective 1996) and Michael Warner's conceptualization of counter-publics (Warner 2002), I argue that these racialized cultural performances might constitute an alternative public sphere, or counter-public. Cultural performances are always embedded in particular contexts, even as we may view them, and their protagonists may experience them, as translocal and linked to similar practices and performances in other places. I then trace the evolution of Afro-Cuban cultural performance, first in Havana and then New York, highlighting the counter-public aspects. In the final part of the chapter, I examine how the historic construction of rumba as a threat to the social order has shaped contemporary attitudes and policies in both Cuba and New York City. Without collapsing Havana and New York into a single, homogeneous entity, I suggest how we might think of an Afro-Cuban public sphere, or an Afro-Cuban counter-public, that is multi-sited, multiethnic, and translocal.

Setting the Stage: Performing Cubanness in New York

On a warm Sunday afternoon in May 2002, New York City's annual Cuban Day Parade filled the Avenue of the Americas with high-school marching bands, salsa ensembles, and floats.[1] In the complex ethnoscape (Appadurai 1993) of New York, such public rituals are important "performances of identity" for an ethnic or national group (Kasinitz 1992). Obtaining parade permits—especially in the post-9/11 metropolis—is not easy, and diaspora communities and other interest groups often spend years lobbying to be recognized with a day and a parade. The fact that the Cuban community, whose numbers have been shrinking since the 1990s, is able to claim such a central and visible location says something about its economic and political weight (or the perception thereof) and its leaders' negotiating skills.

Since nearly all ethnic parades in New York have marching bands, beauty queens, and delegations of elected officials, on a superficial level there is little to distinguish the Cuban parade. As Richard Wilk notes, ethnic groups or nations use a limited repertoire of strategies to demonstrate their "uniqueness." However, for those who could read beyond the "systems of common difference" (Wilk 1993), this year's parade had something different: a sizeable contingent of mostly black dancers and musicians churning out rhythms and steps of the *comparsa* music from Cuba's "black" Carnival tradition.[2] To many onlookers this may not have seemed especially noteworthy, but for the performers and many black Cubans along the sidelines, this was a seismic shift, as this was the first time in the parade's history that distinctly black or Afro-Cuban music and dance were included.

The floats and bands turned west when they reached the José Martí monument on Central Park South; the contingents disbanded; and most parade-goers went home. However, part of this "folkloric" contingent and its supporters among the bystanders continued straight into the park to continue the festivities in a different form.

The "parade within a parade" snaked its way through the park until it arrived at a nondescript grassy area near the lake, where many Cubans were already gathered and the air was pungent with the smells of savory food, alcohol, cigars and generously applied cologne. A small knot of mature men, nattily attired down to the light-colored or two-toned shoes, stood on a slope overlooking the crowd, calling out to their acquaintances and commenting on the proceedings. This site, unremarkable to most park visitors, is known among New York's black Cuban and other communities as "the Central Park rumba." Here, for several decades, people have gathered to play, sing, and dance rumba, a form of music and dance that evolved in Havana and Matanzas, Cuba in the nineteenth century. On a typical Sunday, the Central Park rumba draws a mixed

FIGURE 6.1   Friendly face-off between African American (left) and Cuban (right) *rumberos* in New York's Central Park. *(Photograph by the author.)*

crowd including many Puerto Ricans, other Latinos, some African Americans, and whites, and Cubans are often in the minority. On this afternoon, however, the air was thick with Cuban Spanish, as people who had come to New York thirty years ago or more rubbed shoulders with more recently arrived compatriots. Most were black and had arrived in the 1980 Mariel boatlift or later.

Traditional rumba only uses percussion instruments, and the song, musical accompaniment, and dance all involve improvisation. The performative aesthetics draw on *guapería* ("tough guy" posturing), and *rumba de la calle* (street rumba) like this one often seems like it is about to veer out of control, and it sometimes does. In the late afternoon, police arrived and told participants that since there was no permit for the performance, we would have to disband. However, a compromise was reached: the police agreed that we could stay where we were until 6 p.m., and then move to another part of the park (see Figure 6.1).

The Cuban parade was suspended in 2005, and its future seems uncertain. However, during its lifespan many black Cubans had an ambivalent relationship to the parade and saw the rumba as an antidote to the parade's whiteness and the "exile" mentality it reflected. Some went to the parade in an effort to resist invisibility, and then went to the rumba because it was a more comfortable and "safe" space. Others avoided the parade entirely but went to the rumba on the day of the parade because they knew that on that day, in that place, they would find a distinct node of Cubanness. For these Cubans, the rumba became an alternative stage on which to enact what it means to be Cuban.

On another Sunday, a few miles west of Central Park, another kind of cultural encounter took place at a Cuban restaurant in Union City, New Jersey. From 1996 until 2004, La Esquina Habanera (Havana Corner) hosted weekly "rumba Sundays." Black Cubans who had arrived in 1980 or later always formed the core audience at La Esquina, much more so than at Central Park. In comparison to Central Park, these performances were more controlled and staged spectacles, although the threat of chaos and disorder was never far off. On this particular evening, passions were high because Los Muñequitos de Matanzas, a famous folkloric group from Cuba, were performing. The owner of La Esquina, Tony Zequeiros, was worried because there had been complaints—racially motivated, in his view—about noise, and since Union City is home to many right-wing Cuban exiles, he often received threats when musicians from Cuba are scheduled. When things got rowdy he abruptly turned up the lights and told people to leave.

These two events and sites suggest how racialized cultural practices such as rumba become flashpoints for defining and contesting what it means to be Cuban in New York. These negotiations and controversies have a dynamic relationship to the Afro-Cuban cultural sphere of contemporary Havana. Separated by geography and politics, these cities are nonetheless connected through a constant and bidirectional flow of goods, practices, and people. At the same time that the New York-area Afro-Cuban cultural community engaged in struggle to preserve and make visible its manifestations, and the post-Mariel and black Cubans in particular to have their presence acknowledged, *rumberos* (rumba performers, although the term also applies to rumba enthusiasts more generally) in Havana (as well as proponents of other racially defined cultural practices such as rap) found themselves waging similar battles with symbolic, discursive, and spatial dimensions.

The struggle to legitimize rumba and other Afro-Cuban musical forms in both New York and Cuba includes securing places where people can gather to play and enjoy rumba free from disturbance by disciplinary mechanisms of the state and the dominant culture. This disciplining includes both direct policing and discursive means. Although rumba is not exclusively enjoyed or promoted by blacks, these struggles have a distinctly racial character, tempered by ideologies of gender and class.

Afro-Cuban Culture, Race and National Identity

Rumba evolved in the mid- to late nineteenth century in the densely populated *barrios marginales* ("marginal" neighborhoods) of Havana and Matanzas. It is not a re-creation of a specific African musical genre but a New World hybrid of West African and Central African and Spanish influences. Since that time, rumba and associated cultural practices have been constructed, alternately and simultaneously, as primitive and indecent or colorful and uniquely Cuban. This dualism surrounding rumba mirrors a larger racial ambivalence at the heart of nationalist discourse. While colonial authorities restricted and banned drumming at times, even the independence forces were divided over whether there was a place for blacks in "Cuba libre" (Ferrer 1999; Helg 1995; Scott 1995), and evocations of *Cubanidad,* or Cubanness, have thus both embraced and distanced cultural practices identified as "black" or "Afro-Cuban." In the twentieth century, some nationalist elites began to promote African-derived cultural forms—usually cleaned-up versions of black vernacular musics—as the essence of Cubanness, since they contained the fewest foreign influences. This dualism can be seen in Cuban social sciences—notably, in the work of Fernando Ortíz, whose early studies, principally a three-part study titled *La Hampa Afrocubana* (The Afrocuban Underworld) were influenced by criminological views of African retentions (Ortíz 1998 [1906], 1986). However, Ortíz later allied himself with the *afrocubanismo* cultural movement and devoted himself to documenting, promoting and thus legitimating Afro-Cuban practices.[3] At the same time, commercial entertainers who catered to middle-class audiences developed aestheticized versions of rumba that often bore little resemblance to the original form; the label "rumba" (or "rhumba") was applied almost indiscriminately as a marketing device. People in popular neighborhoods continued to hold traditional rumbas in communal courtyards known as *solares,* but *rumba del solar* but was still viewed by many, including the black middle class, as dangerous and an obstacle to black advancement.[4]

This racial ambivalence was not erased by the Cuban Revolution. Officially, the revolution abolished racial discrimination. Talking about race or singling out blacks was viewed as creating a problem where one did not exist (de la Fuente 1998; Moore 2006). Afro-Cuban culture was again partially inscribed within a new discourse of national identity. Rumba formed part of an endangered national heritage that needed to be preserved but also "cleaned up" and turned into a vehicle for the transmission of socialist values. Racial difference was collapsed under the banner of national unity, and culturally specific forms were turned into national commodities (Hanchard 1994: 181).[5] The state took over the process of "folkloricization" to spread Afro-Cuban folklore beyond the marginalized milieu in which it originated (Hagedorn 2001; Velez 2000). The state underwrote professional folkloric companies and established a "folkloric" curriculum at the National Art School; these initiatives allowed many "culture bearers" to earn salaries as performers and teachers.[6] Locally based community cultural centers called *casas de cultura* (houses of culture) sponsored *aficionado* (amateur) folkloric groups. However, rumba and Afro-Cuban religion were still viewed by many as *cosas de negros* (black people's stuff) and thus slightly dangerous and in need of control. Informants who grew up in the 1960s and 1970s reported that the police often broke up informal rumbas in people's homes or on open-air patios.

Since the early 1990s, when the government embarked on an ambitious tourism-development program to cope with the economic crisis left by the collapse of the Soviet Union, Afro-Cuban folklore has been revalorized as valuable social capital. State-sponsored folkloric companies offer dance and drumming classes for tourists; old and new folkloric groups compete for slots at hotel cabarets; and there are several outdoor locales to hear rumba. Being a *folklorista* (folkloric performer) or a *santera* (Santería priestess) now seems like an attractive career option, since these offer contact with tourists and the possibility of hard currency or even a trip abroad. There are still rumbas or *peñas* (a generic term for a small-scale live music event) held in their "original" settings, in semi-public locations such as patios or on the street, but there is an almost inexorable pressure for these locales to "touristify" themselves (see Figure 6.2).

FIGURE 6.2 Tourists at weekly rumba performance in Havana's Callejon de Hamel.
(Photograph by the author.)

Cultural Performance and Public Space

For communities that have been constructed as marginal or outside of the dominant culture, formal public cultural performances such as parades, processions, and carnivals are important manifestations of their presence (see Kasinitz 1992; Regis 1999). These cultural performances never exist in a sociopolitical vacuum; they are always configured around axes of power and inequality.

Michel de Certeau (1984) argues that, in a class-stratified society, people who have been made marginal make creative use of mundane activities—workplace behavior, talking, storytelling, walking—to address, subvert, or resist their marginality. For de Certeau, in a capitalist society, space—and especially urban space—is never neutral but always a site for the assertion and contestation of power. The powerful use the means at their disposal (which de Certeau labels "strategies") to impose a certain order. This order is never absolute but partial and porous. Instead of passively accepting the established "proprieties," the "weak," however, develop imaginative ways (which de Certeau calls "tactics") to insert and insinuate themselves into spaces that they do not control.

But both kinds of activities—those that take place within institutionally defined constraints and those that are grassroots, spontaneous, unplanned—engage in a politics of visibility and are, I argue, ways of staking larger claims for recognition. These claims may not be shaped or articulated in an overtly political way—that is, they may not be formulated as demands for specific social resources or political representation—but they are political nonetheless.[7]

Public Culture, Public Spheres and Counter-Publics

Jürgen Habermas introduced the concept of the public sphere to describe that aspect of bourgeois society where citizens engage in social and political discourse. For Habermas, the public sphere helps constitute civil society; it does not belong to the state, the church, or the realm of economic production. His ideal example was the seventeenth-century London coffeehouse. Other theorists have criticized Habermas for reproducing the hierarchies of bourgeois society (Negt and Kluge 1993 [1972]). A given society does not have a single, homogeneous public but multiple, often competing publics. The bourgeois public sphere excludes those who are marginalized by race, gender, age, class, ethnicity, or immigrant status, who therefore create their own public spheres, often in the interstices of the dominant culture. These "parallel discursive arenas" are places "where members of subordinated social groups invent and circulate counter-discourses to formulate oppositional interpretations of their identities, interests, and needs" (Fraser 1993: 12). Counter-publics do not appeal to universality but affirm their specific difference(s). For Warner, belonging to a counter-public is active and not simply a reflection of structural social position (Warner 2002: 61). Participating in a counter-public is itself transformative, creating new forms of solidarity and identification.

Counter-publics are often defined in political terms: they are seen as "deriv[ing] their 'counter' status . . . from varying degrees of exclusion from prominent channels of political discourse and a corresponding lack of political power" (Asen and Brouwer 2001: 2–3). However, counter-publics are not solely focused on interventions in the political arena; the state may not even be an object of their attention.

Race and the Afro-Cuban Public Sphere in Cuba

Roger Bastide's study of Afro-Brazilian religions is pertinent to theorizing the evolution of a racially defined counter-public in colonial and postcolonial societies. While not overly oppositional, Candomblé, for Bastide, is not just a set of religious beliefs, or a response to the psychic traumas of slavery and less-than-full citizenship. It contains elements of an alternative socioeconomic system that functions on individual, domestic, and communal levels (Bastide 1980).

The historical work on Afro-Cuban life in the nineteenth century is also suggestive in this regard. Segregation and exclusion from social and political institutions forced or permitted Africans and their descendants to develop their own collective cultural life, both informally and through semiautonomous institutions such as *cabildos* (mutual-aid societies, nominally under the leadership of the church), the Abakuá secret society (an all-male sodality ostensibly re-creating traditions from the Calabar region of what is now Nigeria; see Palmié 2002; Routon 2005), and *casas de santo* (literally, "houses of the saint"—ritual kin groups in Santería). As noted earlier, although many blacks participated in the wars of independence, their presence was viewed with ambivalence by some *independentistas,* who were uneasy about the role of blacks in "Cuba libre" (de la Fuente 1998; Ferrer 1999; Scott 1995). Even after the abolition of slavery, prior to the Cuban Revolution in 1959, black and mulatto Cubans were relegated to second-class status (Fernández Robaina 1990). People of color created a parallel social infrastructure, including newspapers and magazines and social and cultural clubs known as *sociedades de color* (literally, "societies of color"). There was even one short-lived political party, the ill-fated Partido Independiente de Color (Independent Party of Color), or PIC (Helg 1995). Tellingly, not only was the PIC brutally suppressed (thousands of supporters were killed), but it was effectively erased from Cuban historiography until fairly recently.[8]

These institutions can be viewed as constituting a black/mulatto or Afro-Cuban counter-public that developed alongside of—and to some degree,

FIGURE 6.3   Afro-Cuban religion at home: offering for the *orishas,*
Central Havana. *(Photograph by the author.)*

intersected with—an emerging "bourgeois" or official public sphere. However, this more formal Afro-Cuban counter-public sphere is connected to an informal public sphere of Afro-Cuban religion and racialized culture. Afro-Cuban religions are largely decentralized and were able to survive periods of repression by remaining in the interstices of Cuban society, along with street rumba (see Figure 6.3). Sites of popular entertainment, such as dance halls and movie theaters, which also reflected widespread patterns of racial and class segregation, were also important arenas of solidarity and identification by working-class blacks.[9] These Afro-Cuban counter-publics were also informed by translocal and international currents; many black Cubans saw links between their struggles and those of other African diasporic peoples.[10] There were specific linkages between the informal Afro-Cuban counter-public in Cuba and its counterpart in New York.[11] Since the revolution, Afro-Cuban cultural practices have been partially incorporated into the official public sphere of the state but have retained some of their autonomous status and association with marginality and blackness. They are also tied to translocal circuits and the informal economy. The line between official public sphere and informal counter-public is thus unstable and blurred, since individuals move between those spheres and can be said to "belong" to both.

Counter-Publics and Public Spheres in Havana

From this perspective, we can productively re-examine the life worlds and daily circuits of several of my informants. On a Sunday in late January 1999, I ran into the musicians Stanley, Armando, Omar, and Gerardo at the Sunday rumba at Callejon de Hamel in the Cayo Hueso neighborhood of Central Havana. Hanging around the fringes of the rumba, talking, and drinking with one's colleagues is part of "representing" as a folkloric performer. It is a way of identifying oneself with a particular version of blackness and black masculinity. Very often, émigré musicians who are back in Cuba for visits will stop by the Callejon de Hamel or other rumba locales. Mixed in with the gossip and playful banter is news about groups that have disbanded and newly formed, new performance opportunities and auditions. This informal networking is vital, since most of this information is not widely disseminated. However, Stanley and the others had been contracted to play at a religious ceremony in Habana Vieja, and as the rumba wound down, they loaded their instruments onto a rickety hand truck and set off (see Figure 6.4). They were hurrying because after the ceremony, three of them had to be on time for their "day jobs" playing a theatricalized set of Santería music in the nightly cabaret spectacle at the Hotel Nacional. Similar juxtapositions occur in New York's Afro-Cuban cultural sphere.

Afrocubanidad and the New York Cuban Community

In the first half of the twentieth century, New York housed the largest Cuban community in the United States (Poyo and Diaz-Miranda 1994). New York was especially attractive to black Cubans because they saw it as more racially hospitable than Southern cities, and its cosmopolitanism made it a logical choice for musicians (a disproportionate number of whom were black). Cuba's racial politics were replicated in the diaspora, and many of the Cuban social, political, and cultural organizations were effectively or explicitly "white only." In response, black Cuban immigrants in New York followed the practices of the emerging black middle class in Cuba and founded autonomous organizations such as the

FIGURE 6.4   The informal public sphere: playing for the saints,
El Cerro. *(Photograph by the author.)*

Club Cubano Interamericano, which helped shape an Afro-Cuban counter-public sphere in New York.[12]

Cubans settled throughout the five boroughs, mostly in or near black and Puerto Rican neighborhoods. So while there were dispersed "pockets" or "clusters" of Cubans in areas such as Elmhurst, Queens, and Washington Heights—often marked by Cuban restaurants or other small businesses—there was not a single, concentrated Cuban neighborhood. In the 1940s and '50s, African American, white, and Puerto Rican New Yorkers flocked to the Palladium or the Club Cubano on 125th Street to hear Cuban stars such as Arsenio Rodríguez. After the dance music, there would be a rumba. Or musicians congregated at Cuban-owned restaurants, private homes, or after-hours clubs. Afro-Cuban culture was a familiar part of the life world for African American musicians like Teddy Holliday and Gene Golden, or Nuyoricans like Felix Sanabria, who grew up alongside Cubans in Harlem, El Barrio, the Bronx, and Washington Heights and later became rumba musicians, *santeros* (initiated priests of Santería), and *babalawos* (ritual diviners). The Afro-Cuban cultural sphere in New York was thus multicultural from its inception. The Club Cubano Interamericano, for example, counted the Puerto Rican activist Jesús Colón among its founding members.[13]

Following the revolution, Cuba's support of anticolonial struggles and a cultural policy that foregrounded African roots made Afro-Cuban culture a "space" where many Puerto Ricans and African-Americans could construct counter-hegemonic and nationalist imaginaries. In the 1960s, the informal and after-hours rumbas moved outdoors. Aspiring *rumberos,* mostly Puerto Rican and African American, began to congregate every Sunday afternoon by Bethesda Fountain in Central Park, a highly visible and public location. However, by the 1970s the *rumberos* had gravitated to the nearby lakeshore, because it was more secluded and less likely to draw unwanted police scrutiny: many recognized that as a cultural performance coded as black, male, and lower class, the rumba was certainly subject to scrutiny and disciplining.

The rumba caught the attention of cultural reporters, who wrote favorable articles in the *New Yorker* magazine and other publications (see, e.g., Hiss 1976). The Central Park rumba was even written up in Spanish-language newspapers in Florida Guidebooks directed tourists to visit the rumba on their trips to Central Park (Paula Ballan, personal communication). However, even as its popularity grew, the rumba remained resistant to institutionalization. No one "ran" the rumba. There were acknowledged informal leaders, respected for their musicianship. But no one wanted to take responsibility for logistical details and supervising people's behavior.

The context changed dramatically after the 1980 Mariel boatlift, which included some of Cuba's pre-eminent folkloric performers. Many black Cubans, *folkloristas,* and *santeros* opted for New York. The new Cuban migrants soon heard about Central Park, but their arrival produced varied reactions by the New York *rumberos.* The rumba in Central Park was one of many informal meeting places for Cubans, while it continued to attract non-Cubans.

Some appreciated the musical expertise and expanded song repertoire; others resented the newcomers and challenged their knowledge and credentials. The usual homosocial *guapería* took on ethnic and generational overtones. Cubans complained under their breath that Puerto Ricans and Dominicans did not really understand rumba. Older Cubans grumbled that their younger or more recently arrived compatriots were deviating from "classic" or "correct rumba" and simply "inventing." Some Cubans felt that the rumbas at Central

Park and other outdoor locations were too anarchic and undisciplined (and again, aesthetic and ethnic criteria are often confused or intertwined); eventually, the desire to create a more authentic, correct, and Cuban rumba found expression in the establishment of the Sunday rumbas at La Esquina Habanera in 1996. However, the transformation of La Esquina into a site for the promotion of culture associated with Cuba's racialized "urban underclass" has led to occasional conflicts with other residents and local authorities, many of whom are Cuban, and associate rumba with antisocial behavior and criminality.

There is a cyclical and circuitous relationship between the evolution of the Afro-Cuban cultural sphere in New York and the complex social changes under way in Cuba, which I can only briefly hint at here. The "traffic in culture" (Marcus and Myers 1995) between Cuba and the United States has intensified in recent years through tourism to Cuba, return visits by émigrés, U.S. visits by Cuban musicians (during which one or more performers often stay behind), and continued immigration from Cuba—the *balseros* (rafters) of the early '90s; the 20,000 or so who win spots in the annual immigration lottery; and a small number of secondary migrants who came to the United States by way of Europe, Mexico, or elsewhere in Latin America.

An analysis of the composition of the group Raices Habaneras encapsulates the historical trajectory of this sphere while exposing some of these fault lines (although La Esquina Habanera is now closed, the group still performs occasionally at other locales). Vicente has never returned to Cuba after leaving in 1980 and argues that rumba has been debased in Cuba; for Román, who came in 2000, Cuba is the cradle and the living fountain, and he struggles to remain true to his foundations after several years in "*la yuma*," as many Cubans colloquially refer to the United States. Gene Golden is an African American who was first exposed to Cuban music in the 1950s and first visited Cuba in the 1970s. There are more non-Cuban musicians now than in 1996, but the dancers are all Cuban. The only non-Cuban who regularly sings is Chino, a Venezuelan immigrant; he started to hang out at the Central Park rumba before the Marielitos arrived and counts Julito Collazo, a Cuban musician who emigrated in the 1950s, as a mentor.

The musicians negotiate between the performative codes of a folkloric spectacle (presenting a polished show that demonstrates their professionalism and mastery of the genre) and those of a street rumba (no clear lines between audience and performer, open-ended improvisation) that some in the audience prefer. This is played out, to a degree, in the discourse among participants in the Afro-Cuban counter-public sphere as they evaluate the various rumba locales. Some never went to La Esquina Habanera because it cost money, the show did not contain enough variety and is too top-down. Others avoid Central Park because it is too unpredictable and threatens to veer out of control.[14]

The Afro-Cuban Counter-Public in New York: Counter to What?

For Cuban immigrants in New York, the Afro-Cuban cultural world of rumba and Santería is a way to connect with their "roots" and construct a Cuban identity in the diaspora by means of a racialized cultural practice. But how can we conceive of this as a counter-public? To what is it an alternative? I argue that it is an alternative to both the dominant U.S. public sphere and the Cuban American mainstream.

Cuban immigrants in the United States participate in several counter-publics, some of which engage more directly in traditional "political" activities and others that function more informally. There is a Cuban American "exile" counter-public that includes organizations such as the Cuban-American National Foundation, media outlets, and small businesses.[15] The controversy over the return of Elián González to Cuba displayed both the power and limitations of this counter-public.[16] Other Cuban American counter-publics, distinguished by politics, cultural preferences, or generation articulate a Cuban American identity not wholly shaped by hostility to Fidel Castro—for example, those who promote dialogue or scholarly exchange with Cuba.[17] On a less overtly political level, young Cuban Americans, recent émigrés, and non-Cuban music lovers have combined to form an active audience for contemporary music from Cuba, supporting the record stores, radio stations, dance clubs, and concert promoters who cater to this growing market.[18]

Many of the Cubans who emigrated in 1980 or later do not see themselves as political migrants or refugees; they left for economic or personal reasons or because of general dissatisfaction or frustration, not because of overt political opposition. Some go to lengths to distance themselves from politics and from the "exile" leadership. But maintaining contact with other Cubans is vital. Some have re-created parts of the social networks they had in Cuba. Leonardo Wignall, a *marielito* (Cuban who arrived in the 1980 Mariel boatlift) who lives in West Harlem, travels to Union City, New Jersey, every two weeks to get his hair cut by the same barber he patronized in Havana.

The social spaces of Afro-Cuban culture in New York (rumba and the African-based religions of Santería, Palo Monte and Abakuá) are not solely Cuban spaces, but they provide a hidden infrastructure that allows Cuban immigrants to New York—and especially, but not exclusively, black Cubans—to maintain a connection with each other and, increasingly, to everyday life and cultural practices on the island. Rumbas, *toques de santo,* or concerts by touring Cuban musicians, whatever else they may be, are temporary portable homelands for Cuban immigrants.[19] In all of these settings, Cubans, like the Korean Americans studied by Nancy Abelmann and John Lie, enact "a carnival

FIGURE 6.5   Creating Cuban spaces in the multicultural metropolis: alongside the rumba in East Harlem, summer 2005. *(Photograph by the author.)*

of the display of [Cuban] difference" (Abelmann and Lie 1997: 85). In this informal public sphere (Zdravomyslova and Voronkov 2002) they meet old friends; engage in both licit and illicit business; demonstrate their affinity for, and knowledge of, Cuban music, religion, and culture; and exchange news and information about their families "back home" in Cuba and mutual friends throughout the diaspora (see Figure 6.5).

Cuban life in New York is doubly de-territorialized, for there is not a single geographic community or enclave. However, Cubans have become adept at carving out their counter-publics within the interstices of other ethnic and racial communities. Through word of mouth, new Cuban arrivals acquire a cognitive mapping of New York in which the dispersed residences of relatives and friends and centers of religious and cultural activity form coordinates on a particularly Cuban geography of the metropolitan area. As Leonardo Wignall (introduced earlier) described "his" Cuban New York:

> La Esquina Habanera, Central Park, 135th and Broadway in the middle there, all those places, La Flor de Broadway [a Cuban Chinese restaurant in Manhattan], simply is [sic] a little piece of Cuba. The rumba, the drum ceremonies they give here, represent Cuba in that moment that you went and threw yourself into a rumba.[20]

For Leonardo and others, almost any "gathering in diaspora" (Warner and Wittner 1998) evokes (idealized) memories of Cuba:

> We used to share that emotion of the rumba. We used to share that stage of the drum ceremony. We used to share an Abakuá presentation in a patio. La Esquina Habanera represents that. . . . We see so-and-so that we haven't seen for years, a point of meeting, of brotherhood, of contact, a point of understanding, it is so, so, so much that it represents. That it's not La Esquina Habanera, but rather Prado and Neptuno [an intersection along one of Havana's main boulevards], La Engañadora [a popular Havana nightclub in the 1960s and 1970s]. What it represents is so much.[21]

Special occasions like the after-party of the annual Cuban Day Parade are dense with cross-generational introductions and acquaintances. On the Sunday in May 2002 described at the beginning of the chapter, Felix de Jesús, a *marielito* who has frequented the rumba and dance music scenes for more than twenty years, walked around introducing his cousin, who had come only a few years earlier. Mirta and Ñico, both from the Mariel cohort, tried to outdo each other with tales of their recent trips to Cuba. Several acquaintances asked me when I would take my next trip: non-Cubans who visit Cuba may be incorporated into these circuits and frequently serve as surrogates (see Knauer 2005). Even those Cubans who do not visit the Central Park rumba or other locations know about them through their Cuban social and conversational networks.

And as more Cuban émigrés visit the island, their eyewitness accounts of daily life in Cuba form part of the discourse of the émigré community. Most travelers are keen observers, and woven into the *chisme* (gossip) and complaints about delayed flights are richly detailed analyses of changes in the built environment and the social, cultural, and economic life: what necessities are readily available and what a visitor should take for his or her family; what can be bought with Cuban pesos and what is only available at the dollar stores. While supplying practical advice for those who plan to travel or send remittances, these ethnographic narratives serve as a living newspaper, producing a flow of independent information about the homeland.

This Afro-Cuban counter-public sphere, it should be noted, is multi-vocal and poly-cultural, and sometimes fault lines and fissures emerge along migratory generational lines, between those who have traveled back and those who have not, or between Cubans and non-Cubans over authenticity, authority, and interpretation.[22]

Central Park and the Public Sphere

At the time the Central Park rumba began, New York City's Upper West Side was undergoing a major wave of urban renewal under the direction of Robert Moses. The governing logic decreed that the public interest would be best served by replacing unsightly old buildings with gleaming new construction. The cornerstone of Moses's plan was a monumental performing arts center to establish New York's reputation as an international cultural capital. Moses had assembled a tight coalition of business, government, and arts leaders, who sold Lincoln Center (literally) to the public (Fitch 1993). Swaths of tenement houses were declared blighted and replaced with middle-income and luxury high-rises. Low-income residents were pushed toward Harlem or displaced to more distant locales as the frontier of urban change edged northward. The cultural logic governing the construction of Lincoln Center—and the shift it signaled in the city's political economy—set the stage for successive waves of economic restructuring and gentrification.

After losing 400,000 manufacturing jobs in the 1975 fiscal crisis, New York was remade into a "globally oriented center for post-industrial services" (Fitch 1993: 14). The city was also reconfigured socially and demographically. New immigrants arrived from Asia, Latin America, and the Caribbean, many to work in the growing low-wage sector of the service economy. At the same time, the new "post-" industries gave rise to new professional and managerial elites. However, the city experienced a net loss of jobs during the 1980s. The richest 20 percent of New Yorkers saw their incomes grow, while the bottom 20 percent became poorer (Mollenkopf and Castells 1991). The city became increasingly stratified, as class and occupational divisions hewed pretty closely to racial and ethnic divisions. This stratification took a spatial form: recent immigrants changed the character of existing ethnic and working-class neighborhoods while new areas were cleared for upper-middle-class residences, employment, and zones of entertainment and consumption. The arts became a marker of prestige (Bourdieu 1984), and policies and planning initiatives favored "cultural strategies of redevelopment" (Zukin 1995), which involved historic preservation and the creation of historic districts, "improving" existing public spaces, and promoting existing cultural institutions.

As New York became a global center for financial capital, communication, and information, the cultural industries came to play a correspondingly important role in the city's symbolic and "real" economy. Yet with cuts in public funding for the arts, cultural institutions began to adopt more market-like strategies (Zukin 1995).

Although New York continued to be a magnet for new immigrants (Foner 2001), gentrification continued to both rework areas already "colonized" and push into new neighborhoods such as Harlem and El Barrio. For the remaining low-income tenants on the Upper West Side, and the predominantly black and Latino residents of Harlem and El Barrio, gentrification was a mixed bag: while it brought some real improvements, it also threatened to make the areas unaffordable and change the communities' cultures (Dávila 2004).

At the same time, public services in the city increasingly were put under private control. Those who oversaw and promoted the state's retreat from the public sphere sought justification in the fiscal crisis of the city and state governments. These intertwined processes of unfettered development, gentrification, and privatization, often described as neoliberal urbanism, have continued to shape New York's landscape and population since the events of September 11, 2001.

The Central Park Conservancy

This sketch of how private entities have tried to cultivate the public whose interest they claim to serve helps frame the current dynamics at work in Central Park. Public cultural expression—from murals to graffiti, from booksellers to live music—has been subjected to different forms of legal restriction, policing, and harassment in New York City (Erzen and McArdle 2001). Not all spaces are equal, however (de Certeau 1984; Lefebvre 1995) and not all forms of public culture are seen as equal. Race, class, and gender help shape what is viewed as "culture" and what types of public cultural expression are acceptable in what kinds of places—in effect determining who has a "right to the city" (Lefebvre 1991) or to particular parts of the city.[23] Musicians and other street performers have been tolerated—within limits—in some public locales. However, the "publicness" of those public spaces has often been hotly contested.[24]

When Central Park was proposed in the nineteenth century, it was envisioned not only as a respite from the hustle and bustle of urban life, but also as a spiritual benefit for those unfortunates crowded into New York's slums. Much as the great public museums were seen as helping turn immigrants and workers into good citizens (Bennett 1995; Duncan 1995), in the park the working classes would observe how the wealthy comported themselves and thus be socialized into compliance with middle-class behavioral norms (Rosenzweig and Blackmar 1992). Parks would provide a wholesome alternative to Bowery beer halls and other "low-life" entertainments (Boyer 1983). Frederick Law Olmstead's early plans for Central Park included concerts and theatrical performances, originally designed with the moneyed classes in mind.[25] Free band concerts were inaugurated in 1859, but attendees were not allowed to sit on the grass. Tens of thousands of ordinary New Yorkers stood while the wealthy watched from their carriages (Stewart 2000). However, for the first half of the twentieth century, municipal authorities paid little attention paid to performing arts in the park. As Parks Commissioner from 1934 to 1960, Robert Moses focused on playgrounds and playing fields in city parks, but not "the arts."

By the 1980s, many city parks were in sad shape, due in part to the municipal fiscal crisis of the 1970s, exacerbated by the cuts in federal and state aid, which put additional pressure on the city's resources. But efforts to "improve" parks and other public spaces were also motivated by "quality-of-life" concerns voiced by new and traditional elites. Parks had become havens for homeless people and others judged to be unruly and therefore undesirable by virtue of their age, race, gender, or preferred forms of recreation (Deutsche 1998). In the late 1980s, a private group was allowed to take on the "restoration" of Midtown's Bryant Park (Zukin 1995).

The Central Park Conservancy (CPC) was born when a group of well-meaning (and relatively well-heeled) city residents got fed up with "lawless, unmanaged and unmanageable" condition of Central Park (CPC n.d.), and the city's inability to fund or manage restorations and upkeep. The CPC would seek private funding and work together with the city to develop a long-range plan for the park.

The CPC spearheaded several widely publicized restorations of existing landmarks in the park, such as the Delacorte Theater and the lawns, trees, and gardens (Harden 1999; Naumberg Orchestral Concerts n.d.). The CPC and the city have set up information kiosks and expanded and regulated commercial activities both inside and on the borders of the park. This was in line with strategies to crack down on the informal economy and gain public revenue by controlling consumption: independent entrepreneurs are replaced by "branded" and licensed vendors. In 1998, amid concerns about the encroachment of private interests into the public sphere, the CPC was awarded a four-million-dollar annual city contract to run the park.

The CPC is caught in a contradiction, however, between its *mision civilizatrice* and the ostensibly democratic mission of a public park. It has come under fire for closing public access to some heavily used areas so that private philanthropies can rent facilities for lavish fundraisers (Trebay 1998). Harlem residents argued that the CPC's efforts amplified existing inequalities by focusing primarily on the area below 96th Street.

The CPC's stewardship of Central Park needs to be seen in the context of other changes in the way public culture and urban publics are viewed. In the vacuum left by the apparent failure of liberal social policy, proponents of gentrification and "new urbanism" adopted the rhetoric of "restoring civility" from the "broken windows" thesis (Kelling and Coles 1996). This thesis found its expression in the "zero tolerance" policy promoted by former Mayor Rudolph Giuliani, whose electoral base was middle-class and upper-middle-class whites concerned about crime and social disorder. Giuliani's notorious Police Directive No. 5 targeted "quality-of-life (QOL)" crimes such as public urination, turnstile jumping, and panhandling and enlarged the scope of public behaviors that were considered criminal. Giuliani's often belligerent pronouncements attempted to garner public support for increased surveillance and policing of public spaces by appealing to middle-class notions of decorum. Although their promoters presented QOL campaigns as neutral, democratic, and embodying universal values, the types of behaviors and bodies that were considered an affront to the QOL were racialized, gendered and classed (Deutsche 1998; Erzen and McArdle 2001).

These revanchist policies had an impact on street life and public culture in New York. Giuliani's police department began to harass cultural petty entrepreneurs such as artists, artisans, and booksellers who marketed their wares on sidewalks and in other public places. Little-used city ordinances and Parks Department regulations were dusted off and enforced with vigor. Special attention was paid to zones with a lot of tourist traffic and areas targeted for redevelopment or undergoing gentrification

The Rumba and Public/Private Authority in the Park

Since at least the mid-1980s, Central Park has been a popular site for itinerant performers, particularly the area around 72nd Street, which has a dense flow of foot traffic on weekends. The rumba is distinctive in that it is deliberately held in a less trafficked area, and there is little effort to entertain bystanders. For most of its forty-year history, the Central Park rumba took place with only occasional interference from the public authorities.

In the late 1990s, as the CPC stepped up its efforts to spruce up the park, the rumba and some other musical gatherings became subject to more vigorous policing. Starting in 1998, there were a series of confrontations with the police, who often cited complaints from residents of nearby apartments about the noise. A well-known percussionist was arrested for urinating in the bushes. In September, police told the crowd to disperse because there was no permit. Several of the *rumberos* argued with the police, who then arrested one man and confiscated some instruments (Kirby 1998). For the remainder of that "season" and into the next year, from week to week no one knew if the rumba would be able to continue. In late July 1999, the police arrived one Sunday and stopped the rumba. After several such incidents, the Central Park rumba more or less dispersed, and participants gravitated to other locales. Rumba in New York has always been multilocal (Owen 2002): the Central Park rumba has had a dynamic relationship with other rumba locales in the area, and most participants knew where they would be freer from the forces of law and order.

However, there was anger and resentment among the participants. Many saw the police actions as unfairly singling out the rumba or as racially motivated.[26] "Es porque somos negros y somos inmigrantes que nos tratan así (It's because we're black and immigrants that they treat us this way)," some said. Others were angry that a cultural form that had been marginalized in Cuba was suffering the same treatment in the United States, and they talked openly about the parallels with bitter irony. Some of the non-Cuban participants with more social capital strategized to "save" or defend the rumba by mobilizing support from journalists, elected officials, and cultural institutions.

By the time of the events recounted at the beginning of this chapter (May 2002), New York City had a new mayor and a more relaxed attitude among the police and Parks Department officials, and the *rumberos* had reestablished their claim to Central Park. However, these events do mark a cleavage over the meaning of public space, which kinds of public culture are appropriate, and who makes those determinations. The differences do not hew entirely to class or racial lines; there are plenty of affluent tourists and white Upper West Side residents who criticize the Parks Department and the Central Park Conservancy for valuing horticulture over human culture.[27]

La Esquina Habanera also felt the sting of changing demographics and racialized constructions. There were constant tensions with the landlord and the neighbors. While some were predictable for any place that serves food and liquor and has live music (too much noise), many felt that there were racial and political agendas at play. Tony came under fire for bringing musicians from Cuba such as Los Muñequitos de Matanzas and co-sponsoring a concert with Los Van Van, but he feels that the political criticism was racially motivated. The Cuban population of Union City declined as some moved to the suburbs or to South Florida and "new Latinos"—immigrants from El Salvador, Honduras, and other Latin American countries—moved in. With less demand for Cuban food and Cuban music, La Esquina closed in the summer of 2004.

In response to these events, the *rumberos* and the Afro-Cuban cultural community developed a heightened sense of themselves as a community or a counter-public and began to engage in a discourse about cultural rights in which the history of rumba in New York became an important part of the narrative. In discussions with the police, or among themselves, Cubans who had been in the United States for a short while often cited the forty-year presence of the Central Park rumba. To legitimate their claims, Cuban émigrés situated themselves within the expanded historical narrative of rumba in New York City rather than simply collapsing the New York rumba scene into the larger narrative of rumba originating in Cuba, thus acknowledging the important contributions made by the *boricuas, afro-americanos, y judios* (Puerto Ricans, African Americans, and Jews) and others who had shaped the early Central Park rumba. The Cubans have increasingly deployed the language of rights alongside that of "roots," although many of them have not become citizens, and some remain resistant to the norms and governmentalized procedures demanded by the Parks Department regulations. There is also an awareness of the ways in which standards of taste, and the boundaries of acceptability, are shaped by class and race (see Figure 6.6).

Rumba, Race, and Social Disorder in Havana

The policing and disciplining of the Central Park rumba are paralleled, in some ways, by the ambivalent status of rumba and other racialized cultural forms in contemporary Havana. Although New York and Havana are situated within countries with apparently very different socioeconomic and political systems, and they occupy very distinct locations within global hierarchies of power, there are striking similarities in some of the cultural logics at work. For reasons of space, this brief sketch is merely suggestive of some of the parallels.

Rumba was viewed with a degree of suspicion and hostility in the years following the Cuban Revolution. Although Afro-Cuban cultural practices were not outlawed, there were efforts to confine or discipline them (Hagedorn 2001; Velez 2000). The creation of institutional settings and elaborated, theatrical productions such as those of the Conjunto Folklórico Nacional was accompanied by constraining the popular, home-grown versions. Informants recalled that into the 1970s it was not uncommon for the police to break up a rumba on the street or in someone's home, often on the grounds that it was too disruptive. By the time I started visiting Cuba in the 1990s, the Conjunto Folklórico Nacional was solidly established and hardly controversial. The sedate character of the Saturday performances in its patio, however, do not hint at the opposition that Rogelio Martínez Furé encountered when he first attempted to establish the *sabados de la rumba* (rumba Saturdays) to showcase both the genre and its proponents (Rogelio Martínez Furé, personal communication). Likewise, when the poet Eloy Machado proposed a weekly *peña* featuring rumba at the headquarters of the Artists and Writers Union (UNEAC) in the 1980s,

FIGURE 6.6   Performing black masculinity in New York's Central Park. *(Photograph by the author.)*

the leaders of UNEAC were hesitant precisely because they feared opposition from the neighbors (Eloy Machado, personal communication; Moore 1997). These fears were not ill-founded. When I visited acquaintances who lived across the street from UNEAC in the summer of 1998, they complained about the noise and unsavory crowds at the rumba.

In both cases, the opposition was shaped in part by the historically racial-ized and class-defined geography of Havana. While poor whites lived alongside blacks in the *barrios marginales,* before 1959 the more exclusive neighborhoods were virtually all white. The abolition of legal segregation, the departure of much of the elite, and the revolution's housing policies allowed blacks and people of modest means to move into former elite strongholds. While white areas became more mixed, the former *barrios marginales* (where rumba and other "folkloric" genres had been born and flourished) remained predominantly black. Whites, in other words, did not flock into formerly "black" areas. Many Cubans still cognitively map the city into *caliente* (hot), or marginal, areas and "good" neighborhoods. Both the Conjunto Folklórico Nacional and UNEAC are located in El Vedado, formerly a middle-class suburb of Havana. Its broad, tree-lined streets are filled with elegant dwellings set back from the sidewalk. Although El Vedado is no longer an exclusive middle-class enclave, many residents were still uncomfortable with the idea of rumba events in their "backyard," so to speak. I experienced the effects of this racialized and gendered urban imaginary when acquaintances discouraged me from traveling to what they viewed as questionable neighborhoods (where the majority of my informants lived) to conduct research.

The ascendance of tourism as a prime motor of economic revival in Cuba has helped shape urban (and national) planning. "Cultural strategies of redevelopment" are deployed in Havana, and international capital plays an important, if not a leading, role. To make Havana attractive to foreign visitors and investors, a mixture of historic preservation, renovation, and new construction are reshaping the built environment. Several streets in the colonial city have been turned into pedestrian malls, lined with upscale boutiques, cafes, and bars. In some areas, such as the Plaza Vieja, the original residents have been relocated to create more housing for tourists and other foreign visitors (Hill 2004).[28] While a handful of Cuban urbanists and others have called for tourist development that is less geographically concentrated and not solely focused on elite travelers (Coyula 1995), most of the tourist infrastructure to date has focused on luxury hotels and resorts. The "touristification" of Havana is reminiscent of gentrification in New York. Residents in tourist-heavy areas complain that a disproportionate share of resources (electricity, water, building materials) is siphoned off for hotels, leaving Cubans with crumbling homes and inadequate services.

Cuba has also had to allay foreigners' concerns for physical safety, and increased tourism has meant more vigorous policing of public spaces. Street crime (primarily mugging and pickpocketing) is on the rise in Havana, especially in tourist zones. More vigorous policing, however, has resulted in race, age, and gender profiling: just like in many U.S. cities, young black men, especially if they are in the "wrong" part of town, are likely to be stopped and asked for identity papers.[29] Black male bodies are seen as a potential threat to the social order, and every black male I met in Cuba was well aware of this. Police patrol tourist zones but also sites of black cultural performances, including not only rumba events, but also rap concerts.[30]

Rumba remains a highly racialized cultural performance in both New York and Havana. On the rhetorical level, rumba and other Afro-Cuban cultural

FIGURE 6.7   Folkloric dancers, Havana. *(Photograph by the author.)*

forms, such as Carnival, are declared to belong to all Cubans. It is possible to study Afro-Cuban music and dance at one of Cuba's prestigious performing-arts schools. But the rhetoric and institutionalization have not succeeded in desegregating the performers or the audiences. In 1989, thirty years after the revolution, researchers determined that rumba was still concentrated both geographically (in the *barrios marginales*) and demographically (among blacks and those occupying the lower socio-occupational strata; Álvarez Vergara 1989). The overwhelming majority of folkloric performers, professional and amateur, were black (see Figure 6.7).[31]

A decade later, when I started doing fieldwork, the situation did not appear to have changed. There are very few white folkloric singers, dancers, or musicians. In addition, the Cuban public for these performances is also largely—if not quite so disproportionately—black. Most of the white faces at Callejon de Hamel and UNEAC belong to tourists. The demographics are similar at other rumba locales. To a degree, this reflects the historical patterns of residence discussed earlier. Many rumba locales are located in areas that were historically considered *barrios marginales*. In fact, there have been several efforts to "revive" rumba locales in "traditional" areas, such as the famous Solar California, the courtyard of a large housing complex in the neighborhood of Belén.

The construction of these areas as "marginal" and "black" is not simply a discursive flourish. A study on race and inequality by the Centro de Antropología, found that "inherited inequalities" still shape patterns of residence: blacks and *mestizo* or "mixed-race" people predominate in the most deprived neighborhoods (i.e., those with the most crowded, dilapidated housing and fewest amenities). Even within the same neighborhood, blacks and mestizos occupy worse housing than whites (Espino Prieto and Rodríguez, 2006).

But the skewing of audiences is not simply because of location. Although most Cubans will affirm that rumba belongs to all Cubans, they also see it as a black thing (both affirmatively and negatively) or something that would interest tourists. In the summer of 2002, the police forced the closure for several months of a popular weekly rumba event held in a communal residential courtyard (*solar*) in Habana Vieja. This rumba was eventually stopped, more or less for good, in 2005. The Solar de la Cueva del Humo (Courtyard of the Smoky Cave) is located on the same block as a popular tourist attraction, La Bodeguita del Medio, whose fame derives from its association with Ernest Hemingway. Here, as through the Centro Histórico (historic center) of Habana Vieja, foreign visitors with cameras and sun visors, souvenir vendors, and hustlers jostle against neighborhood residents.

For decades, this courtyard—shared by inhabitants of six or seven apartments—was known to local residents as a place where people gathered to play rumba. Indeed, several of my New York-based informants recalled attending rumbas there. In the late 1990s, the *solar* resident Felicia Alfonso and her son Miki established a cultural project focused on the rumba in the *solar* with the support of a foreign nongovernmental organization and public authorities, articulating a rhetoric of cultural preservation along with community improvement. They tried to regularize, professionalize, and promote the rumba. When I first visited in 2000, there was a half a crumbling staircase on one side of the courtyard leading up to one of the roofs and very little seating. By the next summer, the staircase had been torn down, and the sides of the long, narrow patio were lined with benches, leaving a thin strip of concrete floor for dancing There was a small bar along one side selling beer, shots of rum, and mojitos and one or two female vendors emerged from their kitchens with heaping platters of deep-fried *croquetas* (croquettes). Unlike some other rumba performances in Havana, the rumba at the Solar de la Cueva del Humo was not tightly programmed with time-restricted sets by a succession of groups. Well-known figures such as Juan de Dios Ramos, Miguel Angel Aspirina, Luis Chacon (often called by the nickname "Luis Aspirina")—all of whom were among the early members of the Conjunto Folklórico Nacional—came regularly, but none came every week. Audience members frequently took the mike or, occasionally, the drums and were treated with respect.

As more tourists learned about the rumba, they came to make up around a third of the audience. The rest were local residents, Cuban rumba fans from other areas, and the hustlers who frequent such locales. Occasionally, people got drunk or a little rowdy. However, the organizers and many performers were clearly conscious of the social construction of rumba as a threat to the social order and worried about participants' behavior perpetuating stereotypes that would threaten the rumba's future. On several occasions when the crowd seemed unruly, the veteran performer Luis Chacon grabbed the microphone and exhorted people to counteract the negative image of rumba by behaving properly.

As the tourist traffic increased, so did the scrutiny of the police—and thus, the organizers' anxiety. I heard conflicting reports about what prompted the police to shut down the rumba. Initially, a musician told me that a tourist had been robbed at the rumba and complained to the police. Others later reported that the tourist actually had been robbed in front of La Bodeguita, but either he claimed it had taken place at the *solar* or the police presumed some connection and ordered the rumba shut (Carlos Casanova, Luis Chacon, personal communications). It reopened several months later. However, by the time I visited again in early 2004, it had been closed again—apparently for a similar reason. By the summer of 2007, the mural marking the street entrance was no longer visible, and both musicians and friends who live nearby reported that there had not been any rumbas there for a long time.

Even before the closing of the Solar de la Cueva del Humo, many folkloric performers in Havana expressed concern that rumba still occupied a somewhat precarious spot in the cultural landscape. Informants continually fretted about the future of the genre. They were worried not that people would stop playing and enjoying rumba but that it would not be accorded the respect it deserved. They saw themselves engaged in a struggle to maintain rumba's visibility. Some argued that while the state paid lip service to rumba, rumba did not receive the kind of support and promotion that other cultural forms and musical genres did. The success of the Buena Vista Social Club raised the hopes of many Cuban musicians regarding their own prospects for global success; folkloric musicians have long hoped that their genre would be the next one to take off.

Although the official discourse that being Cuban transcends black and white persists, many black Cubans will privately acknowledge not only that has race not been transcended, but that the issue is in some ways more insidious than during the period of legal discrimination. Song lyrics have begun to address the association of blackness with criminality and the links between racial and economic inequality (more obliquely in rumba, more directly in dance music and rap), and what these portend for Cuba's future.[32] Although Cuban research on these issues is still limited in scope (see Fernández 2001;

Hernández-Reguant 2005), during the past several years there have been some important developments, including the publication of findings from a highly publicized study on racial attitudes by the Centro de Antropología (Espino Prieto and Rodriguez 2006) and the establishment of a commission to commemorate the centenary of the founding of the still controversial Partido Independiente de Color (Heredia 2008).

In each place, varied social actors negotiate authority and authenticity within the social spaces of Afro-Cuban culture while simultaneously struggling to enlarge those spaces. In New York, the cleavages are between Cubans of varied migratory cohorts, but also between Cubans and non-Cubans. In Cuba, the market, tourists, and Cuban émigrés all play a role in shaping the terrain.

However, authority and authenticity increasingly are negotiated not in but between New York and Havana. That is, due to the frequency and intensity of the multiple translocal flows between Cuba and the United States that I noted earlier, many participants in the Afro-Cuban counter-public spheres in Havana and New York are aware of the tensions and controversies in both places. Many, further, see themselves as part of the same translocal community—one that is not limited to New York and Cuba but includes other cities in the United States, as well as Cuban immigrant clusters in Spain, Mexico, and elsewhere.[33] Each "side" looks carefully (sometimes critically, sometimes appreciatively) at what the other is doing. This translocal imagining is facilitated by the multidirectional circulation of commercial and home-made video and audio recordings, as well as continued migration and occasional visits to the island by Cuban immigrants and others. In these ways, rumba enthusiasts in New York and Havana remain aware of, and exchange songs, rhythms, styles, and gossip on "the other side." Competence and social capital are frequently established transnationally (see Knauer 2008a, 2008b).

This also suggests that Cuban émigrés involved in Afro-Cuban culture feel a kind of "long-distance nationalism" (Glick Schiller and Fouron 2001) that differs from that of self-identified "exiles." Moreover, their participation in a counter-public that is not solely "Cuban" suggests the need for further analysis of the kinds of identifications shared among Cuban and non-Cuban rumba enthusiasts (and Santería devotees) in New York and elsewhere. In other words, as James Lorand Matory (2005) suggests in his study of Afro-Brazilian religions, diasporic Cubans belong to an imagined community (Anderson 1991) or overlapping imagined communities that are not limited to the nation-state or even to the "nation and its fragments," to borrow a phrase from Partha Chatterjee (1993).[34] Cuban *rumberos* on the island and elsewhere, along with non-Cuban rumba enthusiasts, constitute an Afro-Cuban cultural community or, to adopt a concept from hip-hop culture, a "rumba nation" (see Figure 6.8). Non-Cuban rumba enthusiasts in New York and elsewhere often view Cuba as a "Mecca" or

FIGURE 6.8   Blurring the lines between spectator and participant at the Central Park rumba. *(Photograph by the author.)*

a cultural "homeland" of sorts; many visit Cuba or articulate a desire to do so. The translocal and multicultural character of this "counter-public" offers possibilities for alliances and engagements that transcend the realm of cultural performance, in which the political cleavages between the Cuba and the United States are not insignificant, but are seen an impediments or obstacles to maintaining and developing channels of communication that are multilayered, informal, and not necessarily directed at political ends in either country.

Notes

1. An early version of this article was presented at the June 2003 conference "Translocal Flows/Flujos Translocales: Migrations, Borders and Diasporas in the Americas," co-sponsored by the Social Science Research Council and the Facultad Latinoamerica de Ciencias Sociales, Santo Domingo, Dominican Republic, and at a 2005 conference on immigrant social and political expression sponsored by the International Migration, Integration, and Social Cohesion research network. Participants at both conferences offered useful feedback, including O. Hugo Benavides, Marco Martiniello, and Kevin Yelvington. Thanks also to Mark Reinhardt at Williams College for pointing me to Warner's work on counter-publics. The editors of this volume also gave helpful suggestions for revising the article. Subse-

quently, I developed some of these ideas in my doctoral dissertation (Knauer 2005: esp. chap. 6). I draw upon some of this same material in Knauer 2008a.

2. Cuba, for much of its history, had distinct "black" and "white" Carnival traditions: see Moore 1995; Ortiz 1984.

3. Ortiz produced an extensive catalogue of work, including hundreds of short articles for the popular press and dozens of scholarly publications. Some of the best-known works on Afro-Cuban culture are *La Africania del la Música Folklórica Cubana* (1998 [1950]) and *Los Instrumentos de la Música Afrocubana* (1996 [1952]). Following the Cuban Revolution, he helped establish the short-lived Instituto de Etnologia y Folklore and held seminars whose participants included many of Cuba's leading scholars on Afro-Cuban culture, including the late Alberto Pedro, Natalia Bolivar, and Rogelio Martinez Furé. For critical appraisals of Ortiz, see, among other works, Bronfman 2004, Hernandez-Reguant 2005, and Moore 1997, 2006, as well as Fernando Coronil's introduction to *Cuban Counterpoint: Sugar and Tobacco* (Ortiz 1995).

4. The brief summary in this paragraph draws on Fernández Robaina 1990; Hagedorn 2001; Moore 1997; Velez 2000; and conversations with Rogelio Martínez Furé, Leonardo Wignall, Stanley Insua Hernández, and Tomas Fernández Robaina.

5. Starting in the 1960s, the Cuban government arranged international tours by performing artists, from ballet dancers to the Conjunto Folklórico Nacional: see Hagedorn 2001.

6. The Conjunto Folklórico Nacional was established not by the state but by researchers and traditional performers, although it was "adopted" by the state: see Hagedorn 2001; Moore 2006. Some of Cuba's oldest folkloric troupes, such as the Muñequitos de Matanzas and Los Papines, were established before the revolution, but after the revolution they became "incorporated" into the Ministry of Culture, and their members became state employees.

7. In making this argument, I take issue with Nancy Fraser's discussion of distributive justice, which separates the cultural from the economic and political: see Fraser 1993.

8. In February 2008, a Cuban friend called excitedly to tell me he had just read about a new Commission for the Centenary of the Foundation of the PIC: see Heredia 2008.

9. See, e.g., Ariana Orejuela's work on Havana's famous dance hall La Tropical, which is still constructed in the minds of some contemporary Havana residents as black and low class: Orejuela 2002.

10. See Aranda-Alvarado 2001 for a discussion of the relationship between the Harlem Renaissance and the Afrocubanismo Movement, focusing on painters such as Jacob Lawrence and Wilfredo Lam. The essays in Brock and Castañeda 1998 set out to document and analyze the relationships between African Americans and Cubans before the revolution, in arenas as diverse as baseball and literature.

11. Beatriz Morales (1990) and Marta Moreno Vega (1995) note that, in the 1940s and '50s, the New Year's predictions of Havana's *babalawos* (known as the *letra del año,* or letter of the year) were reported at parties sponsored by New York's Club Cubano Interamericano.

12. The Club Cubano Interamericano had an explicitly translocal "mission" from its inception. It was established at the suggestion of a Havana city official who was visiting New York and wanted to strengthen ties between the two communities. Its monthly newsletter frequently reported on members' visits to Cuba and visits to New York by members' friends and relatives in Cuba: newsletters of the Club Cubano Interamericano, 1940s–1950s, Archives of the Centro de Estudios Puertorriqueños, Hunter College, City University of New York.

13. Ibid. For other discussions of the interactions between Puerto Ricans, African Americans and Cubans in New York see Juan Flores (2000) and Vernon Boggs (1992).

14. There are also gendered critiques of rumba that I have not been able to develop fully here. An oversimplified synopsis of these critiques would be: too much macho posturing, drinking, and *delincuencia* (delinquency), almost always coded as male.

15. This counter-public is multi-sited and includes people and places in Miami/Dade County, Florida, and the Union City/New York metropolitan area.

16. The Cuban American "power structure" was able to influence the government's actions through publicity—lobbying, protesting, editorializing—and delayed but did not prevent Elián González's return to Cuba.

17. Elements of these other counter-publics include groups such as the Antonio Maceo Brigade, progressive young Cuban Americans who visited Cuba in the early 1970s; journals such as *Areito*; the "*dialogueros*" (Cuban émigrés who supported "dialogues" with the Cuban government starting in the late 1970s); and, more recently, magazines such as *ñ* and clubs such as Café Nostalgia and Hoy Como Ayer. The political/intellectual counter-public finds institutional expression in places like the Cuban Research Institute at Florida International University and the Cuba Project at the City University of New York: see Lulo 2000.

18. In the eyes of the right-wing militants, supporting contemporary Cuban cultural production is highly political. For decades, no Cuban groups performed publicly in Florida, and international salsa stars who attended festivals or performed in Cuba were boycotted. In the 1990s, a disc jockey who played current Cuban music at a Miami radio station received death threats, and the station was pressured to cancel his show. A shift started in the late 1990s and although there were still protests and pressures, Cuban musical groups such as Los Van Van performed in Florida without incident. However, during the second term of George W. Bush's presidency, the pendulum swung back in the opposite direction, and virtually no cultural exchange visas were granted to Cuban performers—including several Grammy nominees who were unable to attend the awards ceremonies. Scholarly exchanges were also impeded as Cuban researchers were routinely denied visas to the United States.

19. *Toques de santo,* or "playing for the saints," are drum ceremonies that are an integral part of all Afro-Cuban religious practices.

20. "La Esquina Habanera, Central Park, la 135 y Broadway en el medio allí, todos estos lugares, La Flor de Broadway, simplemente es un pedacito de Cuba. La rumba, los toques de santo que se dan aquí, representa Cuba en el momento aquel donde tú ibas y te metías en una rumba": Leonardo Wignall, interview, July 2004.

21. "Compartíamos esa emoción de la rumba. Compartíamos ese escenario de toque santo. Compartíamos en el pátio una presentacion de abakuases. La Esquina Habanera representaba eso. . . . Vemos a un fulanito que hacia años no lo veíamos, un punto de reunión, un punto de fraternidad, un punto de contacto, un punto de entendimiento, es tanto y tanto y tanto y tanto, lo que representa. Que no es la Esquina Habanera, es decir, Prado y Neptuno, La Engañadora. Es tanto lo que representa": ibid.

22. I have witnessed numerous arguments between Cubans in New York about details of daily life in Cuba, ranging from the prices of basic goods to government policy regarding apartment swaps. Conversely, I have also witnessed debates among Cubans on the island regarding living conditions in the United States.

23. There is, of course, an equally complex and lengthy history surrounding the relationship between racially or ethnically marked cultural forms—many of which, like rap music and graffiti, had their origins in marginalized public spaces—and "polite society."

Duneier 2000 explores how race and class shape the treatment and perception of sidewalk booksellers in Greenwich Village.

24. Washington Square Park, for example, has been the site of numerous battles over the governance of public space, policing, redevelopment plans, and appropriate forms of cultural activity. These have involved community residents, the city, and New York University, which has steadily purchased most of the real estate surrounding the park and thus claims the park as part of its campus.

25. "Perhaps Olmsted and Vaux envisioned New Yorkers promenading up the Mall, stopping occasionally to socialize as they proceeded to the Concert Ground. The music would lift their minds and spirits from daily worries and prepare them for the inspiration that nature would provide in the views from Bethesda Terrace": CPC n.d.

26. A frequent complaint articulated by many of the Cubans was that the African drummers were not subjected to as much harassment, although they attracted larger crowds and made as much—if not more—noise. However, in 2000 the police also cracked down on the African drummers, citing many of the same reasons they had used to justify their actions against the *rumberos*: noise, complaints by neighbors, and the lack of a permit: Siegal 2000.

27. One parent from the Upper West Side quoted in the *New York Times* (Stewart 2000) charged that the CPC had turned the park into a "grass museum."

28. In contrast to what has occurred in many urban renewal programs in the United States, the residents have been re-housed. Most were moved to Alamar, a Soviet-built development on the eastern outskirts of Havana. While the housing stock in Alamar in many ways is in better condition than much of the "unimproved" housing found in the old parts of the Havana, Alamar is physically distant and was designed as a bedroom community, and there are virtually no jobs there. Most Plaza Vieja residents must commute to Havana to work, which means spending time and money dealing with a public transportation system that has not recovered from the economic crisis: Hill 2004.

29. This is not to say that no "white" Cubans are ever stopped, but every black man I met under forty (and many over forty) had been stopped by the police numerous times, sometimes more than once in a day. Age, clothing, body language, and hairstyle seem to play some role in determining whom the police stop but are not completely decisive.

30. I was not able to find statistics to corroborate the anecdotal evidence on racial profiling. This may be due in part to a continued discomfort in addressing questions of race. Cuba's insistence on "race blind" policies means that official police statistics do not take race into account. According to Centro de Antropología 2003, opinions about whether race and racism are problems vary widely; race and age seem to be important factors, as is how racism is defined. Those who had a narrow definition of racism (racial violence, institutional discrimination) were more likely to say that racism was not a problem; those who had a broader definition perceived a greater problem. The study has never been published as such but has been summarized in conference presentations and articles by some of the researchers (see Espino Prieto and Rodriguez 2006) My observations square with reports from other foreign researchers (see Fernandes 2006; McGarrity 1992; Moore 2006; Perry 2004; Safa 2008, among others) and are confirmed by conversations with Cuban researchers and Havana residents. However, others downplay the racial aspects of tourism or refuse to see these incidents as typical or racially motivated.

31. My estimate, based on sixteen visits to Cuba between 1993 and 2007, is that about 5 percent of the professional folkloric performers are white. By "professional," I mean performers who belong to either established folkloric ensembles that are part of the Ignacio

Piñeiro *empresa* (the cultural *empresas,* or enterprises, are state-run organizations that combine the functions of a booking agency and a craft guild), or aficionado groups affiliated with a *casa de cultura.*

32. Several dissertations, articles, and books explore the Cuban hip-hop scene as a space for, among other things, an articulation of black identity and a critique of Cuban racial politics: see, among others, Fernandes 2006; Perry 2004.

33. Scholars inside and outside Cuban are increasingly focusing on Cuban immigrant or diaspora communities and their transnational ties to the island. See, e.g., the essays in Fernández 2005.

34. This theme is addressed extensively by J. Lorand Matory (2005) in his provocative and exhaustive analysis of the transnational evolution of "Afro-Brazilian" Candomblé between the late nineteenth and early twenty-first centuries.

References

Abelmann, Nancy, and John Lie. 1997. *Blue Dreams: Korean Americans and the Los Angeles Riots.* Cambridge, Mass.: Harvard University Press.

Álvarez Vergara, Rosa Esther. 1989. "Caracterización de las agrupaciones de rumba de la Ciudad de La Habana." Trabajo de diploma, Instituto Superior de Arte, Facultad de Música, La Habana, Cuba.

Anderson, Benedict. 1991. *Imagined Communities.* London: Verso.

Appadurai, Arjun. 1993. "Disjuncture and Difference in the Global Cultural Economy." Pp. 269–296 in *The Phantom Public Sphere,* ed. Bruce Robbins. Minneapolis: University of Minnesota Press.

Aranda-Alvarado, Rocio. 2001. "New World Primitivism in Harlem and Havana: Constructing Modern Identities in the Americas, 1924–1945." Unpublished Ph.D. diss., City University of New York.

Asen, Robert, and Daniel C. Brouwer, eds. 2001. *Counterpublics and the State.* Albany: State University of New York Press.

Ballan, Paula. N.d. Untitled document [statement supporting application for a permit], typescript. Photocopy in author's files.

Bastide, Roger. 1980. *The African Religions of Brazil: Toward a Sociology of the Interpenetration of Civilizations,* trans. Helen Sebba. Baltimore: Johns Hopkins University Press.

Bennett, Tony. 1995. *The Birth of the Museum: History, Theory, Politics.* London: Routledge.

Black Public Sphere Collective. 1996. *The Black Public Sphere: A Public Culture Book.* Chicago: University of Chicago Press.

Boggs, Vernon. 1992. *Salsiology: Afro-Cuban Music and the Evolution of Salsa in New York City.* Westport, Conn.: Greenwood Press.

Bourdieu, Pierre. 1984. *Distinction: A Social Critique of the Judgment of Taste.* Cambridge MA: Harvard University Press.

Boyer, M. Christine. 1983. *Dreaming the Rational City.* Cambridge, Mass.: MIT Press.

Brock, Lisa, and Digna Castañeda, eds. 1998. *Between Race and Empire: African-Americans and Cubans before the Cuban Revolution.* Philadelphia: Temple University Press.

Bronfman, Alejandra. 2004. *Measures of Equality: Social Science, Citizenship and Race in Cuba 1902–1940.* Chapel Hill: University of North Carolina Press.

Central Park Conservancy (CPC). N.d. "Then and Now: Central Park History." Available online at http://www.centralparknyc.org/thenandnow/cp-history.

Chatterjee, Partha. 1993. *The Nation and Its Fragments: Colonial and Postcolonial Histories.* Princeton, N.J.: Princeton University Press.

Coyula, Mario. 1995. Talk on tourism, preservation, and development in Cuba, at CUNY Graduate Center. Author's notes.

Dávila, Arlene. 2004. *Barrio Dreams.* Berkeley: University of California Press.

de Certeau, Michel. 1984. *The Practice of Everyday Life.* Berkeley: University of California Press.

de la Fuente, Alejandro. 1998. "Race, National Discourse, and Politics in Cuba: An Overview." *Latin American Perspectives* 25, no. 3: 43–69.

Deutsche, Rosalind. 1998. *Evictions: Art and Spatial Politics.* Cambridge, Mass.: MIT Press.

Duncan, Carol. 1995. *Civilizing Rituals: Inside Public Art Museums.* New York: Routledge.

Duneier, Mitchell. 2000. *Sidewalk.* New York: Farrar, Straus and Giroux.

Erzen, Tanya, and Andrea McArdle, eds. 2001. *Zero Tolerance: Quality of Life and the New Police Brutality in New York City.* New York: New York University Press.

Espino Prieto, Rodrigo, and Pablo Rodríguez Ruiz. 2006. "Raza y desigualdad en la Cuba actual." *Temas* 45 (January–March): 44–54.

Fernandes, Sujatha. 2006. *Cuba Represent!* Durham, N.C.: Duke University Press.

Fernández, Damián J., ed. 2005. *Cuba Transnational.* Gainesville, Fla.: University Press of Florida.

Fernandez, Nadine. 2001. "The Changing Discourse on Race in Contemporary Cuba." *International Journal of Qualitative Studies in Education* 14, no. 2: 117–132.

Fernandez, Nadine. 2006. "A Racial Geography: The Meaning of Blackness in a Havana Neighborhood." *Islas* 1, no. 2: 13–20

Fernández Robaina, Tomas. 1990. *El Negro en Cuba 1902–1958.* Havana: Editorial de Ciencias Sociales.

Ferrer, Ada. 1999. *Insurgent Cuba: Race, Nation and Revolution, 1868–1898.* Chapel Hill: University of North Carolina Press.

Fitch, Robert. 1993. *The Assassination of New York.* New York: Verso.

Flores, Juan. 2000. *From Bomba to Hip Hop: Puerto Rican Culture and Latino Identity.* New York: Columbia University Press.

Foner, Nancy, ed. 2001. *New Immigrants in New York.* New York: Columbia University Press.

Fraser, Nancy. 1993. "Rethinking the Public Sphere: A Contribution to the Critique of Actually Existing Democracy." Pp. 1–32 in *The Phantom Public Sphere,* ed. Bruce Robbins. Minneapolis: University of Minnesota Press.

Glick Schiller, Nina, and Georges Fouron. 2001. *Georges Woke up Laughing: Long Distance Nationalism and the Search for Home.* Durham, N.C.: Duke University Press.

Hagedorn, Katherine. 2001. *Divine Utterances.* Washington, D.C.: Smithsonian Institution Press.

Hanchard, Michael. 1994. "Black Cinderella? Race and the Public Sphere in Brazil." *Public Culture* 7: 165–185.

Harden, Blaine. 1999. "Rich Donors Revive Central Park." *Houston Chronicle,* December 6, 4.

Helg, Aline. 1995. *Our Rightful Share: The Afro-Cuban Struggle for Equality.* Chapel Hill: University of North Carolina Press.

Heredia, Fernando Martinez. 2008. "La diversidad social no es una debilidad de la nación sino una instancia muy importante de su riqueza." *La Jiribilla* 35, no. 2 (February 2–8). Available online at www.lajiribilla.cu/2008/n352_02/352_12.html.

Hernandez-Reguant, Ariana. 2005. "Cuba's Alternative Geographies." *Journal of Latin American Anthropology* 10, no. 2 (November): 275–313.

Hill, Matthew J. 2004. "Globalizing Havana: World Heritage and Urban Redevelopment in Late Socialist Cuba." Unpublished Ph.D. diss., Department of Anthropology, University of Chicago.

Hiss, Tony. 1976. "Drums." *New Yorker,* September 29, 41.

Kasinitz, Philip. 1992. *Caribbean New York: Black Immigrants and the Politics of Race.* Ithaca, N.Y.: Cornell University Press.

Kelling, George L., and Catherine M. Coles. 1996. *Fixing Broken Windows.* New York: Free Press.

Kirby, David. 1998. "Police Officers Put Abrupt End to Rumba Beat." *New York Times,* October 11, sec. 14, 6.

Knauer, Lisa Maya. 2005. "Translocal and Multicultural Counterpublics: Rumba and Santería in and between New York and Havana." Unpublished Ph.D. diss., New York University.

Knauer, Lisa Maya. 2008a. "The Politics of Afrocuban Expression in New York." *Journal of Ethnic and Migration Studies* 46, forthcoming.

Knauer, Lisa Maya. 2008b. "Audiovisual Remittances and Transnational Subjectivities." In *Cuban Culture of the Special Period,* ed. Ariana Hernandez-Reguant. New York: Palgrave, forthcoming.

Lefebvre, Henri. 1991. *The Production of Space,* trans. D. Nicholson-Smith. Cambridge, Mass.: Blackwell.

Lefebvre, Henri. 1995. *Writings on Cities,* ed. Eleonore Kofman and Elizabeth Lebas. London: Blackwell.

Lulo, Sara. 2000. "Off-Shore Politics: Changes within the Cuban Exile Community." In *Cuban Transitions at the Millennium,* ed. Eloise Linger and John Cotman. Largo, Md.: International Development Options.

Marcus, George, and Fred Myers, eds. 1995. *The Traffic in Culture: Refiguring Art and Anthropology.* Berkeley: University of California Press.

Matory, James Lorand. 2005. *Black Atlantic Religion: Tradition, Transnationalism, and Matriarchy in the Afro-Brazilian Candomblé.* Princeton, N.J.: Princeton University Press.

McGarrity, Gayle. 1992. "Race, Culture and Social Change in Contemporary Cuba." Pp. 193–206 in *Cuba in Transition: Crisis and Transformation,* ed. Sandor Halebsky and John M. Kirk. Boulder, Colo.: Westview Press.

Mollenkopf, John, and Manuel Castells, eds. 1991. *Dual City: Restructuring New York.* New York: Russell Sage Foundation.

Moore, Robin. 1997. *Nationalizing Blackness: Afro-Cubanismo and Artistic Revolution in Havana, 1920–1940.* Pittsburgh: University of Pittsburgh Press.

Moore, Robin. 2006. *Music and Revolution: Cultural Change in Socialist Cuba.* Berkeley: University of California Press.

Morales, Beatriz. 1990. "Afro-Cuban Religious Transformation: A Comparative Study of Lucumi Religion and the Tradition of Spirit Belief." Unpublished Ph.D. diss., City University of New York.

Moreno Vega, Marta. 1995. "Yoruba Philosophy: Multiple Levels of Transformation and Understanding." Unpublished Ph.D. diss., Temple University, Philadelphia.

Naumberg Orchestral Concerts. N.d. "The Naumberg Bandshell in Central Park: A Brief History." Available online at http://naumburgconcerts.org.

Negt, Oskar, and Alexander Kluge. 1993 (1972). *Public Sphere and Experience: Toward an Analysis of the Bourgeois and Proletarian Public Sphere.* Minneapolis: University of Minnesota Press.

Orejuela, Ariana. 2002. "La Tropical. Bitácora de la música popular cubana del siglo XX." *Clave: Revista Cubana de la Música* 4, no. 1.

Ortiz, Fernando. 1984. "La antigua fiesta Afrocubana del día de los reyes." Pp. 41–78 in *Ensayos etnográficos,* ed. Miguel Barnet and A. L. Fernandez. Havana: Editorial de Ciencias Sociales.

Ortiz, Fernando. 1986. *Los Negros Curros,* prologue and editorial notes by Diana Iznaga. Havana: Editorial de Ciencias Sociales.

Ortiz, Fernando. 1995. *Cuban Counterpoint: Sugar and Tobacco.* Durham, N.C.: Duke University Press.

Ortiz, Fernando. 1996 (1952). *Los Instrumentos de la Música Afrocubana.* Madrid: Música Mundana.

Ortiz, Fernando. 1998 (1950). *La Africanía de la Música Folklórica de Cuba.* Madrid: Música Mundana.

Ortiz, Fernando. 1998 (1973, 1906). *Los Negros Brujos.* Miami: Ediciones Universal.

Owen, Bruce McCoy. 2002. "Monumentality, Identity and the State: Local Practice, World Heritage, and Heterotopia at Swayambhu, Nepal." *Anthropological Quarterly* 75, no. 2: 269–316.

Palmié, Stefan. 2002. *Wizards and Scientists: Explorations in Afro-Cuban Modernity and Tradition.* Durham, N.C.: Duke University Press.

Perry, Marc D. 2004. "Los Raperos: Rap, Race, and Social Transformation in Contemporary Cuba." Unpublished Ph.D. diss., University of Texas, Austin.

Poyo, Gerald E., and Mariano Diaz-Miranda. 1994. "Cubans in the United States." In *Handbook of Hispanic Cultures in the U.S.: History,* ed. Alfredo Jimenez. Houston: Arte Publico Press.

Regis, Helen. 1999. "Second Lines, Minstrelsy, and the Contested Landscapes of New Orleans Afro-Creole Festivals." *Cultural Anthropology* 14, no. 4: 472–504.

Rosenzweig, Roy, and Elizabeth Blackmar. 1992. *The Park and the People: A History of Central Park.* Ithaca, N.Y.: Cornell University Press.

Routon, Kenneth. 2005. "Unimaginable Homelands? 'Africa' and the Abakuá Historical Imagination." *Journal of Latin American Anthropology* 10, no. 2 (November): 370–400.

Safa, Helen. 2008. "Afro-Cubans in the Special Period." *Transforming Anthropology,* 16, no. 1: 68–69.

Scott, Rebecca. 1995. "Race, Labor and Citizenship in Cuba: A View from the Sugar District of Cienfuegos, 1886–1909." *Hispanic American Historical Review* 78, no. 4: 687–729.

Siegal, Nina. 2000. "African 'Talking Drums' Silenced by Park Visitors Seeking Quiet." *New York Times,* May 28, sec. 14, 6.

Stewart, Barbara. 2000. "Central Park Keepers Struggling to Balance Masses with Grasses." *New York Times,* May 29, A1.

Trebay, Guy. 1998. "No Park-ing Today." *Village Voice,* June 16, 28.

Velez, Maria Theresa. 2000. *Drumming for the Gods: The Life and Times of Felipe Garcia Villamil, Santero, Palero and Abakuá.* Philadelphia: Temple University Press.

Warner, Michael. 2002. "Publics and Counterpublics." *Public Culture* 14, no. 1: 49–90.

Warner, R. Stephen, and Judith G. Wittner, eds. 1998. *Gatherings in Diaspora: Religious Communities and the New Immigration.* Philadelphia: Temple University Press.

Wilk, Richard. 1995. "Learning to Be Local in Belize: Global Systems of Common Difference." Pp. 110–133 in *Worlds Apart: Modernity through the Prism of the Local,* ed. Daniel Miller. London: Routledge.

Zdravomyslova, Elena, and Victor Voronkov. 2002. "The Informal Public in Soviet Society: Double Morality at Work." *Social Research* 69, no. 1: 49–69.

Zukin, Sharon. 1995. *The Cultures of Cities.* Cambridge, Mass.: Blackwell Publishers.

Interviews and Personal Communications

I have benefited from the intelligence, generosity, and critical insights of dozens of people in New York and Havana. Those whose input was especially relevant to the development of the ideas in this article are Paula Ballan (New York), Antonio (Ñico) Cadenón (New York), Carlos Casanova (Havana), Luis Chacon (Aspirina) (Havana), Ogduardo (Roman) Diaz Anaya (New York), Mario Dreke Alfonso (Chavalonga) (Havana), Gene Golden (New York), Ted Holliday (New York), Stanley Insua Hernández (Havana), Rogelio Martínez Furé (Havana), Ariana Orejuela (Havana), Armando Pinillos (Havana), Felix Sanabria (New York), and Leonardo Wignall (New York).

7

The Making of Suriland

The Binational Development of a Black Community
between the Tropics and the North Sea

LIVIO SANSONE

A msterdam is an important city of the region we now know, after Paul
Gilroy (1993), as the Black Atlantic. It has become so relatively recently:
since the mass-immigration of people of (mixed) African descent from
Suriname in the late 1960s and early '70s; the more recent pendulum migration
from the Dutch Antilles; and the even more recent immigration from a variety
of African countries, especially Ghana. These migrations have turned Amsterdam into the European capital with the largest percentage of "black" people—
approximately 7 percent of the 800,000 inhabitants in 2000.[1] In the Black Atlantic, Amsterdam has a special position on the fringe of the English-speaking
ecumenia, in many ways reflecting the position of the Netherlands in relation
to continental Europe and Britain. Most important, Amsterdam is a site of
a process of ethnogenesis that is leading to the transformation of a Creole
Caribbean culture into a new "black culture," whose main actors are the second-
generation sons and daughters of immigrants from Suriname. Over the past
thirty years in the Netherlands, a somewhat traditional, Caribbean-oriented
Creole culture has given way to a cosmopolitan, pan-black, and relatively "modern" black youth culture with a head in Amsterdam but a heart in Paramaribo.

Similar transformations have occurred in Britain and, to an extent, France
(Grosfoguel 1997), where the cultural life of Caribbean immigrants has partially given way to a pan-black culture and identity among the younger generation who have grown up in Europe. These groups have moved, as it were, from
an ethnic condition into a racial condition (even though, admittedly, in these

cases the analytical difference between ethnicity and "race" is even fuzzier than usual). However, the transformation has taken on specific contours in Amsterdam for two related reasons: the rise of multiculturalism, which gained the support of the Dutch state in the 1970s and '80s (it receded in the '90s) and Amsterdam's reputation as a capital of the so-called counterculture that favors so-called alternative lifestyles, such as those of the squatters movement, neo-hippies, new-age movements, Rastafarians, and so on.

Some dimensions of this making of a Dutch black culture have been already highlighted by research, in particular regarding the involvement of a growing section of Creole youth with black youth styles and streetwise lifestyles (Sansone 1990, 1992a, 1994; van Niekerk 2003; Wermuth 1999). This chapter deals with an aspect that has been little explored in social research. It emphasizes how in this process, the place and relevance of Suriname as a homeland, as well as the role and sorts of popular music associated with the making of a Dutch black culture, have changed over time. It describes the modernization of one of the main aspects of traditional Surinamese Creole community life in the Netherlands: the organization of and participation in parties and feasts. In the second section, the chapter expands on the process that is making it possible to envisage a peculiar, magical "bi-nation," Suriland—a country that overcomes the dilemmas of re-migration and homesickness by displacing the very notion of homeland. The transnational Surinamese population is developing new ways to cope with (cultural) colonialism and its aftermath.

I will first provide some basic socioeconomic context. Caribbean migration to the Netherlands can best be described as a movement of people from small countries into another small country. The number of Caribbean migrants to the Netherlands totaled over 360,000 in 1996 (2.4 percent of the total population), of whom approximately 90,000 were from the Dutch Antilles (Curaçao, Aruba, Bonaire, St. Eustatius, Saba, and St. Maarten). The rest were from Suriname.[2] Caribbean immigrants and their offspring also constitute a very large share of the total number of the *allochtonen* (the ethnic minorities who are the result of immigration). They are more urban than most other immigrants, both because they mostly were urban dwellers in the Caribbean (especially the Creoles) and because of where they have settled in the Netherlands. The Surinamese—and, in particular, the Surinamese Creoles—are more heavily concentrated in the main cities than other groups of *allochtonen*. For the Creoles, emigration has been from a city to a city—that is, from Paramaribo to one of the main Dutch cities (van Niekerk 1994: 47–49).

The Creoles are people of African–European and African–Asian descent. In this chapter, I focus on the Creoles, about whom I conducted longitudinal research from 1981 to 1992 (Sansone 1992, 1992b, 1994). The population of Caribbean descent in the Netherlands is heterogeneous in both ethnic and social terms, with relatively poor cohesion and little recognized leadership when compared with other ethnic minorities of immigrant origin, such as the Turks and the Moroccans. In terms of social position, over the past three decades large groups of Surinamese and Antilleans have been marginal to the Dutch labor market. Unemployment rates peaked at more than 50 percent in the late 1980s and have receded ever since. A relatively large minority of lower-class Creoles has never managed to tap into the labor market and lives off welfare checks. This is due to a combination of exclusion, untimely immigration, and the self-exclusion that results from attempts to anticipate racism and other obstacles. This process is imbued with colonial images, which affect both the Creoles' self-image and the image the white majority has of them (Sansone 1999).

However, the Creoles' relatively marginal position in the Dutch labor market—which is associated with a marginal position in Dutch political life—is not necessarily echoed in marginality in other aspects of public life, such as in the leisure arena and in rituals of conspicuous consumption. There, Surinamese and Antilleans are more prominent than most other ethnic minorities. These colonial immigrants and their offspring are a very conspicuous example of selective integration/assimilation; they show that speaking the language of the country of immigration fluently, having Dutch citizenship, and considering themselves better off than other immigrant groups—and being seen as such by outsiders—do not automatically result in better-than-average socioeconomic status. Apparently, the kind of social and cultural capital one needs to climb the ladder of Dutch society is not just the mastering of Dutch ways, as today's prophets of cultural integration at all costs seem to suggest.

All of this said, over the past few years the position of the Surinamese in Dutch society seems to have improved in a number of areas. Educational levels are higher, particularly among those who were born or entirely educated in the Netherlands. Even more pronounced is the social advancement of the majority of children of mixed Surinamese-and-white-Dutch marriages (van Heelsum 1997). Participation in the labor force has increased as part of a general trend toward reduction in unemployment and increase in the number of flexible jobs available for the poorly skilled, even though those jobs offer little chance for a career. In addition, black people in the Netherlands more generally have become more assertive and aware of their rights as *burger* (citizens) and consumers.

Whether because of their relative marginality to the labor market or because of their tropical traditions, a certain picture of young blacks has become hegemonic in the local leisure arena. In Amsterdam, Creole young people, it is commonly said, like to hang around in groups and are keen on youth culture, dancing, music, and fashion. They are also more active than their white contemporaries in creating youth styles of their own, such as the *wakaman* (the streetwise womanizer/hustler), as well as mixed black youth styles for which they use English names, such as disco freaks, Rastas, electric-boogie dancers, and, lately, hip-hoppers. Young Creoles have also developed their own version of street gangs with names inspired by U.S. movies, such as the Warriors, Cobras, Mafia West, and Black Brothers. A certain emphasis on the centrality of public leisure is very much a part of the self-image of these young black people. Indeed, since the mass-migration of Surinamese to the Netherlands began, young Creoles—especially young, lower-class males—have created a series of youth styles that have been conspicuous in the leisure arena. It is my impression that some of the most recent styles, such as hip-hop, affect more than 50 percent of Creole youth. A minority of these young people participate directly and intensely, while a larger group participates in a more detached fashion as fans, music and fashion consumers, and media audiences, often through small peer groups that might remind one of the bedroom subculture of working-class British girls in the 1970s (McRobbie and Garber 1976).

Predictably, these conspicuous youth styles have attracted the attention not only of Dutch popular mass media, but also of academic publications on race relations and black cultural creativity. When researching these areas, however, one must keep in mind a number of problems that relate to stereotyping as well as self-image. Because of the selective media coverage of cultural production among black youth, media portraits have been heavily based on this "spectacular" streetwise youth style, which has had an influence on racial stereotyping of young black people. The selective media coverage and racial stereotyping in turn has deeply influenced the self-image of the silent majority of Creole youth.

The centrality of conspicuous youth style and the public dimension of leisure in the life of Creole youth raises two further questions. First, is the investment in public leisure an effort to relax and reduce strain, a protest, or even a means to gain greater acceptance in mainstream Dutch society? And second, to what extent does such investment result from what can be seen as an obsession with spectacular and aestheticized forms of black cultural creativity on the part of social research—a bias that has been associated with a relative lack of concern for other, subtler and less straightforward combinations of blackness with tradition and modernity?

Surinamese Partying and the Creole Pleasure Circuit

Black clubs and venues such as *negercafes* (black men's bars) already existed in Amsterdam before World War II (Kagie 1989). They grew in importance and popularity in the 1950s and became a real circuit soon after the mass-immigration from Suriname began in the early 1970s, when the Creole inhabitants of Amsterdam started to see themselves as representing a sizable ethnic community. The 1970s and '80s saw the growth of Surinamese welfare organizations, which in their heyday, when the Dutch state was still in a state of shock over the decolonization of Suriname, were generously funded. Those decades also saw the rise of a plethora of Surinamese leisure impresarios such as record producers, music agents, choreographers, rally organizers, and, to a certain extent, religious leaders. In Amsterdam, these frantic and often competing activities produced an atmosphere (*surinnaamse sfeer*) in which the large Surinamese population could revive memories of their tropical homeland—that is, relax, feel at ease, and forget that they were in fact in a foreign country, even though the overwhelming majority of Surinamese had always had Dutch citizenship. The leisure facilities that grew up around these developments came to known as *zwarte uitgangsgelegenheden* (black leisure facilities) among native white Dutch social workers and youth workers.

Today, the vast majority of young Creoles in the Netherlands spend at least part of their leisure time on this pleasure circuit. In particular, those who grew up in Suriname and migrated to the Netherlands in their teens, especially those of lower-class and lower-middle-class status,[3] often prefer Creole parties and black facilities to mixed leisure facilities. It goes without saying that their degree of involvement has varied to a great extent. When their goal is to get to know their own ethnic community, these youths' involvement has been more intense; when the priority is exploring the metropolis, they have drawn on the Surinamese pleasure circuit more episodically.

The Surinamese pleasure circuit consists of large dance parties where Creole pop dance music (better known as *kaseko* or *bigi poku*[4]) is played; contribution parties (*bijlegfeesten*); Surinamese "happenings" such as bus and boat excursions (which are often floating parties); family parties, often held because of a *winti* religious ritual or on a birthday; and *pese-pese* parties (home bingo). One can also add to that circuit what insiders and outsiders see as a re-creation of Paramaribo lower-class street life in the Netherlands: a couple of street markets; some patches of the Chinese quarter; the public squares of the high-rise neighborhood of Zuidoost;[5] and even a few McDonald's restaurants near the street markets. Most Surinamese I interviewed agreed that this was the closest one could get to a tropical atmosphere in the Netherlands. They also added that it was particularly Creole and, even more so, *volkscreool* (lower-class Creole). An informant, in fact, once told me that he preferred Amsterdam to other Dutch cities because it was "the most American city in the Netherlands." By "American," he meant open-minded and easygoing.[6]

For most members of the first generation of young Creoles who arrived in the Netherlands, this "Creole atmosphere" was the only place they felt at home. Going out basically meant visiting places where *bigi poku* was played; those who considered themselves more enlightened combined *bigi poku* with visits to salsa and soul clubs—places where black people, and mostly black men, controlled the dance floor. "That's real having fun Surinamese style, because at Dutch parties people sit down all the time," I was told. In 1982, a young adult man described a "typically Creole" weekend to me this way: "dancing, a quick stop at home for freshening up, new clothes on, going somewhere dancing, back home again, and the whole thing all over again." Older young men visited discos where a lot of Surinamese went with (mostly English) names such as Ebony and Caribbean. Some of them simply did not feel comfortable in places where only white people could be seen: "among black people I feel I am somebody (*een mens*)."

Family parties may be the most important meeting places for the Surinamese; they are the backbone of the ethnic community. They offer people with little disposable income the opportunity to go out. Single mothers and young couple can bring children to these parties: kids are welcome even at dance parties, whereas, the Surinamese complain, native Dutch people are friendlier to dogs than they are to young kids at parties. Especially for young single mothers, children's birthday parties represent a proper network where tips on possible odd jobs, informal economic activities, and baby products are exchanged. Baby products and women's fashion are often also for sale, usually for a low price or on installment plans. Young mothers can chat while kids play with one another. Moreover, men sometimes attend these children's parties. They tend to stay by the kitchen entrance, where booze is served or sold. At some point during most of these parties, the music changes from children's songs to dance music. Women start dancing, first with one another, then with the men (when they are available). Organizers sometimes invite bands to play at children's parties, but according to most of my informants, that practice was becoming less common because of the rising costs of hiring musicians.

Throwing a party can be expensive. In 1988, a children's party cost 250–500 guilders (for comparison, the supplementary benefit for a single mother with one child was about 1,450 guilders, or about 1,000 U.S. dollars). A party for a teenager could easily cost 1,000 guilders. That is a lot of money for someone on the dole, as the majority of lower-class Creoles were in the 1980s and early '90s. Sometimes people borrow money from friends and relatives, or they draw on the rotating credit system called *kasmoni*. One has to pay for food (usually a member of the family cooks, but sometimes a professional cook is hired), liquor, and music. When records are played, the disc jockey is usually a family member. At larger parties, the music is mostly live, especially in Zuidoost, where the flats are larger and neighbors do not tend to complain about loud music. A band costs 200–250 guilders and plays for one hour at the end of the party. In most cases, such bands consist of reduced formation of three to six musicians, who often also play in larger bands.

At certain parties—particularly birthday parties for senior citizens—a choir is hired to sing church songs, which are popular especially among the members of the traditional Moravian church, but also among people of other Christian faiths. At other birthday parties, certain *winti* rituals are carried out. In fact, throwing a (large and loud) party can be one of the obligations of your *winti*, or soul, often suggested in a session with a *bonoeman*, or healer (Venema 1992). The borderline between a party and a *wintipré* (*winti* ceremony) can be rather thin. The religious ritual flows into a party, or the party is interrupted to practice a *winti* ritual, after which the party continues. Apparently, this borderline has become even thinner in the Netherlands, where the practice of *winti* has become more open and accepted than it was in Suriname, largely thanks to the incorporation of *winti* into the universe of "other religious practices" that form the mosaic of ethnic-minority culture through multiculturalism and its institutions, including schools, nongovernmental organizations, and television programs. Meanwhile, Creoles in the Netherlands and, albeit to a lesser extent, in Suriname have been experiencing a degree of secularization. Religion is less a structuring factor of their social life. In 1990, a *bigi poku* musician described the change this way:

Fifteen years a ago you had people who asked you to play a whole string of churchly songs. Nowadays they expect you to play just about two choral tunes right in the beginning, to make grandma happy. Then they want you to play *kaseko,* for dancing and the rest. Toward the end, they expect a cultural number [a piece of *kawina* music] so that they feel they are concluding the party in peace with their culture [*winti*].

The opinion that these family parties represent a sort of a liminal space contributes to their popularity. People from different social backgrounds can attend the parties. Even white people like to come and enjoy the frolicking Creole atmosphere. Often the person who is throwing the party makes a special effort to invite better-off Creoles or even white people, such as relatives with good jobs or managers of Surinamese welfare organizations. The presence of these "better" people gives the party status: it can provide opportunities to make interesting contacts, and it is said to be a good antidote against violent brawls, because even the toughest *wakaman* (street hustler) would not show much aggression in the presence of these higher-status people. For their part, the higher-status people also like to attend parties with different groups of Surinamese, either because they feel emotionally involved with the Creole culture and traditions or because they believe that *winti* practices are more effective when exercised in a lower-class milieu. (Traditions and magic powers are said to be stronger among the poor.) When it comes to a *winti* ritual or to a night of *bigi poku* dancing, middle-class Creoles admit, they prefer to move socially "downward." At those times, lower-class Surinamese are said to be the real "pleasure people (*pleziersvolk*)."[7]

In fact, better-off Creoles maintain a kind of borrowing relationship with the lower-class Creoles. The *volkscreolen* and *bosnegers* are regarded as the conservators of the Creoles' roots.[8] They are visited and consulted on certain occasions, but participation in their social network is kept to a minimum, because intensive involvement with the network and the close system of reciprocity of the *volkscreolen* would not fit easily with the demands of Dutch modernity and social mobility in daily life. Better-off Creoles (their number is usually estimated as approximately a third of the Creole population in the Netherlands) have created their own, more discreet network that is less exposed to the stereotyping gaze of Dutch popular culture and media. They tend to hold "cooler" parties, with less *ondroberedansi* and no drumming music (*kawina*).[9] Light, older *kaseko* and, especially, soka, merengue, and salsa are preferred.

Nonetheless, the relatively high degree of social mixture at parties held by lower-class Creoles shows the important function of such parties and the strength of the flexible family networks that are important in assisting new immigrants. This commitment in moments of relative social mixture among individuals from both the middle class and the lower class explains the absence of class discourses among the Creole in the Netherlands, as opposed to in Suriname, as well as the fragility and uncertainty of the middle-class status of the better-off third of the Creole population in the Netherlands.[10]

During the period of my research, from 1981 to 1991, the party circuit experienced dramatic changes. In the last years, the popularity of Creole parties, especially the commercial ones, had decreased, despite the constant in-flow of newcomers from Suriname, who in most cases entered the Netherlands on tourist visas and then, with their families' help, tried to obtain residence permits. Newcomers, of course—especially those of the lower classes—tend to be consumers of the Creole leisure circuit, but they are also willing to explore "new things." In many ways, they come precisely to experience the modernity they associate with life in the Netherlands. Many of them associate the image of wealth and modernity with just two countries: the Netherlands, to which they have relatively easy access, and the United States, which they know mostly from a distance.

Further, most of the first-generation Surinamese immigrants in the Netherlands are no longer young and go out less often. Other factors are at play. The generation that has grown up in the Netherlands has more options. According to most of my informants in that group, especially those considered "Dutchified" by the older generation, giving a feast "for yourself" (that is, to oblige your *winti*) has become too dear. In the last years of my research, only a couple of informants had given such a party. Most said they had no money for such things or that they had other priorities. A great threat to the Creole pleasure circuit also comes from the white leisure industry, which offers better attractions, frequently for lower prices and in more central locations. Such opinions go hand in glove with a general idea among young Creoles that the Creole pleasure circuit is mostly old-fashioned and provincial. "You bump into the same people all the time," one informant told me. "It's a matter of staring at each other in the doorway because in those *shebeens* there is no real room for dancing." (A *shebeen* in this context is a venue for non-legal parties in the Caribbean or South Africa.) Moreover, they find the social control too strict: the traditional parties are not a good place for flirting. In fact, it has become increasingly important among young Creoles to gain access to the so-called white leisure facilities, where they are convinced they can make better use of their blackness and tropical background (which, they believe, can make them more appealing to certain sections of the white youth, especially those of the opposite sex) than they can while negotiating space in the fairly small and saturated Creole leisure industry. They like the more professional attitude of Dutch musical venues, where shows start on time, there are no fights, and the facilities are generally newer and cleaner. On top of that, white facilities, against the odds, have managed to keep up much better with developments in the musical taste of young Creoles. The best-known hip-hop groups and soul bands, as well as the most popular *bigi poku* bands, tend to play at these white venues, which on these occasions draw overwhelmingly black audiences.[11]

Commercial parties still have an important social function in the Creole community, especially in Zuidoost, for a smaller and older public. For a group of lower-class young adults, they represent a pivotal opportunity for courting. For another group, organizing parties has become an source of extra income. Most young Creoles, however, believe that it is OK to visit these parties from time to time to eat traditional food and get news from Suriname. But if one is interested in contemporary trends and fashion, then one is much better off in the larger, more anonymous, and less ethnically tinged leisure facilities downtown.

Also, the musical taste of young Creoles has changed. In the years of my research, *bigi poku* lost some of its popularity among young Creoles in favor of other sorts of black music that, unlike *bigi poku*, attract and are consumed by a large section of the urban white youth. The young men who had grown up in Suriname and migrated to the Netherlands in their early twenties saw this as a sell-out to the Dutch. Indeed, a survey I took in 1982 on musical taste among one hundred young Creole visitors to the youth club United World, where I did volunteer youth and social work, showed that they preferred to buy disco and reggae records rather than *bigi poku* records. Most of them argued that *bigi poku* was for family or community parties and that somebody in their family already had those records. Disco and reggae music, they added, was more modern and trendy. The decrease in interest in traditional Creole pop music and the pleasure circuit did not mean, however, that they opposed Creole parties and *bigi poku*. Neither did it mean that these traditional forms of lower-class Creole cultural production were static. In fact, the last round of interviews, held in 1991–1992, demonstrated that even those young Creoles whom the older generation considered more Dutchified, attended Creole parties, especially those held within the family, and that "in due time" they would also properly dance to *bigi poku*.

The orientation of young Creoles toward musical styles other than *bigi poku* can be seen as an attempt to differentiate themselves from the older young men who are more oriented toward Suriname—who, in fact, said that they worked hard to have fun, "just as it was back in Paramaribo." Members of the younger generation show a more varied pattern of consumption in the leisure arena. They insist on having individual(ized) opinions on musical styles and consumption, often resisting attempts by outsiders (media, teachers, youth workers) and by older member of the Creole community to influence their tastes and fashions. Young Creoles tend to be well informed about white and black musicians, bands, live shows, and venues in Amsterdam and other large Dutch cities. Music magazines are well read, and musical programs on radio and television are well followed.

Music also plays an important role as an ethnic marker, whatever the borders of one's own ethnic group might be. In certain situation, blackness can even include a couple of non-black peers with whom one shares neighborhood life. In Oud West, the other region of Amsterdam in which I lived and conducted fieldwork, youth and community centers experienced a true "music war" in the early 1980s:

> We were [white and black] skas and DJed in the Witte Brug [a youth club within a community center]. Everything was going fine until those heavy young [white] men from the Wachttoren [a nearby youth center catering to young men with drinking or hard-drug problems] came along. They could not stand any black music. One of them put his revolver on the forehead of Freddy, the DJ, and ordered him to play André Hazes [a folksy pop singer]. When he refused, they smashed the head in of one of us.

Even though young Creoles want to be and feel musically modern, they also have been engaging in a process of rediscovering certain musical traditions associated with their roots—identified as a combination of authenticity with down-to-earth, vibrant percussion. Accounting for this phenomenon requires providing some details on the dynamics within Creole pop music. As is the case with music in general, and with Caribbean music in particular (Bilby 1985), Creole pop music is constantly experiencing change in the Netherlands, as well as in Suriname (Weltak 1990: 67–84). On the one hand, developments in the Netherlands reverberate in Suriname, where *bigi poku* and *kawina* groups pay increasingly attention to Western pop music and modern music technology. Musical traditions and modern technology are mixed wittily to create new tonalities, whose aim is to get the performers invitations to tour the Netherlands. On the other hand, the Surinamese community in the Netherlands looks up to music groups based in Suriname. The most exclusive and expensive musical shows revolve around a Suriname-based band as the main act. There is, therefore, reciprocal influence. Surinamese bands are inspired by the "modern things" they can capture from the way Netherlands-based bands play; Dutch Surinamese musicians are inspired by the "original and deep" forms of playing music and singing back in Suriname. There is a also a division of roles. New arrangements and instruments are developed mostly in the Netherlands, where musicians supposedly have access to better and more advanced technological equipment. Developments and new trends in lyrics and singing techniques come mostly from Suriname, where musicians supposedly are endowed with more creativity and can draw on "purer" voices, especially *bosneger* voices.

This representation, of course, reveals a polarity in which Suriname is perceived as closer to nature, purer, and more creative, and the Netherlands is perceived as closer to technology, a place where things can be mixed and where technological skills are available. In fact, this reciprocal transatlantic influence has been going on for more than two decades and in many ways is constitutive of the cultural creativity and sociology of Surinamese pop music. *Bigi poku* groups from Suriname visit the Netherlands often—touring there makes them more important, and thus more expensive to hire, in Suriname. To a lesser extent, mostly because there is less money to pay bands from abroad, Dutch Surinamese bands also tour Suriname. Playing in Suriname also confers credit with the band's "home" audience in the Netherlands. In the period from 1986 to 1992, travel to and from Suriname increased a lot, largely due to a very favorable exchange rate that enabled even poor Surinamese who depended on Dutch welfare checks to travel. During this period, Suriname came to be seen not as a poor homeland to which emigrants had an obligation to return but, instead, as a second, tropical-holiday homeland in which one could spend time and invest. As in the case of music, it became increasingly difficult to detect which of the two countries was influencing what.

Over the years of my research, developments in *bigi poku* in the Netherlands were going in two directions. A number of groups, such as the renowned Trafassi, were playing increasingly "classical" *bigi poku* aimed at an older, nostalgic audience. They purged their lyrics of "raw" words, played less syncopation, and brought percussion down to a minimum—percussion being associated with mostly disreputable, lower-class *volkscreolen* and sometimes with *winti*. Other groups, by contrast, played *plat,* or raw, music. Ganzensound and Jongoe Bala, for example, followed a development that had been under way for years in Suriname. There, a number of bands under the leadership of the famous band Soekroe Sani (Sweet Thing) were rediscovering "deep" forms of *kawina* music, especially those played by the *bosnegers,* which featured uncensored lyrics, so-called *bosneger* vocals, and the percussion beat of *kawina* music.

At the same time, these groups introduced new instruments, especially of the electronic sort, in *kawina* music. In the early 1990s, a specific sort of music from Suriname that one could call "electro-*kawina*," began to acquire great popularity, which it has maintained ever since, especially among the second generation in the Netherlands and among young people in Paramaribo. Electro-*kawina* is a very danceable and mostly sung in Saramakaan rather than in Sranan Tongo.[12]

In the Netherlands, the groups that play raw music aim at a younger and more Western-oriented audience that is also keen on hip-hop. Indeed, they are the same young people who considered traditional *kawina* old-fashioned and slow just a few years ago. I heard some of them call the music of Jongoe Bala "punk *bigi poku*." This rediscovery of *bosneger* roots and *kawina* has been spreading. In 1990, Ganzensound, which was probably the best-known *bigi poku* band in Amsterdam in the 1980s, sensed the change. It sought to attract the young generation by moving in two directions: first, by making its lyrics and music increasing raw, and second, by turning the act into a complete show. At large parties, for example, Ganzensound started with a "playback" show (playback singing, or singing to a tune that is being played) is a popular activity among Surinamese children and adolescents); then came a hip-hop group, followed by the first *bigi poku* tunes. During the break, a dance group demonstrated a combination of jazz ballet and Latin American and African dances. The hip-hop got all of the children and teenagers dancing; the *bigi poku* and electro-*kawina* got everyone in the hall off their seats.

One Homeland?

Attitudes toward Suriname and toward cultural production originating in Suriname have varied largely based on the number of years of residence and the part of one's life spent in the Netherlands. Thus, one can say that attitudes have varied according to generation. Generally, one can say that the experience of Surinamese—and Antilleans—and their offspring in the Netherlands can be seen as part of different processes: transnationalism, diasporization, and the formation of an ethnic minority (the Surinamese/Antilleans) and of a racialized group (the blacks). All three of these processes are present, depending on the one's point of view and on the degree of generalization.

The position of Surinamese and Antilleans in the Netherlands cannot be understood outside their status as special colonial migrants. The political status of these immigrants and their offspring is essential to the understanding of their situation, and sets them apart from other immigrant groups. Suriname and the Dutch Antilles were Dutch colonies. In 1954, they were given a came under a special statute known as "Autonomy within your own country (Autonomie in eigen land)." Today, the Dutch Antilles is part of the Netherlands as a Rijksdeel, but it is not a province. The Dutch Antilleans have a parliament of their own and can vote for the Dutch parliament only when they are residing in the Netherlands. They are Dutch citizens, with Dutch passports (Schuster 1999). The situation of the Surinamese is different. Surinam obtained independence in 1975, and on the eve of independence, the Surinamese were allowed choose their nationality. Approximately 40 percent chose Dutch nationality either because they had already migrated to the Netherlands or because they had planned to do so. At present, 90–95 percent of the people of Surinamese origin in the Netherlands are Dutch citizens.

For colonial migrants, push and pull factors are related to a high degree of political, economic, and cultural interaction between the metropole and the (neo)colony. Hence, these push and pull factors are more culturally laden than for other groups of migrants. Cultural motives such as fear of social and racial unrest, as well as the attractiveness of the "bright lights of the city" (which has a high-brow as well as a low-brow version), have always been present, as both push and pull factors in emigration from Suriname and the Dutch Antilles. The special relationship between these countries and the (former) metropole since the early 1990s has resulted in a sort of collective international adoption by Dutch society of certain social groups that experience hardship in the homeland (mostly because of lack of public-health provisions, psychological stress, educational problems, trouble with the police or criminals, and harassment on ethnic grounds).

Re-migration, or what I call "commuting," has always been strong among the Dutch Antilleans, probably stimulated by the absence of restrictions on travel to Europe and by better unemployment benefits and medical care in the Netherlands. In 1993, departures were more numerous than arrivals in the Netherlands. In 1996, arrivals were slightly higher.

A circular movement of some sort linking the Netherlands with the homeland through flows of people, goods, opinions, sounds, and tastes also exists for the Surinamese. Cash flows seem to be more intense than for the Antilleans, possibly because of the much greater disparity in living standards between the Netherlands and Suriname than between the Netherlands and the Dutch Antilles. Surinamese support relatives in Suriname almost as often as do the other main immigrant groups.[13] Surinamese also buy land and property in Surinam, which is made easier by the favorable exchange rate.

Re-migration, except among the older generation, is largely a dream; part and parcel of the ethnic ideology of the Surinamese and Dutch Antilleans. Nevertheless, in opinion polls Surinamese and, even more so, Dutch Antilleans state more often than Moroccans, Turks, and southern Europeans that they want to go back to the homeland (Martens and Verweij 1997: 102).

In fact, the whole notion of homeland has become rather relative for a large number of these Caribbean emigrants, mostly for the Antilleans, who have developed a transnational lifestyle, which exists in both a lower-class and a middle-class version. The Netherlands and the homeland have become two extremes of a continuum.

In terms of belonging to a country or a particular place, we can speak of multiple allegiances. The ingredients of this complex system of allegiances can be Suriname, the Antilles, the Netherlands, the urban Western world, the Black Atlantic, and, for the Hindustani, the Indian diaspora. The Surinamese and Dutch Antillean communities are strongly bi-national: the Surinamese community spans two nation-states, and the Antillean community spans two parts of the same nation-state. However, in both cases the two ends of the bi-national whole have different power, status, cultural, and emotional importance for the people involved, depending on the duration of their stay in the Netherlands and on the time of life when they migrated.

Among the Surinamese there are a variety of subgroups with different geographic horizons, from the small-scale "own place" back in the Caribbean to the Black Atlantic or simply the "dead ordinary" Western world as it is perceived through life in a Dutch city. For sure, explicit diaspora ideas and practices concern a minority. Yet for everybody, settling in the Netherlands has offered more scope for the cultivation of diaspora ideals and for the maintenance of international links with the Black Atlantic (the United States, the United Kingdom, the Caribbean writ large, and, to a lesser extent, Africa), India, or China. The perception of this process, and of the modern "transnation" and its benefits for life in the Netherlands, depends largely on gender, age, ethnic origin (Hindustani, Creoles, or Chinese), and life orientation.

Some Surinamese Creoles started relating to English-speaking black culture—for example, in terms of musical taste—soon after World War II while U.S. troops were stationed in Suriname. The influence of English-speaking black culture has increased ever since. Emigration to the Netherlands has multiplied the opportunities for direct contact with different black subcultures from all over the world, and from the United States in particular. The Netherlands is better connected than Suriname with the international media and the leisure and music industry. In the Netherlands, orientation toward the mythical "super blacks," or blacks with high spending patterns as they are perceived from movies and video clips, particularly in the United States, is a way to become modern and to differentiate oneself from white Dutch people. One of the results of this is that, particularly for the Creoles who have grown up in the Netherlands, English-speaking African America is becoming a cultural point of reference. Besides these cultural contacts with English-speaking African America, a large group of first-generation Creoles have maintained close social and cultural ties with Suriname. A part of this group has actually developed a transnational lifestyle by commuting between Suriname and the Netherlands (Sansone 1992b). In effect, the international orientations toward African America and Suriname tend to complement rather than combat each other. This adds to the complexity of Creole-black culture in the Netherlands, where locals and cosmopolitans coexist along with different degrees of Suriname-ness, ethnic allegiances, and cultural influences.

In fact, for an increasing section of the population of Caribbean origin, the Netherlands is, if not a new fatherland, at least home. For this group, silent or visible displays of affection for the place of origin, the symbols of the diaspora, and ethnic identity are ways to cope with life in the Netherlands and even to liven up certain aspects of this European experience.

Life in the Netherlands is leading to a transformation of ethnic identity, to a process of de-provincialization and de-territorialization of both social networks and symbolic horizons. Among the Creoles, a new black identity is in the making. At he same time, a section of the Hindustani population is starting to identify strongly with India, without necessarily scorning its Surinamese origins. These are largely generational trends, and they are more pronounced among those who have grown up in the Netherlands.

All of this fluidity notwithstanding, however, the Dutch system of race relations and the state's attitude toward Surinamese and Antilleans foster the continuation of ethnic difference and of its spectacular performance. The system of pillarization (verzuiling), through which the Dutch establishment has managed national social and confessional tensions, has had a profound influence on the creation of a system of ethnic and race relations that is specifically Dutch. The attitude of the Dutch state toward ethnic difference and the politics of ethnic identity among ethnic minorities has changed over time, from antagonistic toward minorities' ethnicity; to stating that ethnic identity is the precondition for participation on an equal basis in the majority society; to the more relativist position that minority ethnicity is fine but ought not affect the duties all citizens have toward society; all the way to strongly emphasizing assimilation to the social mores of mainstream Dutch society (whatever they might be).[14] Special social services for Caribbean migrants were created at first, mostly on the eve of mass-immigration, but have been dismantled in recent years. Also, although the official terminology for defining different categories of (black) foreigners have changed over time, categories remain, underlining the continuous existence of ethnic difference. Currently, the most used term is *allochtoon* (something like "of foreign origin"), which applies to people who are born abroad and in the Netherlands, to first- and the second-generation immigrants,[15] to "full-blooded" as well as "half-blooded" citizens, and to people with Dutch citizenship as well as foreigners. To be an *allochtoon*, one needs to look different or practice a culture that supposedly originated abroad. It goes without saying that this term—which is often used from a relativist perspective to express respect for "different" or "minority" cultures—draws somewhat on the one-drop-of-blood rule, because symbolically it denies biological and cultural mixing. One can be an *allochtoon* even if only some of one's ancestors were of foreign origin and even if one's family has lived in the Netherlands for three or more generations. In addition to the official terminology and classifications, of course, there is popular use of racial or ethnic terms, which depend not on descent but on perceived differences in culture or phenotype along the gradient from *donker* (dark-skinned) to *blank* (white).

Interestingly, in times of collective and individual conflict, Creoles claim civil rights as *autochtonen* or as *allochtonen*, depending on the group they are competing with and other circumstances. Their political status as Creoles offers more options to manipulate ethnicity than the more univocal status that the other main immigrant groups in the Netherlands have at their disposal.

Conclusions

The cultural production involved in the making of a new black culture in the Netherlands relates to a set of multiple ethnocultural allegiances—to Suriname (Paramaribo and the "bush"), to African America, to lower-class urban Dutch white urban culture, and to youth culture. In many ways, such multiplicity explains both the attractiveness of so-called black culture for certain groups of non-blacks, who view that culture as having managed to combine modernity with being "natural" and in opposition to humdrum Western culture.

Most of the cultural interaction and production described in this chapter does not occur in the shadow of the state or of official, and pretty stiff, multiculturalism. The combination of new technology, media, and leisure activities more than formal education and state-sponsored activities—the privileged site for official multiculturalism—have been playing a pivotal role in this process. This combination of factors has had a double function. On the one hand, it has forced dramatic changes even on traditional forms of Surinamese music and dance. On the other hand, together with the new channels offered by the trans-nationalization (a de facto bi-nationalization), it has created new opportunities for the rediscovery of the "authentic," "deep," and "ancient" Surinamese cultural production. It has also helped to change the general impression in Dutch public opinion that Surinamese Creole culture, and black cultural forms more gener-ally, lacks authenticity.

The attractiveness and "coolness" of black cultural forms to non-black youth, often of immigrant origin, however, does seem to weaken the claim of many black spokespeople that their culture is an "authentic ethnic culture" within Dutch society. Apparently, the condition sine qua non for official recog-nition by the Dutch state and in multicultural education is the intrinsic degree of originality, distinct visible traits, and authenticity of the cultural expression of a recognized ethnic minority. In the opinion of Dutch policy, claims that the Surinamese Creole (who are sometimes described as *onze negers,* or our own black people) make in this respect score low.

Most likely, it is this feeling of estrangement from official multicultural-ism, a set of practices and narratives that offer little scope for black cultural production—that is, for the making of a Dutch black culture that can largely be understood as a metropolitan reinterpretation of a lower-class Surinamese Creole subculture—that spurs the pursuit of different transatlantic avenues for black cultural creation. It is a spurious universe that, thronged with com-modification and commerce, seems to bestow a certain status on exactly those traits—that is, those that combine blackness with modernity—that otherwise are seen as hybrid and mixed.

The bi-nationalization of the Surinamese community and the globalization of black culture have had great influence on both black cultural production and black leisure in Amsterdam. In turn, such developments have been influencing public leisure and youth culture in Paramaribo. The significance of the catego-ries "youth" and "black" are being redefined in this transnational context and process.

One can certainly read the experience of lower-class Surinamese Creoles in the Netherlands as an example of segmented assimilation (Zhou 1997). In Dutch society, Surinamese Creoles are much more central in the arena of leisure than in that of work. I would suggest we apply this reading to the bi-national context in which a large number of Dutch citizens of Surinamese origin live. Their relative economic marginality in Dutch society is largely counterbalanced by the relatively high status of the Dutch-passport holder in Suriname.

The relationship between Suriname and the large Surinamese community in the Netherlands today cannot be understood outside the context of the colo-nial past. The Surinamese are colonial migrants, and one of Suriname's raisons d'être is its polemical and yet hyper-dependent position in regard to the former "mother country," the Netherlands.[16] However, this neocolonial relationship has offered scope for important transatlantic flows of commodities and cultural artifacts that by now have become part and parcel of certain aspects of urban life in both Suriname and the Netherlands. From Suriname comes the exotic, while from the Netherlands come technology and modernity. This is obvious in the process that has led to the creation of a black youth culture in Dutch cities—largely developing from within the arena of Surinamese Creole cultural creativity—as well as in the dynamics of production and public consumption of different varieties of popular Surinamese music.

Notes

1. By "black" I understand people who consider themselves, and who are seen by others as being, of African or partly of African descent. Negroid phenotype is essential to the definition of both insiders and outsiders. The Dutch equivalent of black, *zwart*, has recently also been used in a series of circles in a different way—to define those who look different from mainstream, native, white Dutch people.

2. The multiethnic origin of the Surinamese population is reflected in the migration. According to my estimates, one-third of the population registered as of Surinamese origin in the Netherlands (that is, those who have at least one parent who was born in Suriname) is Hindustani; one half is Creole; 10–15 percent are of Javanese origin; and the rest are either of mixed origin or of Chinese, Portuguese, or Lebanese descent.

3. Roughly, one can say that, in recent years, one-fifth to one-third of the Surinamese are middle class.

4. In this essay, I use these two terms as equivalent, as my informants did. For a very good account of music in Suriname and its dance version, see Weltak 1990, 1999.

5. This large high-rise neighborhood, which is well served by the subway and has a lot of green areas and parks, was built for the upper middle class, but since the early 1980s it has become home to the largest and most "problematic" concentration of lower-class Creole immigrants and their offspring in the country.

6. It is commonly understood that Amsterdam is a "*Creool*" city, whereas The Hague is a "Hindustani" city. Politically, Amsterdam is progressive; The Hague, the former imperial capital, is more conservative. A large number of Eurasian immigrants from Indonesia arrived in The Hague in the 1940s and '50s.

7. This attitude is much more explicit in the Surinamese community in the Netherlands than in Suriname itself, which tends to be much more conscious of social hierarchy and ethnic differences. In fact, the relative lack of hierarchy among the Surinamese in the Netherlands is said to be one important push factor in the continuing popularity of emigrating to that country.

8. This is the native, emic term for the Bush Negroes, or Maroons. In Suriname, Creoles from the coast and the city, Paramaribo have been insisting that the term "*boslandcreolen*" (Creoles from the forest region) be used instead. I argue that this is an attempt to get Bush Negroes counted as Creoles, because Suriname's Creoles feel outnumbered by the Hindustanis, who have higher fertility rates and are said to be (and who represent themselves as)

more successful as entrepreneurs, whereas Creoles have made public-service jobs and the army their main labor niches.

9. In colloquial Sranan Tongo, *ondrobere* (lit., that which is below the navel) means something like intense, gutsy, deep, and typical Creole. It is what you feel when you are excited and while participating in your culture.

10. Because of the mass character of migration from Suriname and the Dutch Antilles, in which all levels of society participated enthusiastically (with an over-representation of the better-educated strata in the first waves and of the poorer strata in the more recent waves), people of Caribbean origin have much more representation in the middle class than do other immigrant groups. In fact, there is a stronger class divide among the people of Caribbean origin (and even more so among the Antilleans) than for the other main immigrant groups in the Netherlands.

11. Musical venues and other leisure facilities are defined as white (*blank*) when they are owned and managed by white people. Over the past few years, however, these white managers have begun to hire large numbers of young Creole and Moroccan young men and attractive Creole girls, possibly to add a certain ethnic flavor to the facilities.

12. Saramakaan is a Creole language that has incorporated a sizeable Portuguese lexicon. It is spoken by a large section of the *bosnegers*. It is very different from the Creole language of Suriname, Sranan Tongo, which, though often associated with lower-class urban *volkscreolen,* is the language of markets, neighborhoods, and street life. Urban Creoles have ambivalent attitudes towards the *bosnegers*: they respect then for their bellicose and brave past of resistance to slavery but scorn on them for their present condition, which is deemed backward and inherently un-modern. As part of this ambivalence, Saramakaan-speaking singers and religious healers are deemed more powerful because they live closer to nature, one of the roots of Surinamese Creole culture (Bilby 1999; Reijerman 1999).

13. Among the Surinamese, Hindustanis are more likely than Creoles to support parents who are still living in Suriname (Martens and Verweij 1997). This has to do with the more close-knit Hindustani families and with their shorter average stays in the Netherlands.

14. This new assimilationist policy, called *inburgering* (lit., becoming a citizen), has been gaining political and popular support especially since the assassination of the populist and racist politician Pim Fortuin and of the filmmaker Theo van Gogh.

15. It is a matter of speculation how the third generation and successive generations will choose to identify themselves and will be seen by others. As black Dutch, perhaps?

16. After all, as often noted, Dutch newspapers traditionally place news about Suriname on the home-news page (*binnenland*) rather than on the page dealing with international news.

References

Bilby, Kenneth. 1985. "The Caribbean as a Musical Region." In *Caribbean Contours,* ed. Sidney Mintz and Sally Price. Baltimore: John Hopkins University Press.

Bilby, Kenneth. 1999. "Aleke: Nieuwe muziek en nieuwe identiteiten." *Oso* 10, no. 1: 49–60.

Gilroy, Paul. 1993. *The Black Atlantic.* London: Verso.

Grosfoguel, Ramón. 1997. "Colonial Caribbean Migrations to France, the Netherlands, Great Britain and the United States." *Ethnic and Racial Studies* 20, no. 3: 594–612.

Kagie, Rudi. 1989. *De eerste neger.* Amsterdam: Het Wereldvenster.

McRobbie, Angela, and Jane Garber. 1976. "Girls and Subcultures: An Exploration." Pp. 209–222 in *Resistance through Rituals: Youth Subcultures in Postwar Britain,* ed. Stuart Hall et al. London: Hutchinson.

Martens, E. P., and A. O. Verweij. 1997. *Surinamers in Nederland. Kerncijfers 1996.* Rotterdam: Institute for Socio-Economic Research.

Reijerman, Mieke. 1999. "'Sranakondre a no paradijs'. De constructie van localiteit in de populaire muziek van de Saramaka." *Oso* 10, no. 1: 50–82.

Sansone, Livio. 1990. *De boot gemist. Over Surinaamse jongeren, werk en werkloosheid.* Amersfoort: Acco.

Sansone, Livio. 1992a. *Schitteren in de schaduw. Overlevingsstrategieën, subcultuur en etniciteit van Creoolse jongeren uit de lagere klasse in Amsterdam 1981–1991.* Amsterdam: Het Spinhuis.

Sansone, Livio. 1992b. *Hangen boven de oceaan. Het gewone overleven onder Creoolse jongeren in Paramaribo.* Amsterdam: Het Spinhuis.

Sansone, Livio. 1994. "The Making of Black Culture: The New Subculture of Young Lower-Class Blacks of Surinamese Origin." *Critique of Anthropology* 14, no. 2: 173–198.

Sansone, Livio. 1999. "Small Places, Large Migrations: Notes on the Specificity of the Population of Surinamese and Antillean Origin in the Netherlands." *Review* 22, no. 4: 471–501.

Schuster, John. 1999. *Portwachters over immigranten. Het debat over immigraties in het naoorloogse Groot-Brittannië en Nederland.* Amsterdam: Het Spinhuis.

van Heelsum, Anna. 1997. *De etnische-culturele positie van de tweede generatie Surinamers.* Amsterdam: Het Spinhuis.

van Niekerk, Mies. 1994. "Zorg en hoop. Surinamers in Nederland nu." Pp. 45–80 in *Het democratische ongeduld: De emancipatie en integratie van zes doelgroepen van het minderhedenbeleid,* ed. Hans Vermeulen and Rinus Penninx. Amsterdam: Het Spinhuis.

van Niekerk, Mies. 2003. *Premigration Legacies and Immigrant Social Mobility: The Afro-Surinamese and the Indo-Surinamese in the Netherlands.* Oxford: Lexington Books.

Venema, Tijno. 1992. *Famiri nanga kulturu. Creoolse sociale verhoudingen en Winti in Amsterdam.* Amsterdam: Het Spinhuis.

Weltak, Marcel. 1990. *Surinaamse muziek in Nederland en Suriname.* Utrecht: Kosmos.

Weltak, Marcel. 1999. "Afrikaans-Surinaamse muziek." *Oso* 10, no. 1: 39–48.

Wermuth, Mieke. 1999. "Ritme in de diaspora. Surinaamse jongeren en popmuziek." *Oso* 10, no. 1: 122–136.

Zhou, Min. 1997. "Segmented Assimilation: Issues, Controversies, and Recent Research on the New Second Generation." *International Migration Review* 31, no. 4: 975–1008.

III

Incorporation, Entrepreneurship, and Household Strategies

8

Cubans and Dominicans

Is There a Latino Experience in the United States?

John R. Logan and Wenquan Zhang

What we call the Hispanic population in the United States is actually a mixture of many different groups from around the world whose common link is language. As Hispanics become the nation's largest minority (up from 22.4 million to 35.3 million in the past decade alone), it is increasingly important to understand not only the similarities but also the differences among them. This chapter focuses on Hispanic immigrants from the Caribbean and the two largest of these groups, Cubans and Dominicans. It compares them in broad strokes to other Hispanics and then focuses on their situation in their principal settlement areas of Miami and New York. We emphasize their socioeconomic position and their residential patterns in these metropolitan regions, as revealed in the most recent census data.

Counting Hispanic National Origin Groups

Census 2000 did an excellent job of counting Hispanics but performed poorly in identifying their origin. In previous years, a single "Hispanic question" on the census has served reasonably well to distinguish Hispanics from those of different national origins. In the last two decennial censuses, people who identify as Hispanic were asked to check one of three boxes (Mexican, Puerto Rican, or Cuban) or to write in another Hispanic category. In Census 2000, no examples of other categories were provided to orient respondents. It is likely that this caused an unprecedented number of Hispanics to provide no information or only the broad category of "Hispanic" or "Spanish." As a result, 6.2 million, or 17.6 percent, of all Hispanics were counted in census reports as "Other Hispanics." This represents nearly double the share of the Other Hispanics category in the 1990 census.

There is good evidence that the sharp jump in the Other Hispanics category has to do with the change in the wording of the question itself. A census study conducted in 2000 (Martin 2002) compared results from a questionnaire using the old and new wording. Using the new wording, 20.1 percent of Hispanics gave responses that had to be coded "Other Hispanics." Using the old wording, only 7.6 percent gave such responses. The result is a severe underestimate of the numbers of specific Hispanic groups in 2000. National studies that rely solely on the Hispanic origin question of the decennial census find only modest growth for major sources of Hispanic immigration such as El Salvador (up 16 percent) and Colombia (up 24 percent). States and metropolitan areas where Latino immigrants from sources other than Mexico and Puerto Rico are particularly concentrated are dramatically affected by this problem. In the State of California, for example, the census estimated the number of Salvadorans in 1990 as 339,000; ten years later, the estimate is only 273,000. In Miami, the census counted 74,000 Nicaraguans a decade ago, but only 69,000 in 2000. It is implausible that these groups actually decreased in this period of intensified immigration.

This chapter uses improved estimates of the size of every Hispanic group compared with those relying solely on the Hispanic origin question in Census 2000 (these are referred to as the Mumford estimates; see Logan 2001). Our procedure uses the Current Population Survey, which has the advantage of being conducted in person or by telephone, as the basis for determining the percentage of Hispanics who "really" should be classified as Other Hispanics. We then apply this target to Census 2000 data at the level of census tracts. Where the census has an excessive number of Other Hispanics, we allocate them across specific national-origin groups according to a pre-established formula. Details of the procedure for 1990 and 2000 are documented in the appendix. For comparison, Table 8.1 also provides the Census Bureau's alternative estimates, prepared in 2003 and taking into account additional information on people's country of birth and ancestry (Cresce and Ramirez 2003). These are described by the authors as "simulated" counts, and they have not replaced the bureau's official numbers.

Table 8.1 provides a detailed breakdown of the Hispanic population at the national level (not including Puerto Rico) in 1990 and 2000. In absolute numbers, the Mexicans are the group most affected by our reallocation of Other Hispanics, increasing by 2.4 million from the census count. In proportion to their number, however, it is the New Latinos for whom the figures

TABLE 8.1   ESTIMATES OF THE HISPANIC POPULATION IN THE UNITED STATES, 1990 AND 2000

	Mumford Estimates			Census Reports		
	1990	2000	Growth	1990	Original 2000	Simulated 2000
Hispanic total	21,900,089	35,305,818	61%	21,900,089	35,305,818	35,305,818
Mexican	13,576,346	23,060,224	70%	13,393,208	20,640,711	22,338,311
Puerto Rican	2,705,979	3,640,460	35%	2,651,815	3,406,178	3,539,988
Cuban	1,067,416	1,315,346	23%	1,053,197	1,241,685	1,312,127
Dominican	537,120	1,121,257	109%	520,151	764,945	999,561
Central American	1,387,331	2,863,063	106%	1,323,830	1,686,937	2,435,731
South American	1,095,329	2,169,669	98%	1,035,602	1,353,562	1,847,811
Other Hispanic	1,530,568	1,135,799	−26%	1,922,286	6,211,800	2,832,289

changed the most. Taken together, the Mumford estimates show that New Latinos more than doubled their number, compared with an increase of about a third reported by the Census Bureau. We calculate more than 350,000 additional Dominicans and Salvadorans, 270,000 additional Colombians, and 250,000 additional Guatemalans.

- By all estimates, Mexicans are by far the largest Hispanic group: about two-thirds of the total and still growing rapidly. They number over 23 million, an increase of 70 percent in the past decade.
- Puerto Ricans and Cubans remain the next largest Hispanic groups, but their expansion is now much slower, up 35 percent and 23 percent, respectively, since 1990.
- The largest newer groups are Dominicans and Salvadorans, both of whom have doubled in the past decade and have now reached over 1.1 million. Salvadorans are listed in the table with other Central Americans, who now total nearly 3 million. Guatemalans (over 600,000) and Hondurans (nearly 500,000) are the next largest Central American groups.
- South Americans are also growing quickly, doubling to over 2 million. The largest numbers of these are Colombians (nearly 750,000), and Ecuadorians and Peruvians are quickly approaching the half-million mark.

These numbers place Hispanic immigration from the Caribbean into a wider perspective. On the one hand, they make clear that Mexico continues to be by far the major origin of Hispanic Americans in the United States. On the other hand (and this is why it is so important for the census figures to be corrected), there are more than a million Hispanics from each of several different origins, and these smaller groups are increasingly important—particularly outside the Southwest, where Mexicans are most highly concentrated. Among these groups, Cubans represent an older immigration that has at least temporarily slowed; Dominicans represent a newer and faster-growing Hispanic community.

The Hierarchy of Success

This chapter will first describe the many Hispanic groups in broad strokes. We will examine the extent to which Cubans' current experience matches their usual portrayal as one of the country's most successful immigrant groups. They certainly benefit from their development of an enclave economy based on entrepreneurial activity in the Miami region (Portes and Bach 1985). However, the distinctions between different generations of Cuban immigrants, particularly between early exiles and more recent economic refugees, are also significant (Portes and Stepick 1993), and there is evidence that many self-employed Cuban workers benefit from the enclave primarily because of its opportunities for long working hours (Logan et al. 2003). The more difficult incorporation of Dominicans into U.S. society has been analyzed by numerous scholars, though here also there are distinctions to be made among cohorts of immigrants (Grasmuck and Pessar 1991; Pessar 1995). We also compare these groups' residential patterns, looking for additional indicators of their incorporation into mainstream society. Have Cubans succeeded in part by establishing unusually separate community areas, or is greater residential separation more clearly a reflection of failure of economic mobility?

Our best current information about people in each group is from the Current Population Survey, because this data source allows us to use their parents' birthplace as part of the identification of national origin. To maximize the size of the sample on which they are based, our figures here are pooled estimates from the Current Population Surveys conducted in March 1998 and 2000 (see Table 8.2).

Nativity and Year of Entry

Puerto Ricans are considered by definition born in the United States. The majority of Cubans are foreign-born (68 percent), though relatively few of those entered the country in the past ten years (27 percent). They mainly represent a pre-1990 immigration stream. In contrast, only about a third of Mexican Americans (36 percent) were born abroad, but nearly half of these (18 percent) arrived in the previous ten years.

The newer groups are like Cubans in having a majority of foreign-born people, ranging from 63 percent for Dominicans to over 70 percent for Central

TABLE 8.2 SOCIAL AND ECONOMIC CHARACTERISTICS OF HISPANICS, BY NATIONAL
ORIGIN (pooled estimates from Current Population Survey, March 1998 and March 2000)

	% Foreign-Born	% Post-1990 Immigrants	Years of Education	Mean Earnings	% Below Poverty Line	% Un-employed	% Public Assistance
All Hispanics	38.5	17.2	10.7	$9,432	25.2	6.8	3.0
Mexican	36.5	18.0	10.2	$8,525	26.3	7.0	2.6
Puerto Rican	1.3	0.3	11.4	$9,893	30.4	8.3	7.3
Cuban	68.0	18.2	11.9	$13,567	18.3	5.8	2.2
Dominican Republic	62.7	28.4	10.8	$7,883	36.0	8.6	8.2
Central America total	71.3	34.3	10.3	$9,865	22.3	6.4	2.4
South America total	73.6	32.7	12.6	$13,911	13.6	4.3	0.8

Americans and South Americans. But they are like Mexicans in that they represent the most recent wave of immigration—generally close to half of their foreign-born arrived in the past ten years.

Education

Mexicans are the least educated of the older Hispanic groups, with an average education of only 10.2 years (for those age twenty-five and older). Puerto Ricans average 11.4 years, and Cubans 11.9 years. Central Americans and Dominicans have the least education (fewer than 11 years). But Hispanics from South America are better educated than Cubans, averaging 12.6 years.

Income

Compared with Puerto Ricans and Mexicans, Cubans in the United States have always been regarded as economically successful. The mean earnings of employed Cubans are above $13,500, compared with about $10,000 for Puerto Ricans and $8,500 for Mexicans. Only 18 percent of Cubans fall below the poverty line, compared with 26 percent of Mexicans and 30 percent of Puerto Ricans.

Among the newer groups, Dominicans stand out for their very low income: mean earnings below $8,000 and more than a third in poverty (36 percent). Central Americans are roughly equivalent to Puerto Ricans in average earnings, although they are less likely to fall below the poverty line. Hispanics from South America do considerably better: on average, they earn more and have lower poverty rates than do Cubans.

Unemployment and Public Assistance

Levels of unemployment among Hispanic groups are generally consistent with their average earnings. Dominicans have higher-than-average unemployment, and they are the group most likely to receive public assistance (above 8 percent). In fact, in both of these respects, they are less successful than Puerto Ricans. Those from South America have the lowest levels of unemployment and are even less likely than Cubans to receive public assistance.

Thus, a new and wider range of social and economic characteristics accompanies the growing diversity of national origins among Hispanics in the United States. It is becoming harder to view Hispanics as one group. As their growth and diversity continues, we must recognize that there are many Hispanic situations in America, apparently creating a continuum with Cubans and South Americans at one end and Dominicans at the other.

National Trends in Hispanic Segregation

Another way to assess a group's experience in the United States is to ask where its members live and, especially, to what degree they live in different neighborhoods from the non-Hispanic white majority. Hispanic segregation, as measured by the Index of Dissimilarity (reported in Logan et al. 2004), is intermediate between that of blacks (who have values about 14 points higher) and Asians (about 9 points lower). These figures were calculated by computing levels of segregation in every metropolitan area, then taking a weighted average, giving more weight to areas with more group members. We can use the same procedure for individual Hispanic groups, with one provision. The 1990 Census reported counts for Dominicans, Central Americans, and South Americans only for a one-in-six sample of persons. This means that there is sampling error, especially at the census-tract level. In metropolitan areas with fewer than 25,000 group members, we believe that the 1990 indices for these groups are unreliable. Therefore, we limit our calculations for both 1990 and 2000 to those metropolitan regions with larger numbers of group members. (In the case of Dominicans, this means that only the New York metropolitan area is included.)

Table 8.3 shows that there is considerable variation in Hispanic groups' settlement patterns at a national level. Consider first segregation from non-Hispanic whites (the Index of Dissimilarity). The index ranges from 0 to 100, giving the percentage of one group who would have to move to achieve an even residential pattern—one where every tract replicates the group composition of the metropolis. A value of 60 or above is considered very high. Values of 40 to 50 are usually considered moderate levels of segregation, while values of 30 or less are considered low.

The national average for all Hispanics in 2000 is 51.5—meaning that 51.5 percent of either Hispanics or whites would need to move to a different tract for the two groups to become equally distributed. Three groups have substantially higher levels of segregation from whites: Dominicans (the extreme, measured

TABLE 8.3   METROPOLITAN SEGREGATION OF HISPANICS: NATIONAL AVERAGES FOR
1990 AND 2000

	Population		Segregation from Whites		Segregation from Blacks	
	1990	2000	1990	2000	1990	2000
Hispanic total	21,900,089	35,305,818	50.6	51.5	54.0	49.2
Mexican total	13,576,346	23,060,224	51.4	53.1	53.4	49.3
Puerto Rican total	2,705,979	3,640,460	61.9	56.5	56.0	50.2
Cuban total	1,067,416	1,315,346	55.4	49.5	76.1	71.5
Dominican total	537,120	1,121,257	82.0	80.8	69.7	64.3
Central American total	1,387,331	2,863,063	67.2	64.1	63.8	56.3
South American total	1,095,329	2,169,669	51.4	47.8	73.0	68.8

	Group Isolation		Exposure to Whites		Exposure to Hispanics	
	1990	2000	1990	2000	1990	2000
Hispanic total			41.8	36.5	42.4	45.5
Mexican total	40.3	38.7	40.2	35.0	46.7	49.5
Puerto Rican total	19.1	14.0	42.1	42.4	33.5	31.6
Cuban total	29.8	26.2	37.6	34.5	51.9	52.8
Dominican total	24.1	19.5	16.3	12.7	56.2	57.4
Central American total	12.0	7.9	27.9	23.6	47.6	50.4
South American total	7.2	7.4	46.8	38.4	34.3	39.6

for New York only, at 80.8), Central Americans (64.1), and Puerto Ricans (56.5).
South Americans and Cubans, by contrast, have segregation levels below 50.
The national average increased very slightly in the last decade, while segre-
gation declined for every group except Mexicans. This illustrates the impor-
tance of the Mexican experience, since two-thirds of Hispanics in the United
States are Mexican. It also reflects the fact that the two most segregated groups—
Dominicans and Central Americans—grew faster than the others.

Segregation from (non-Hispanic) African Americans is another important
feature of the Hispanic experience. Overall, Hispanics are about as segregated
from blacks as they are from whites. In fact, although many Dominicans and
Cubans classify themselves in the census as non-white, they are more segregated
from African Americans than are Mexicans. Nevertheless, segregation from
blacks has declined 5 points for each Hispanic group, so the trajectory is clearly
downward.

Table 8.3 also shows levels of group isolation (the percentage of same-group
members in the census tract where the average group member lives). This is an
indicator of the extent to which a group has developed residential enclaves in
metropolitan areas. Mexicans, who make up less than 10 percent of the nation's
population, live on average in neighborhoods that are almost 40 percent Mexican and nearly 50 percent Hispanic. Cubans, not even 1 percent of the nation's
population, live in neighborhoods were more than a quarter of residents are
Cuban and more than half are Hispanic. Every group has a similar experience.

Of course, the smaller the group, the lower is its isolation. But even the smaller groups, such as Central Americans and South Americans, whose neighborhoods are only 7–8 percent Central American or South American, live in neighborhoods that are half, or nearly half, Hispanic. There is a high degree of residential mixing among these groups: each tends to concentrate in its own specific neighborhoods, but the presence of people from other Hispanic national origins reinforces the Hispanic character of those neighborhoods.

Conversely, exposure to whites (defined as the percentage of non-Hispanic whites in the census tract where the average group member lives) is lower and has fallen over time for every group except Puerto Ricans. Dominicans have the lowest exposure to whites; the average Dominican lives in a neighborhood where only one of eight residents is a non-Hispanic white.

Miami and New York

We now take a closer look at Cubans and Dominicans in the two metropolitan regions where they are found in the largest numbers, Miami and New York. Table 8.4 lists several social and economic characteristics of group members and provides a comparison with the total Hispanic population in each metropolis. Cubans represent just above half of Miami's Hispanic residents; Dominicans now are over a quarter of New York's Hispanics, where a majority are Puerto Rican. (These data are from the Census Bureau's Summary File 3 and Summary File 4. Note that the census population estimate for Dominicans, which is the basis for this table, is fewer than half a million.)

Cubans are significantly older than other Hispanics in Miami, with a median age of nearly forty-four years, and they include a smaller share of recent

TABLE 8.4   CHARACTERISTICS OF PERSONS AND HOUSEHOLDS IN THE MIAMI AND NEW YORK METROPOLITAN REGIONS, 2000

	Miami		New York	
	Cubans	Hispanics	Dominicans	Hispanics
Population (census estimates)	656,751	1,291,681	444,174	2,341,108
Median age	43.8	36.9	29.9	29.3
% English only	5.3	5.6	6.2	13.0
% Foreign-born	79.3	71.4	68.7	41.8
% Post-1990 immigrant	22.8	25.3	28.6	18.7
% College educated	10.5	11.0	6.1	7.0
% Below high school	14.9	13.4	15.2	13.4
% Unemployed	7.8	8.6	14.5	13.2
Median household income	$33,427	$33,536	$26,218	$28,791
% in poverty	15.6	17.5	32.1	29.8
% Households with public assistance	7.9	6.9	18.2	14.5
% Female-headed households	13.4	15.6	37.7	29.1

TABLE 8.5   SEGREGATION OF CUBANS AND DOMINICANS,
1990 AND 2000

	Miami Cubans		New York Dominicans	
	1990	2000	1990	2000
Population	563,979	681,032	351,377	602,714
Segregation from whites	59.8	53.6	82.0	80.8
Segregation from blacks	82.4	81.3	69.7	64.3
Isolation	50.3	46.3	24.1	19.5
Exposure to whites	20.4	16.4	16.3	12.7
Exposure to Hispanics	73.5	76.5	56.2	57.4

immigrants. In other respects they are very similar to Hispanics from other national origins in the Miami region.

Compared with other Hispanic New Yorkers, Dominicans stand out most prominently for their high percentage of female-headed households—just under 40 percent. This level is high for New York and more than double the figure for Miami. Dominicans are less likely than other Hispanic New Yorkers to speak only English at home, and they have somewhat lower education and income levels. But in these respects also the greater contrast is between New York and Miami as contexts of reception: Hispanics in New York are much younger and more likely to be recent immigrants than Hispanics in Miami; they are also considerably less educated, less likely to be employed, poorer, and more likely to receive public assistance. This means that when we compare Cubans and Dominicans in the United States overall, we need to be aware that a very large share of them live in parts of the country where the Hispanic community as a whole has a different character.

One would expect that Cubans, given their age, longer average residence in the United States, and greater human capital resources, would be more fully integrated with other groups than are Dominicans at the neighborhood level. This is only partly the case. Table 8.5 shows that Cubans in Miami have become less segregated from non-Hispanic whites in the past decade, from a level that most would consider "high" in 1990 (59.8) to a more moderate level in 2000. Yet there are other population dynamics at play. Cubans are unusually highly segregated from Miami's black minority (the value of the Index of Dissimilarity [D] is over 80). Also, because Hispanics are actually a majority of metropolitan residents, they live in neighborhoods with relatively little exposure to non-Hispanic whites (20.4 percent on average), where Cubans are a near-majority and Hispanics are three-quarters of the population. Cuban Miami is very Cuban and even more Hispanic.

Dominicans in New York (as noted earlier) have a different pattern. They are remarkably segregated from non-Hispanic whites (D over 80), though more intermixed with blacks. The average Dominican lives in a census tract where

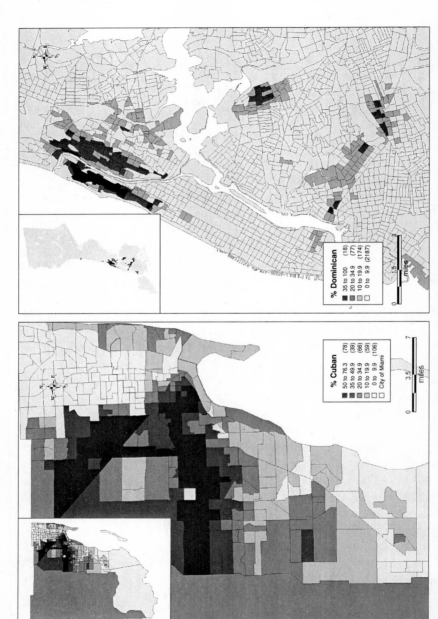

% Cuban
50 to 76.3 (78)
35 to 49.9 (39)
20 to 34.9 (66)
10 to 19.9 (59)
0 to 9.9 (106)
City of Miami

0   3.5   7
miles

% Dominican
35 to 100 (18)
20 to 34.9 (77)
10 to 19.9 (174)
0 to 9.9 (2187)

0   1.5   3
miles

FIGURE 8.1   Concentrations of Cubans in Miami (left) and Dominicans in the New York metropolitan region (right), 2000.

only one in five residents is Dominican but a majority is Hispanic. Their residential mixing with other Hispanics is especially pronounced in the western portions of the Bronx, formerly dominated by Puerto Ricans, where Dominicans have recently been moving.

These differences are represented in part by maps of Miami and New York that show how each group is distributed across census tracts (Figure 8.1). The map of Miami shows that relatively few tracts have fewer than 10 percent Cuban residents (the legend notes that the number of such tracts is 106), and nearly as many tracts (78) have a Cuban majority. Cuban settlements extend from the southwestern corner of the city, where Little Havana is located, across the Miami city line in both a western and northern direction. A large concentration of African Americans is found to the northeast, and whites are settled in the very high-income neighborhoods along the coast to the south of the Cuban area.

The map of New York, in contrast, shows that most of the metropolitan area has very few Dominican residents—indeed, more than 2,000 census tracts are less than 10 percent Dominican, and only 97 tracts have as high as 20 percent Dominican residents. Dominican neighborhoods are highly clustered in upper Manhattan (the area known as Washington Heights) and in adjacent portions of the Bronx. There are smaller but well-known clusters of Dominicans in Corona (Queens) and in northeastern sections of Brooklyn that border on Queens.

A final step that we can take is to describe the social and economic characteristics of these ethnic neighborhoods and assess what living in a distinctively Cuban or Dominican neighborhood means for members of each group. We are guided here by expectations about spatial assimilation of ethnic groups in American cities (Massey 1985). Cities like Miami and New York have both grown mainly by attracting newcomers, whose customs or language often set them apart from the majority population—never more so than in the current period of intensive immigration. Concentrated immigrant settlement areas seem to be a permanent feature of cities, but the predominant view among social scientists is that they are also transitional places. People live in them as long as they need the affordable housing, family ties, familiar culture, and help in finding work that they provide. They search for areas with more amenities as soon as their economic situation improves and they become better able to function without assistance from co-ethnics—that is, they assimilate. An alternative view is that members of some groups seek ways to sustain a strong ethnic identity even as they move to neighborhoods with a better environment and greater community resources. We would expect Dominicans as a newer and less affluent minority to be more likely to manifest the traditional pattern in which group members who live in ethnic neighborhoods are not only less integrated with other racial and ethnic groups, but also are limited to areas with substantially more newcomers and lower socioeconomic standing.

Do Cuban neighborhoods in Miami also resemble such immigrant enclaves? To answer this question, we use new spatial-analysis techniques that have been developed to determine the extent to which an aerial characteristic is spatially clustered (Logan et al. 2002). Geographers have developed several indicators of the extent to which the spatial distribution of place characteristics departs from a random pattern. Luc Anselin (1995) has extended this work to a class of "local indicators of spatial association" (LISA), which offer a measure for each place of the extent of *significant spatial clustering* of similar values around it. In brief, LISA indicators identify "hot spots" that take into account not only unusually high or low values in a single place (such as a census tract) but also the values in nearby places. Such spatial clustering provides a method for identifying ethnic neighborhoods. This approach takes advantage of an underlying statistical theory through which only sets of tracts that depart significantly from a random distribution are assigned to clusters.

A majority of Miami Cubans (56 percent) live in the Cuban neighborhoods that we identified in this way, as do 60 percent of Dominicans in New York. But this means that substantial minorities live outside ethnic clusters. Table 8.6 summarizes the characteristics of census tracts where group members live (i.e., they are averages that have been weighted by the number of Cubans or Dominicans who live in each tract), classified as Cuban/Dominican or mainstream neighborhoods.

Cuban neighborhoods are defined by the presence of Cubans, so it is not surprising that, on average, 61 percent of residents are Cuban, compared with 27 percent in the mainstream neighborhoods where Cubans also live. Cuban neighborhoods are almost entirely Hispanic (one in eight residents is black or non-Hispanic white). Almost 70 percent of residents are foreign-born and nearly a quarter are recent immigrants, and only 10 percent of residents speak only English at home. Mainstream neighborhoods have a less pronounced ethnic character, but even these are nearly two-thirds Hispanic. Mainstream neighborhoods have a higher share of English-only speakers and a lower percentage of immigrants than do Cuban neighborhoods.

There are systematic differences in socioeconomic standing, and these mostly favor mainstream neighborhoods. For example, the median income of mainstream neighborhoods is nearly 20 percent higher than that of Cuban neighborhoods. This means that moving away from Cuban areas of Miami does represent social mobility as well as increased exposure to other groups. It should be noted, though, that there is a socioeconomic gradient within the heavily Cuban portion of the region, and it is also possible to move to a somewhat more affluent but still Cuban neighborhood beyond the city limits.

TABLE 8.6   CHARACTERISTICS OF CUBANS' AND DOMINICANS' NEIGHBORHOODS

	Miami Cubans		New York Dominicans	
Neighborhood type:	Cuban	Mainstream	Dominican	Mainstream
Group total (Mumford estimate)	383,427	298,036	351,456	251,297
Race and ethnicity				
% Non-Hispanic white	11.5	23.0	6.1	21.9
% Black	2.0	12.4	22.4	28.3
% Hispanic	86.7	63.0	70.6	39.3
% Group	63.3	28.7	40.0	9.0
Language and nativity				
% English only	10.2	28.3	26.6	47.0
% Foreign-born	69.6	52.2	46.0	34.6
% Post-1990 immigrant	23.2	19.2	20.7	15.3
Socioeconomic status				
% College+ educated	9.6	14.7	7.2	11.9
% Below high school	14.5	10.5	14.8	11.5
% Unemployed	8.5	8.2	16.5	12.5
Median household income	$36,303	$42,545	$25,347	$33,331
% Below poverty line	11.6	12.6	26.6	20.5
% with public assistance	7.7	5.4	17.2	11.0
% Female-headed households	15.7	15.2	32.5	24.8

Dominican neighborhoods of New York are less intensely ethnic than are these Cuban neighborhoods. Table 8.6 shows that they average 29 percent Dominican, well above the 6.5 percent level in mainstream neighborhoods but still definitely a minority of residents. But Dominican neighborhoods are over 70 percent Hispanic, while mainstream areas are only 40 percent Hispanic. Nearly half of residents in mainstream neighborhoods speak only English, which is much more than in Dominican neighborhoods, and they also have a lower share of foreign-born and recent immigrants.

Socioeconomic disparities between ethnic and mainstream neighborhoods are similar and in some respects even more pronounced that what we found in Miami. For example, the median income in Dominican neighborhoods is 30 percent below that of mainstream neighborhoods. In this case, there is also a distinction in household formation, as Dominican neighborhoods also have higher shares of female-headed households. Again we see that moving out of ethnic neighborhoods represents a degree of upward social mobility, as the spatial assimilation model anticipates. More detailed analyses show that there are more affluent sections within Washington Heights, and at a greater distance the Corona neighborhood in Queens is much more middle class, but on average moving up means moving out for Dominicans in New York.

Is There an Average Latino?

The scale of immigration from nontraditional Hispanic sources brings new and less-well-known groups into the United States. Because they are highly concentrated in a few regions, often in a fairly narrow set of neighborhoods, every Hispanic group has local significance. And their growth expands the range of variation in what could be considered the typical Latino experience.

Of the groups studied here, Cubans and South Americans stand out for their high degree of economic success. This success translates into moderate levels of segregation from whites, although members of both groups still tend to live in neighborhoods where non-Hispanic whites are outnumbered by Hispanics. They are also the most segregated from African Americans, although this dimension of separation is on the decline. On the other hand, two of the newer and fastest growing groups—Dominicans and Central Americans— lag behind in economic standing. Dominicans are clearly the least successful as well as the most segregated. These differences show up even more clearly when we study these groups in places like Miami and New York where they are most highly concentrated. Looking to the future, it is likely that the Hispanic population will maintain or accentuate the diversity we see today. Our ability to distinguish among the national-origin groups is therefore crucial to understanding Hispanic Americans. There is no "average Hispanic."

Yet we found some commonalities among Cubans, Dominicans, and other Hispanic groups. The differences between Miami and New York for Hispanics of all national origins are so large that they make variations between groups within these metropolitan regions seem minor. Even Cubans and Dominicans, despite being at polar extremes among Hispanics, have some traits in common. They are both moderately to highly segregated from non-Hispanic groups, and they are very likely to live in neighborhoods where Hispanics are a majority or near-majority. This is especially true in Miami and New York, given the magnitude of immigration in both parts of the country in the last several decades. Regardless of the differences in their socioeconomic background, both Cubans and Dominicans manifest the same process of spatial assimilation. Living in a Cuban or a Dominican neighborhood—as do more than half of group members in these two metropolises—implies not only a particular ethnic character but also substantial socioeconomic disadvantages. When they move to mainstream neighborhoods, members of both groups continue to have high exposure to immigrants, but they achieve greater integration with people of other racial and ethnic backgrounds in addition to improved residential surroundings. The project of assimilation, manifested in the labor market or in space, may be the most significant common denominator of the Latino experience in the United States.

Appendix:
Estimates of Hispanic-Origin Populations

The adjustment procedures described here are analogous to standard techniques employed by the Census Bureau to deal with incomplete census forms. The bureau routinely "imputes" information from other household members or from neighbors to fill in missing data. The difference is that our adjustment is done at the level of the census tract. To the extent that we believe the tract's Other Hispanics population has been overstated, we impute specific national origins to the "excess Other Hispanics" based on the distribution of responses of others in the tract.

Estimates for 1990

We first describe our approach to 1990. The Public Use Microdata Sample (PUMS) from the 1990 Census provides individual-level information for a large national sample on Hispanic origin, country of birth, and ancestry. In the PUMS sample, 8.7 percent of Hispanics are classed as Other Hispanics. If we also use country of birth and ancestry as a basis for determining individuals' specific Hispanic origin, we can reduce Other Hispanics to 7.5 percent. For some specific states or metropolitan areas, however, we can do much better, reducing Other Hispanics to less than 1.5 percent of Hispanics in New York, Los Angeles, and Miami.

We treat these estimates of the "real" size of the Other Hispanics category as targets, setting a specific target for every census tract. For tracts in metro areas with more than 100,000 Hispanics (39 metro areas), we calculate the target from data for the metro area itself. In other cases, we apply statewide figures. For the thirty-one states with fewer than 100,000 Hispanics, we apply the national target of 7.5 percent.

We then turn to the figures from the 1990 Census, comparing our target for every census tract with the number of Other Hispanics reported by the census. If the reported number is equal to or below the target, we make no adjustment. If it is larger than the target, we allocate the number of "excess" other Hispanics to specific national-origin categories based on the reported figures in the tract for those categories.

Analysis of 1990 PUMS data reveals that people of Mexican, Puerto Rican, or Cuban birth or ancestry were much less likely (by a factor of 1:4) to fail to indicate an origin than were Hispanics of other backgrounds, a result that we attribute to the questionnaire format. It is appropriate to allocate some Other Hispanics to these listed groups, but not in the same proportion as for unlisted groups. In allocating Other Hispanics, therefore, we weight members of the listed groups in each tract at .25; this procedure generates national totals that are consistent with the national group populations found in the PUMS.

Estimates for 2000

Our procedure for 2000 follows the same logic but draws on a different source for calculating targets. We use the Current Population Survey, pooling together the samples from March 1998 and March 2000. As a national average, information on the person's country of birth and both parents' country of birth from the Current Population Survey allows us to reduce the target to 3.3 percent—well below the 17.3 percent reported in the decennial census. These targets also vary by state and metro area. For Consolidated Metropolitan Statistical Areas (CMSAs) with more than 400 sampled Hispanics, we use CMSA figures to calculate targets (this covered 67 Primary Metropolitan Statistical Areas, or PMSAs). For other cases, we employ statewide figures or, where a state has fewer than 400 sampled Hispanics, we use the national target. In some cases, the targets are even lower than 3.9 percent: they are 2.4 percent in New York, and 1.1 percent in Los Angeles. This procedure reallocates a very large share of people who were reported as Other Hispanics in Census 2000.

As in 1990, we allocate a substantial number of Other Hispanics to Mexican, Puerto Rican, and Cuban. The weighting factor for these groups is .10, calibrated to yield national totals that are consistent with the Current Population Survey. Substantively, this weight means we are estimating that members of other groups were ten times more likely to fail to indicate their origin, a greater discrepancy than in 1990. The difference reflects the fact that the Census 2000 questionnaire provided no examples to guide respondents from the unlisted groups, examples that proved helpful in 1990.

References

Anselin, Luc. 1995. "Local Indicators of Spatial Association—LISA." *Geographical Analysis* 27: 93–115.

Cresce, Arthur R., and Roberto R. Ramirez. 2003. "Analysis of General Hispanic Responses in Census 2000." Working Paper 72. Washington, D.C.: U.S. Bureau of the Census. Available online at www2.census.gov/census_2000/datasets/Sim_Hispanic_Totals/General_Hispanic_Working_Paper_%2372.pdf (accessed April 29, 2005).

Grasmuck, Sherri, and Patricia R. Pessar. 1991. *Between Two Islands: Dominican International Migration.* Berkeley: University of California Press.

Logan, John R. 2001. "The New Latinos: Who They Are, Where They Are." Lewis Mumford Center for Comparative Urban and Regional Research, September 10. Available online at http://browns4.dyndns.org/cen2000_s4/HispanicPop/HspReport/HspReportPage1.html (accessed April 29, 2005).

Logan, John R., Richard D. Alba, and Brian J. Stults. 2003. "Enclaves and Entrepreneurs: Assessing the Payoff for Immigrants and Minorities." *International Migration Review* 37 (Summer): 344–388.

Logan, John R., Richard D. Alba, and Charles Zhang. 2002. "Immigrant Enclaves and Ethnic Communities in New York and Los Angeles." *American Sociological Review* 67 (April): 299–322.

Logan, John R., Brian Stults, and Reynolds Farley. 2004. "Segregation of Minorities in the Metropolis: Two Decades of Change." *Demography* 41: 1–22.

Martin, Elizabeth. 2002. "The Effects of Questionnaire Design on Reporting of Detailed Hispanic Origin in Census 2000 Mail Questionnaires." *Public Opinion Quarterly* 66, no. 4: 582–593.

Massey, Douglas. 1985. "Ethnic Residential Segregation: A Theoretical Synthesis and Empirical Review." *Sociology and Social Research* 69: 315–350.

Pessar, Patricia. 1995. *A Visa for a Dream: Dominicans in the United States*. Boston: Allyn and Bacon.

Portes, Alejandro, and Robert L. Bach. 1985. *Latin Journey: Cuban and Mexican Immigrants in the United States*. Berkeley: University of California Press.

Portes, Alejandro, and Alex Stepick. 1993. *City on the Edge: The Transformation of Miami*. Berkeley: University of California Press.

9

Dominican Women, Heads of Households in Spain

LAURA OSO CASAS

Introduction

In the late 1980s and early '90s, Southern Europe developed into a new migratory space for immigrant reception. This new space is characterized mainly by the presence of female migratory flows in response to a demand for labor to fill unskilled and poorly paid jobs in the service sector. Unlike industrial activity, domestic service, the catering industry, personal services, and sex work cannot be exported, which leads to a demand for foreign labor and the development of female migratory flows of an economic nature. Parallel to this phenomenon is the international increase in the number of female household heads, or, to put it another way, households that are financially supported by women. The incorporation of immigrant women into the labor market in the receiving countries is often the result of a household-survival or social-mobility strategy in which the woman becomes the principal breadwinner in the transnational household.

The aim of this chapter is to analyze migration to Spain by Dominican women from the perspective of female heads of households and their integration and social-mobility strategies.[1] To do so, I will analyze and interpret qualitative data obtained from in-depth individual and group interviews and discussion groups made up of female Dominican immigrants in Spain held during the course of various periods of research I have undertaken. The first of these took place in 1992, a period characterized by the entrance of large numbers of Dominican immigrants into Spain. The fieldwork was carried out mainly in the borough of Aravaca, Madrid (Oso Casas 1997; Oso Casas and Machín Herranz 1993). The second period of research was undertaken between 1996 and 1997 within the context of a comparative study of immigrant female household heads of varying nationalities (Oso 1998). Finally, data have been taken from in-depth interviews held with Dominican women as part of research carried out into irregular female immigrants for Spain's Instituto de la Mujer (Institute for Women) in 2000 (Oso 2000) and ongoing research into immigrant women and ethnic business (Oso 2003).[2]

First, I will reveal the social-mobility strategies of immigrant Dominican women in Spain by determining whether they are of an individual or family nature. I will then analyze the integration and social-mobility strategies in the receiving society, looking first at these women's occupational strategies (live-in or live-out domestic service). This will be followed by a study of the residential, educational, and marital social-mobility strategies of Dominican women in Spain. Finally, I will assess the impact of these integration and social-mobility strategies on actual social progression, as well as on the role and socioeconomic status of Dominican female household heads in the transnational household.

My theoretical approach to Dominican immigration in Spain from the perspective of female-headed households and these women's integration and social-mobility strategies does not intend to restrict its vision to that of the rational individual. The aim is to draw attention to the fact that these strategies are frequently family-oriented and therefore far from being purely rational decisions. Indeed, imaginary and symbolic components have a considerable impact on strategic behavior. Migratory projects that impel Dominican women to migrate do not necessarily result in corresponding social trajectories. And it is here that my principal interest lies—namely, in highlighting how the goals that are set may result in highly differing social trajectories and on occasion may be quite the opposite of those to which the women aspired. These directional changes may result from structural factors, changes in initial strategies, the strategies of other social actors in the receiving context and the country of origin, or the individual's position in the life cycle. My intention is to highlight the conflicting interests of the various social actors (immigrant women, family members in the country of origin, employers, and the autochthonous population, among others), as well as those that exist between the strategies employed by Dominican female immigrants in Spain for the purposes of integration into the receiving society and the social mobility of the transnational household.

Economically Motivated
Female Migratory Flows into Spain

Spain began to acquire the status of an immigrant-receiving context from the early 1980s onward. By the end of the 1990s, this status had become firmly established. In just over sixteen years, between 1991 and 2007, the total number of foreigners in Spain increased from 350,062 to 4,519,554 (see Table 9.1). In 2007, 47 percent of the foreigners in Spain were women. Although in average terms the male–female balance in Spain tips slightly in favor of male immigration, data reveal the existence of female-dominated migratory flows from Latin American countries such as the Dominican Republic (59 percent), Colombia (56 percent), Bolivia (56 percent), Peru (52 percent), and Ecuador (51 percent; see Table 9.2). We are therefore faced with migratory flows made up of women who act as pioneers in migratory movements. Many of them travel alone, thereby distancing themselves from the stereotyped image of the "regrouped" wife. Traditionally, women have not been seen as actors in the migratory process. The literature has considered men as the initial migrants and women as followers in the context of the family-reunion process (Oso 1998).

It is important to highlight the fact that female Latin American immigrants in Spain are employed mostly in the "service and catering industries, personal and security services, and seller trade" (32 percent), as well as in "non-qualified jobs."[3] Latin American women in Spain are channeled principally toward domestic work.

From 1993 until 1999, the demand for immigrant women for domestic work has been accepted, and even encouraged, by the Spanish government's policy of fixing annual quotas as a means of regulating migratory flows. It

TABLE 9.1 FOREIGN WOMEN IN SPAIN ACCORDING TO PRINCIPAL COUNTRIES OF ORIGIN

Year	Total	Morocco	Romania	Ecuador	Bolivia	Peru	United Kingdom	Colombia	Argentina	Dominican Republic
1991	180,700	12,149	—	—	—	—	28,133	—	10,933	2,370
1996	269,087	32,095	770	—	—	—	36,879	—	9,347	9,999
2000	452,413	63,364	2,893	—	—	—	51,082	—	12,168	18,227
2001	653,820	79,940	12,264	70,529	3,691	21,335	54,888	52,355	16,471	22,233
2002	929,767	101,307	26,254	131,478	7,396	26,468	64,795	110,000	28,070	26,244
2003	1,249,418	123,548	58,517	199,849	15,485	32,051	80,768	139,626	53,636	29,736
2004	1,428,603	141,873	92,826	245,352	29,072	37,745	86,520	141,732	64,580	30,813
2005	1,738,576	170,498	144,050	255,649	54,405	45,729	112,222	153,482	75,388	35,631
2006	1,928,697	191,071	189,476	236,834	78,749	50,350	135,393	150,147	74,221	36,972
2007	2,123,869	207,634	249,061	219,090	113,004	53,511	154,898	147,612	70,306	38,558

Note: — = data not available.

Source: Computed base data on "Censo de población y viviendas," 1991. *Padrón municipal de habitantes* since 1996 to 2006 and advanced results for 2007; Instituto Nacional de Estadística, available online at www.ine.es.

TABLE 9.2   PERCENTAGE OF FEMALE IMMIGRANTS CLASSIFIED ACCORDING TO
PRINCIPAL LATIN AMERICAN COUNTRIES OF ORIGIN, 1996–2007

Year	Ecuador	Colombia	Bolivia	Argentina	Peru	Dominican Republic
1996	—	—	—	52.1	—	77.3
2000	—	—	—	52.1	—	73.4
2001	50.7	60.0	55.8	50.8	61.0	71.4
2002	50.7	57.6	54.7	49.5	59.1	69.4
2003	51.2	57.1	54.5	49.0	57.3	67.1
2004	51.6	56.9	55.5	49.4	55.0	64.2
2005	51.4	56.6	55.5	49.3	53.8	62.4
2006	51.3	56.6	56.3	49.4	52.5	60.5
2007	51.3	56.4	56.4	49.8	51.6	59.2

Note: — = data not available.
Source: Computed base data on "Censo de población y viviendas," 1991. *Padrón municipal de habitantes* since 1996 to 2006 and advanced results for 2007; Instituto Nacional de Estadística, available online at www.ine.es.

implies government acceptance of the existence of a demand for foreign labor to occupy certain jobs that remain unfilled by the autochthonous labor market. However, these quotas mask an annual regularization process. The government establishes a set of requirements each year and quotas that are dependent on the state of the labor market in terms of economic sectors and geographical locations, thereby determining the selection of immigrants. Spain's quota policy especially benefited immigrant women from 1993 to 1999, since in that period domestic service and agriculture were among the major areas of opportunity for employment. In 1993, 84 percent of the favorable quota decisions corresponded to domestic work, while the figures for 1995 and 1999 corresponded to 60.6 percent and 51.6 percent, respectively (*Anuario Estadístico de Extranjería* 1993, 1995, 1999).[4] The political situation, combined with the demand for female domestic workers, facilitated the migration of women to Spain during the 1990s, specifically to Madrid, and has resulted in the consolidation of female migratory flows arriving mainly from Latin America.

Establishment of Social Networks among Female Dominican Immigrants in Madrid

The pioneers in female Dominican migration to Spain came mainly from the southeastern Dominican Republic, and specifically from the borough of Vicente Noble. This led to the later arrival of women from other parts of the country. The survey carried out by the Colectivo IOE among 811 immigrant domestic-service workers in Spain, 166 of whom were of Dominican origin, reveals that 61 percent of Dominican respondents came from the southeastern area of the country (mainly from Barahona, Independencia, and Azúa), while 22 percent came from the eastern regions and 17 percent came from Cibao (Colectivo IOE 2001: 264).

The fieldwork I carried out in Madrid in 1992 with immigrants from the southeastern Dominican Republic revealed low levels of education among these women. They came mainly from rural areas and in many cases had not undergone a process of intermediate migration before traveling to Spain, coming instead directly from Vicente Noble to Madrid. As Carmen Gregorio Gil has noted, these migratory flows originated with the families of commercial airline pilots residing in the Dominican Republic who, on their return to Spain, brought over women to work in domestic service, as well as with nuns in Dominican Republic who looked for contacts for those who wished to travel to Spain to work in private houses (Gregorio Gil 1998). The growth of this immigration was also due to the increased permeability of the border following the commencement of these entry flows. Indeed, until September 1993 Dominican citizens were not required to possess visas to enter Spain as tourists and could then remain for three months. The pioneers of Dominican migration to Spain took advantage of this situation to join the informal labor market. Spain therefore found itself with large numbers of recently arrived female migrants.

The rapid development of flows from the Dominican Republic gave rise to a strongly consolidated structure of social networks based in Corona Boreal Square in Aravaca (which the group referred to as "el parque"), an upper-middle-class residential area on the outskirts of Madrid. Initially, the women working as live-in domestic staff in the area would meet in the public square on their days off (Thursdays and Sundays). The number of people who attended these informal meetings, who mainly were from the southeastern Dominican Republic, continued to grow. The square, which acted as a space for social communication, enabled the women to obtain details about possible opportunities for employment and mechanisms that would allow them to legalize their status. Veteran immigrants would inform more recent arrivals about the vicissitudes of immigration. These networks also acted as a means of obtaining news of family members and as a form of social control, reducing the sense of geographical distance from the country of origin through social and communicational proximity. For example, in interviews, women from southeastern Dominican Republic said:

> When I arrived, I said to X, I haven't got a job. And she replied, go to Aravaca and if you don't find anything there I'll look for an agency for you.

Aravaca is the center; I'd heard about Aravaca before I left my country, because there they tell you about what you should do here. The Dominicans meet in the park in Aravaca; it's the meeting point for Dominicans, the first place they go to when they arrive.

It's as if this park belongs to you, here you feel as if you're in your own country. (Oso Casas and Machín Herranz 1993)

In *el parque,* the women would eat *moro* (a Dominican specialty), play cards, and sell or exchange clothes and other items. Some women held hairdressing sessions. The fact that the Dominicans met in a square, an open and public place, rather than on private premises gave rise to xenophobic reactions that led to an increase in the number of police raids in 1992 and the murder of Lucrecia Pérez, a Dominican immigrant from Vicente Noble. Today, only a few Dominicans continue to meet in *el parque* in Aravaca. The immigrants from the Dominican Republic have gradually spread into other areas of Madrid and are now mainly found in working-class areas of the city, such as Cuatro Caminos, where the cost of housing is lower than in Aravaca. Private spaces (the homes of the immigrants, who formerly resided mainly in their employers' homes, food stores, bars, and hairdressing salons) have gradually replaced *el parque* as meeting places for the Dominican community, who continue to carry out the same activities as before, albeit now removed from the public gaze of the Spanish population.

The situation of Dominican migration today reveals a different reality. The majority of the women I interviewed during the most recent fieldwork I carried out in Madrid (Oso 2000, 2003) had migrated from different regions of the country. The migratory cycle of these women is different from that analyzed during our 1992 fieldwork. These are regular immigrants, and as such their insertion into the receiving society is more stable. Indeed, their main difficulty does not lie in obtaining legal papers. Some of them were pioneers in the family migration process, regrouping their children, for whom they had already "paved the way." Their social relations network was not necessarily restricted to the immigrant community, and many of them had married Spaniards.

Having established the context of Dominican migration to Spain within the framework of the consolidation of Spain's status as a receiving country for immigrants and an upsurge in the demand for domestic workers in Madrid, I will now consider the principal idea I wish to transmit in this chapter: the analysis of female Dominican immigration in Spain from the perspective of social-mobility strategies.

Downward Social Mobility of Female Dominican Immigrants in Spain

According to Pitirim Sorokin, mobility within the geographic space does not necessarily imply social mobility. Two individuals may be physically close, yet at the same time distanced from each other within the social space, as in the case of the master and the servant. Social mobility is the process whereby individuals move within the social space. This author considers that the social space has both a horizontal and a vertical dimension. Vertical mobility brings with it a change in the social hierarchy, whilst horizontal mobility implies a transformation in terms of belonging to a particular group on the same social scale. The former involves a change in social status, which may be either upward or downward on the social scale, and which may also take two forms: the mobility of an individual towards a new social stratum or the joint movement of a whole social group towards higher or lower strata within the structure of society (Sorokin 1964).

The study of migration and social mobility should consider at least two social spaces: the one that the migrant leaves behind in his or her community of origin and the receiving social space. They are governed by different social structures and hierarchies, with the migrant possibly occupying different positions in each. For example, on migrating an individual may descend the social hierarchy in the receiving social space (Spain) while at the same time increase his or her status in the social space of origin (the Dominican Republic).

The Colectivo IOE survey highlighted the mainly rural nature of domestic workers migrating from that country. Indeed, 43 percent of the respondents had come from boroughs with fewer than 10,000 inhabitants. The survey also revealed large numbers of agricultural workers among the relatives of the Dominican immigrant respondents. Forty-two percent of the Dominican domestic workers had only a primary-level education, and 0.6 percent of those interviewed had never been to school. Nevertheless, we must not overlook the fact that 41 percent of Dominican domestic workers in Spain had a secondary-level education, and 17 percent had received higher education. Consequently, and in overall terms, the level of education among Dominican domestic workers is higher than that of their Spanish counterparts, of whom 4 percent had never been to school, 50 percent had only a primary-level education, 30 percent had secondary-level education, and 16 percent had received higher education (Colectivo IOE 2001: 268, 270).

Thus, the migration of Dominican women to Spain can be considered a process of downward socio-professional mobility in the receiving social space compared with the position they occupied in their society of origin. Indeed, some of the immigrants joined the labor market at a lower level than the one they occupied in their home country. Our respondents included women who had worked in professional occupations such as teaching, nursing, and psychology. Some had worked in the retail trade, and others had been registered students. Even those who had worked in agriculture (on small farms) or as housewives perceived working in domestic service in Spain as a step backward on the social scale. While they considered agricultural work or housework to be a "natural" activity, cleaning up "other people's mess" brought with it social devaluation. The women who had worked in domestic service in the Dominican Republic were not subjected to downward socio-professional mobility, although domestic service in Spain cannot be considered a move upward on the social scale.[5] In addition to their labor status as domestic workers, one must also consider their status as "immigrants" and the marginalizing effect this can have within the receiving society. Contrary to the idea that immigrants come to "better themselves," migration can actually mean downward socio-professional mobility or stagnation in the receiving social space. This raises the question: where is the supposed "social improvement" or "bettering" of the migrant?

The answer may lie in the notion of social strategy. Indeed, "If we claim that an individual displays strategic behaviour, we immediately try to show that not only is his behaviour rational, and that he chooses his courses of action according to his interests and the risks involved in certain choices, but that it is also based on the future, opting for lower income today in order to secure greater or more stable benefits tomorrow" (Gresle et al. 1994). This means that the downward socio-professional movement or stagnation of many Dominican women who join the Spanish labor market as domestic workers can be seen as forming part of a social strategy. That is, they are prepared to accept more precarious positions and downward social movement in the receiving social space to ensure the achievement of specific future goals.

Imaginary Social-Mobility Strategies and Migratory Projects of Dominican Women

Dominican Migration to Spain as a Family Social-Mobility Strategy

Female Dominican migration to Spain responds essentially to family projects. Data obtained during the extraordinary regularization process in 1991 revealed that Dominicans ranked first in terms of the number of female migrant workers with dependants (84 percent). It can therefore be claimed that this migration responds to family strategies aimed at supporting the domestic unit at origin, as 76 percent of the dependent family members of Dominican immigrants remained in the country of origin. As we will see later, and as indicated by the statistics discussed earlier, we are faced with female migratory flows with a strong family element and a predominance of female household heads who choose migration as a means of maintaining the transnational household.

A survey carried out by Antonio Izquierdo during the extraordinary regularization process in 2000 also indicated that, of the 1,019 women of varying origin who were interviewed, 58 percent had dependent family members (10 percent had five or more dependants). Furthermore, most of the relatives who were financially dependent on the respondents resided outside Spain, as 77 percent of the women claimed to have no dependent family member with them in the country (Izquierdo 2000). The Colectivo IOE survey of domestic-service workers revealed that 60 percent of the Dominicans interviewed sent more than 20 percent of their income back to the Dominican Republic. Seventy-five percent had children living in the country of origin, a fact that highlights the transnational element of these migratory flows. "Among long-stay immigrants in Spain—notably sectors of the Filipino and Dominican communities—separation from the family unit cannot be considered as a temporary situation, but rather as a perspective that tends to consolidate the existence of permanently separated transnational families" (Colectivo IOE 2001: 280).

The existence of financially dependent individuals in the country of origin can be considered an indicator of family migratory strategies, as from an economic point of view the migration involves various members of the household even though it requires the displacement of only a single member (Oso 1998). This phenomenon was corroborated throughout the course of the fieldwork carried out in 1992, 1996–1997, and 2000–2003 (Oso 1993, 1998, 2003). Indeed, many of the Dominican respondents directed their social-mobility strategy not only at themselves as individuals but also, and on some occasions primarily, at their families.

Migration as a family strategy tends to occur among married, widowed, separated, and divorced migrants, as well as among single mothers who leave their husbands or children behind and who tend to direct family mobility toward the social space of their communities of origin. The social-mobility strategies of these women can be classified into three types. The first covers the daily survival or maintenance of the transnational household and its basic needs (such as food and clothing); the second refers to obtaining some kinds of material goods or assets (savings, a house, consumer goods); and the third is of an intangible nature, principally that of providing children with an education. Occasionally, these strategies become intertwined, or the family social-mobility strategy requires several members of the household—the couple, the mother and a daughter, several sisters—to migrate. This family strategy also exists for some unmarried women without children.

Data from the Colectivo IOE survey once again indicate the magnitude of the phenomenon and the weight carried by the various migratory projects: (1) married female household heads who migrate alone, leaving their husband or partner and children behind in the Dominican Republic; (2) widowed female household heads, single mothers, and divorced or separated women who provide for single-parent transnational households; and (3) single women with no dependants who mainly have individual motives for migrating. Thirty-six percent of the Dominican domestic-service workers were single, while 20 percent had a partner in the country of origin (married household heads), and 16 percent were widowed, separated, or divorced (single-parent household heads). Unmarried stable couples who choose to live together is common practice in the Dominican Republic, which also has high numbers of single mothers. Considering the high percentage of respondents with children in the country of origin (75 percent), it can be assumed that a large number of those who claimed to be single also had children or dependants in the country of origin and were heads of single-parent households or responsible for other members of their family (Colectivo IOE 2001). As a result, in many instances single status included not only individual but also family strategies.

Married Female Household Heads
For the women who leave their husbands and children behind in the country of origin, migration is a family strategy that affects the whole household and that may respond to a range of projects, such as survival, the children's education, or an increase in the family's standard of living and socioeconomic status. The decision to migrate may be adopted by the wife, the husband, or both. These women are motivated principally by the desire to save as much money as possible to enable them to return to the country of origin at the earliest opportunity. Their insertion into the Spanish labor market as live-in domestic workers allows them to achieve this objective.

One of the principal migratory goals of the women we interviewed, in addition to supporting the family, was to build a house or set up a small business in Dominican Republic.

The women who opt to migrate alone, leaving behind husbands and children, become the heads of the transnational household because of the importance of the money they send to support the family members who remain in the country of origin. The children stay with their grandparents or father but are normally looked after by a female family member such as an older sister, aunt, or sister-in-law. Some Dominican women even hire another woman to look after their children. The testimony of some respondents leads me to think that the lack of paternal responsibility that is characteristic of Dominican society causes these women to delegate less to their husbands when it comes to caring for the children. They also tend to set up strategies to control their husbands' behavior, normally through family networks, as one Dominican woman noted in an interview conducted in 1997:

> My husband is back there with the children, and there's someone to look after them, but I'm lucky because our house is next door to my mother's; he can't do anything he shouldn't. He's closely watched, and he'd have to go a long way to do it.

In recent years, there has been a growing trend toward family reunion in which the women are joined in Spain by their husbands and children. The arrival of the family implies a series of additional expenses for the pioneering female immigrant. She must finance the accommodation and maintenance of her children and husband, who in the beginning may encounter difficulties in finding stable employment. This is one of the reasons, as we have seen, that transnational households continue to constitute a major feature of immigration among Dominican domestic-service workers in Spain.

Widowed, Separated, Divorced, and Single-Mother Household Heads

As a result of the high separation and divorce rates in the Dominican Republic, plus the general lack of marital stability and men's frequent abandonment of the home, women are often the principal breadwinners within the family unit. Those respondents and members of the discussion groups who were separated or divorced prior to migrating indicated that, following the separation and in the light of paternal lack of responsibility, they were obliged to taken on sole responsibility for supporting the family. The need to bring up the children turns migration into a survival strategy for the single-parent household, as women in the 1997 discussion group highlighted:

> You know what Dominican fathers are like; they leave you and don't want anything to do with their children.

> I got divorced from my first husband, and I have three children, but it's as if their father had died.

> I used to have a shop over there, selling clothes and food. . . . When I came here I just left the stock, the food, and the clothes. . . . Why did I come? Because my pig of a husband did the dirty on me. . . . I didn't come here to get a house, or furniture, or heating. I didn't come for the money. I came here because of a dirty trick, and I said to myself, I'm not going to get sent to prison. . . . It's not worth it. If I was going to kill one of them, it would be him, not her.

Divorced, widowed, separated, and single-parent female migrants may also become pioneers in family migration. There has also been a growing tendency for separated or divorced Dominican women to bring their children or other family members to Spain. Particularly worthy of mention is the fact that the arrival of the eldest daughters and their integration into the labor market turns them into active members of the household and perpetuates the female migratory chains.

Dominican Migration to Spain as an
Individual Social-Mobility Strategy

An individual social-mobility strategy may be directed at either the social space of origin or the receiving society. Generally, this individual strategy occurs among unmarried women with no dependent family members in the country of origin and whose decision to migrate is motivated by a desire for "personal improvement." As in the previous case, these projects may include a strategy aimed at obtaining material goods or assets (savings, a house, consumer goods) or intangible benefits. This latter strategy is normally motivated by the desire to acquire the education and skills in Spain that will lead to socio-professional progress. Other projects also include the search for "female independence" both in economic terms and in access to public space and decision making; as a means of escape from social control or personal conflict, violence in the family, or an emotional problem caused by a failed love affair; or the desire for new experiences and "adventures."

However, real-life situations often fail to fit neatly into the analytical categories of family and individual strategies, and a combination of the two is not uncommon. Many unmarried women with individual social-mobility projects also consider the possibility of contributing to the social and financial advancement of their family members in the country of origin. Likewise, several of the married, separated, divorced, widowed, and single-mother respondents included an individual component in their family strategies. For some, migration was the result of marital conflict, a search for financial independence, or the desire to have a greater say in family decisions, while for others, migration combined the family project of providing younger brothers and sisters with an education with the goal of building their own homes, as a woman with a husband and children in the Dominican Republic said in 1997:

I know there are lots of people who are much worse off than I am, because I can stay here and make my way, but I also wanted to travel, to get to know another country, to think of myself for once. My whole life was centered on my husband and two children. I never thought of myself. . . . My parents don't have much money, but they live well. I wanted to become independent from my parents, because when I was around them I used to waste money. If I spent all my money, I knew my father would be there with more. I wanted to find out for myself, not to depend on him.

Indeed, for some of the Dominican women we spoke to, leaving the country represented a liberating strategy based on the gradual acquisition of greater authority within the family. Rather than being a mere strategy for survival, migration may in fact be deeply rooted in this type of social factor. Migrating to acquire economic resources is a means of becoming independent from the male spouse, conferring greater autonomy and decision-making capacity on the woman in the transnational household. This turns the migratory process into a way to escape from marital dependence networks, because it means "I am in control of my life; I can live with or without my husband," as one Dominican participant in the 1997 discussion group said. Migration is therefore seen as an exercise in autonomy, in women's independence:

What I want to do now is work in order to save up, to have enough money to go and say to him, "Here I am; are you ready to accept what I say? If you're not, then you can just clear off and leave me with my children." What I really want is to go back with enough money . . . to be able to say to him, I'm my own person. The reason I came here was because I was dependent on my husband.

From Imaginary Projects to Real Social Mobility Trajectories

Having established the family and individual social aspirations of the respondents, I will now discuss the ways in which immigrant women implement their upward social-mobility strategies.

Debt: The First Obstacle in the Race to Social Mobility

The first stage in the migratory project and the corresponding individual or family social-mobility strategy involves acquiring the financial resources necessary for the journey. Only rarely do the immigrants possess sufficient financial resources of their own, and several channels are open to migrants to obtain the amount required. The most traditional methods of obtaining the money is through a mortgage or bank loan or by borrowing the money from a relative, a friend, or other migrants who have been in Spain for some time or from third parties involved in immigrant trafficking (such as private money lenders). The Dominican women we spoke to during the 1992 fieldwork, many of whom came from the southeastern Dominican Republic, frequently resorted to the practice of mortgaging a house (Oso Casas and Machín Herranz 1993).

The corresponding debt frequently constitutes the first obstacle in an immigrant's social-mobility trajectory. The responsibility for repaying the debt places migrants in a particularly vulnerable position, and they will consequently be prepared to accept situations of marginalization and abuse to achieve their objectives, as any failure would affect the third parties who have invested financially in the project. Beyond the will of the individual, micro-structural and macro-structural factors, including migratory policies and the situation of the labor market, may distort the strategies. For example, before Spain established visa requirements for Dominican citizens entering the country in September 1993, Dominicans were allowed entry into Spain as tourists for a maximum of three months. In 1992, however, Dominican women were frequently refused entry and were returned to the Dominican Republic.[6] This resulted in a need to reorient initial strategies to finance a second journey, which doubled the size of the debt and could lead to a family's financial ruin, thereby turning a strategy for upward social mobility into a trajectory of downward mobility. In addition, interest rates on the debt increased, so that the women who had been expelled actually added to the size of the debt. This led to a distortion of the initial objectives, the result of macro-structural factors such as a restrictive migratory policy, or of micro-structural factors caused by the arbitrary decision of an immigration officer at a border control. Other unexpected situations, such as illness or death, can also lead to the abandonment of the migratory project and have the opposite effect from that initially planned. The murder of the Dominican Lucrecia Pérez in Madrid in 1992 and its racist overtones highlighted how the migratory strategy for upward social mobility can have the opposite effect in its most extreme form: the death of the immigrant and the financial ruin of the family in the country of origin, who are forced to accept responsibility for an unpaid debt. As one participant said in a discussion group with four Dominican men:

It takes two years' work to pay off the debt for coming over here, and I got sent back once, so you can just imagine. The thing is that if you take that long to pay it off, the price of money goes up, sale and resale. It's like the hen that lays an egg: the chicken hatches, and it's a female like the hen, so it goes on and on, and there are more [chickens]. As time goes on, the interest becomes bigger than the initial capital, which just grows and grows. If you have a debt and you get stopped at Barajas airport and sent back, just imagine, if you owed 50,000 pesos, then it doubles to 100,000. You have to put up some kind of property as a guarantee before they'll lend you anything, and if you don't repay the debt within a certain amount of time, then the property is handed over to the investor. (Fieldwork by Oso Casas and Machín Herranz; some results of this fieldwork were published in Oso Casas and Machín Herranz 1993.)

Migration is therefore a risk that migrants are forced to take to achieve their desired goals, thereby reinforcing the strategic component of the migratory project. The idea of "sacrifice" to obtain future benefits forms a key part of this social strategy. And the larger the family component of the migratory project, the greater the sacrifice. For those whose migratory strategy is based on individual objectives, the risk is lower in that it essentially affects only the migrant and therefore does not place the financial future of a whole family in jeopardy. The negative impact of failure and the sense of vulnerability that surrounds the idea of "sacrifice" will be reduced if the number of people involved in the family migratory project and the financial liability to third parties or financial institutions are kept to a minimum.

Strategies and Real Trajectories for Social Mobility in the Receiving Social Space

Occupational Strategies

As I have indicated, insertion into the Madrid labor market tends to imply downward social mobility compared with the socio-professional status held by Dominican women in the social space of origin. This is due to the fact that the opportunities for female immigrants in the labor market tend to be limited to occupations that are little valued by society, such as domestic service.

Domestic service did not form part of the migratory project of many of the qualified immigrant women we interviewed. Originally they aspired to practice their professions in Spain. Those with higher levels of education saw domestic service as a merely temporary occupation, part of the "sacrifice" required by any social strategy, and as a means of bridging the gap between the present and future employment in the professional world. However, these expectations of social mobility are frequently thwarted in the receiving society. Indeed, only rarely were our respondents able to undertake a process of labor mobility in Spain, moving from domestic service to other, more socially valued occupations. Once more, factors beyond the control of the social actor constitute an impediment to attaining initial strategies.

Analysis of social-security registers (the difference between initial and current contributions) shows whether a worker has changed activity at least once since he or she registered with the social-security system. The data indicate that Dominican workers, together with Ecuadorians and, to a lesser degree, Filipinos and Colombians, rank at the bottom of the list of nationalities in Spain that have abandoned domestic service (85 percent of the Dominicans remained in domestic service, compared with 88 percent of the Ecuadorians, 82 percent of the Filipinos, and 83 percent of the Colombians). These figures are logical in the cases of Ecuadorian and Colombian workers if one considers that they constitute relatively recent migratory flows and that domestic service is the most easily accessible labor niche during the initial stages of the migratory cycle. However, it cannot be argued that those migrating from the Philippines and the Dominican Republic are new arrivals; instead, they constitute groups whose labor strategy takes place within the domestic-service sector (Colectivo IOE 2001: 258). Consequently, 90 percent of the Dominican domestic-service workers interviewed by the Colectivo IOE have been employed only in this sector, proof of their low levels of socio-professional mobility. In addition, the Dominicans, together with the Filipinos, are the group with the longest-standing tradition in the domestic-service sector (Colectivo IOE 2001: 293).

A series of structural mechanisms determine the insertion of female Dominicans into the lowest occupations on the social scale, such as domestic service. Consequently, the way to achieve upward social mobility in the labor market tends to come from moving from live-in to live-out domestic service. Generally, immigrant women indicate that live-in employment implies the greatest degree of domination and exploitation by employers. All of our respondents rejected this labor option, even though for some immigrants it offers advantages, which frequently results in their accepting live-in work despite the difficult conditions. Curiously, although Dominican immigration has been going on for far longer than other migratory flows, the number of Dominican domestic-service workers who have moved from live-in to live-out positions is surprisingly low. Only 25 percent of the Dominicans interviewed by the Colectivo IOE had changed from live-in to live-out domestic service, and 44 percent of respondents had only ever worked in live-in domestic service (Colectivo IOE 2001: 296). As one woman who had been a teacher in the Dominican Republic but was working in domestic service in Spain told the discussion group for Dominican women in 1997:

I took my letter of recommendation from the school I used to work at and my [curriculum vitae] to a school. They told me I needed papers and that I would have to do another course in education if I wanted to teach. I wasn't prepared to work just to spend it all at university.

The main advantage offered by live-in domestic service is the increased capacity to save money. Board and lodging are provided, which enables the workers to send the whole of their salaries to their country of origin. The live-in option is therefore an excellent alternative for women with families or with debt that requires repayment. It is also the best mechanism for rapid insertion into the receiving society for lone women or pioneers in the family migratory chain. Because of the increased capacity to save and send money back to the country of origin, it is the type of employment best suited to the transnational household.

Live-out domestic workers enjoy greater independence, a clear division between private and working life, longer leisure hours, and less paternalistic and dominant relations between employer and employee. Yet on the downside, it also involves greater living expenses, thereby reducing the capacity to save. Indeed, there tends to be little difference between the wages paid to live-in and live-out domestic workers; the difference lies in the fact that the former have fewer living expenses. It is also more difficult to obtain the corresponding work and residence permits, particularly when working by the hour. Live-out domestic service paid by the hour is attractive from a financial perspective, but it is more tiring and can complicate the immigrant's legal situation. As a result, the women who opt to work in live-out domestic service tend to be those who need a certain degree of freedom and who are under less pressure to save and repay a debt; women in search of a certain degree of independence; and women whose families also reside in Spain.

Many female Dominican immigrants use live-in domestic service as a temporary solution or as a springboard toward another type of employment. They also use live-in domestic service as an initial insertion strategy until they are able to save up a certain amount of money or until their family members arrive. Moving from live-in to live-out domestic service is therefore a means of occupational mobility employed by female Dominican immigrants in Spain. That said, in recent years we have seen rapid growth in the number of ethnic businesses, some of which are owned by Dominican women, including telephone booths, money-transfer services, bars or restaurants selling Dominican specialties, food stores, and hairdressing salons offering special services. These businesses have enabled some Dominican women to abandon domestic service and move upward into other areas of employment, specifically toward ethnic businesses.[7]

Educational Strategies

For Dominican women whose migratory project includes an intangible social mobility-strategy (education or training) in the receiving social space, additional obstacles can stand in the way of upward movement. As we have seen, these projects are usually conceived by young single women whose migratory project is motivated by an individual strategy or by those who combine the quest for family social mobility with a personal goal of upward mobility in the receiving context (a joint family and individual strategy). For the majority of our respondents, factors beyond their control blocked their aspirations for upward social mobility through education. To meet financial needs to survive in Spain, most needed to join the labor market, which, as indicated, tends to be restricted to domestic service, and working conditions in that sector make it difficult to pursue other employment and training. The immigrants are forced to dedicate the majority of their time to their work. Even regrouped young daughters who receive financial support from their mothers, the migratory pioneers established in Spain, may encounter difficulties in carrying out educational projects for social mobility. Additional factors such as their legal position, the validation of diplomas, and so on come into play, as one woman noted in the 1997 discussion group:

> When I first came here I left behind two single daughters. A year later the eldest got married, but the other one was still single, and it bothered me, so I sent for her. I would never have done it if I'd known what was going to happen, because before coming over my youngest was planning to go to university, and that's why I sent for her, not to work, but it was impossible here. My daughter has been here all these years and has ended up without an education . . . because she didn't have a residence permit, and they couldn't validate her studies. My daughter was really smart in Santo Domingo, intelligent and studious, she never wasted a year! Now I'm always saying to myself, I should have stayed there instead of coming to Spain.

The position in the life cycle of many of the Dominican women who migrate with an educational project—namely, young single women—means that finding a partner (regardless of whether they choose to marry) often leads to maternity, which in turn brings a restructuring of their initial objectives. The objectives become family-motivated, directed at supporting and educating the young child. In the case of women whose initial strategy already combined a family-based strategy with an individual educational project, achieving the desired objective is even harder, because family responsibilities often involve "sacrificing" personal goals. One Dominican woman who had migrated while single told the 1997 discussion group:

> I came because my mother sent for me. She came over first, and I stayed behind to look after my brothers and sisters and also to study. During

the first few months, I worked to help my mother out, and at the same time I kept control over my brothers and sisters. But of course, in the end I had to choose between my job and my studies. . . . I started a course in secretarial studies at an academy, but because I was paying for it out of my wages, there wasn't enough money, and I had to give up my studies and keep working.

Once again, it can be seen how a series of determining factors regarding women's insertion into the domestic labor market, their position in the life cycle, family economic needs, and legal issues (residence permits and validation of qualifications) thwart immigrants' educational social-mobility strategies in the receiving social space. The receiving society exerts a series of pressure mechanisms designed to limit the social mobility of Dominican female workers in Spain, channeling them toward the type of employment that is least socially valued in Spain and blocking their educational strategies for upward social mobility. Another woman told the discussion group:

I have no grievances with the Spanish, but I do complain about the system that exists for immigrants in Spain. Why? Because everything's so complicated, they even make it difficult for you to set up your own business. If you want to become an ideal citizen, study for a degree, work, you'll find it impossible. The only option open is going to work in someone's home.

Residential and Marital Strategies

In view of the limited opportunities for socio-professional and educational upward mobility, the only possibilities for improvement left open to female Dominican immigrants in Madrid are often ethnic businesses or residential or marital social-mobility strategies. The most common residential strategy consists of renting a shared flat, which is normally used as the principal home, combined with employment in live-out domestic service, or in the case of live-in domestic workers sharing a flat as a second home for their days off. Renting a flat gives the immigrants greater freedom and their own personal space. Although it is perceived as a strategy for upward social mobility for female Dominican immigrants in the receiving society, renting a flat may also lead to a reduction in their capacity for saving, and thus for upward mobility, in the social space of origin. As a result, the decision to adopt a residential strategy for social mobility will depend on whether priority is given to social mobility in the receiving society or in the country of origin. Single women in search of greater independence and whose migratory project is more individually motivated are therefore more willing to move to live-out domestic work and to set up home in a rented flat, even though this may reduce their capacity to save money, while those with greater family responsibilities in the Dominican Republic or with larger financial liabilities (such as debts) will remain in live-in domestic service, despite the major personal sacrifice required. They will only opt to rent a flat as a second home or to use as a meeting place on days off.

Marital strategies are another option employed by female Dominican immigrants as a means of improving their situation in the receiving social space. Nevertheless, and depending on the type of marriage, this strategy may or may not lead to a real upward social trajectory. Marriage to a Spaniard with a certain degree of purchasing power tends to favor the upward social mobility of Dominican women in Spain from the moment they begin to benefit from their husbands' financial and relational support (i.e., access to the social networks of the autochthonous population). In this case, the marital strategy can provide women with the opportunity to regroup their children and to leave live-in domestic service. It can also contribute to an increase in the amount of money transferred to the country of origin. In addition, marriage to a Spaniard can make it easier for immigrant women to set up their own businesses or buy their own homes, as it can give them greater access to bank credit facilities and administrative procedures.

Strategies and Real Trajectories for Social Mobility in the Social Space of Origin

The mobility strategy directed at family members in the social space of origin tends initially to be combined with a short-term migratory project aimed at saving as much as possible in Spain, with minimum outlay. Achieving these strategic family goals requires insertion into the labor market as a live-in domestic worker. However, a number of mechanisms also exist that may block the social-mobility project directed at the country of origin. The first of these is the risk the immigrant runs of being expelled by the Spanish authorities. The second may be caused by a period of unemployment, which will affect the immigrant's capacity to save money. The third of involves irregularities in the use of the money transfers by the recipient family members, such as husbands spending the money sent from Spain in ways that directly counter the objectives established by their wives (in extreme cases, gambling or going out with other women), or other family members taking the family money for personal use. Our female Dominican informants frequently referred to such irregularities. Such irregularities can lead to the extension of the migratory project to guarantee that the initial objectives are achieved; it can also bring about a reorientation of the initial strategies and the decision to transfer the money to other family members.

The fact that female immigrants are unable to control the real use to which their money transfers are put can block, and may even reverse, their mobility strategies in the society of origin. On occasion, money sent home that was designated to pay for child care was used for purposes, which resulted in downward social mobility for the migrant's children, who suffered the effects of the loss of child care and even of food following their mother's departure. Several informants also referred to the negative impact that the mother's absence may have on the children's education. Consequently, a whole series of micro-structural factors, including decisions made by the recipients of money transfers, and of macro-structural elements such as unemployment or being refused access at the border can block the initially established strategies or even produce the opposite effect. As a result, aspirations for social mobility may in actual fact lead to downward mobility in the society of origin for some members of the household, as women in the 1997 discussion group explained:

> I started off sending the money to my husband and do you know what he used to do? . . . He'd take the money and go after some other woman. . . . When I went back, my fifteen-year-old was as thin as a rake. He said to me, "Mom, the only thing I get to eat is spaghetti, and I can't take it any more, so they give me eggs." And here I was, sending my money back and keeping nothing for myself. . . . I took my kid to my brother's house. . . . I'd sent 16,000 pesos [460 U.S. dollars] back to Santo Domingo in three months.

> I sent some money back to buy some things over there, and do you know what my daughter did? She took the money, bought some of the things I'd told her and used the rest to buy a ticket to Puerto Rico.

The family members who receive the money transfers are the main beneficiaries of the migration process while the woman remains in domestic service in Spain. As can be observed, the family strategy implies a contradiction between those who benefit and those who suffer as a result of downward social-mobility processes. Women are the actors in the family strategy, and for them migration frequently implies a drop in socio-professional status in the receiving society, as well as difficulties in integrating into Spanish society, while other family members experience upward mobility in the social space of origin. As a result, instead of "finding a better life," female immigrants working in domestic service in Spain are forced to observe from a distance how the social position of their dependent family members—particularly the beneficiaries of the money transfers—improves in the country of origin.

Achieving the social-mobility goals established in the country of origin requires a great degree of sacrifice on the part of the immigrant, whose opportunities for social improvement in the receiving context are severely limited. The need to save up and send back as much money as possible will determine the woman's decision to join the live-in domestic-service sector and to endure poor working conditions and domination by her employer. She becomes vulnerable and is forced to cope with situations of marginalization, because losing her job would reduce the money transfers. Her opportunities to integrate into Spanish society and improve her social position by renting a flat are also limited, because it reduces her capacity to save money. Consequently, the female immigrant with major financial burdens in the Dominican Republic tends to sacrifice her personal standard of living in the receiving society to benefit the family members who will be receiving the money transfers. Migration as a family strategy therefore often leads to conflict, as the financial investments do not have an equal impact on the various members of the transnational household.

Conclusions

Analysis of the social-mobility strategies of female Dominican household heads in the receiving society and the social space of origin reveals a series of points. First, rather than being exclusively oriented toward the individual, immigrants' strategies often extend to family projects and have a considerable imaginary element, which contradicts the neoclassical vision of migration centered on the rationality of the individual. Micro- and macro-structural factors often block established goals or reverse immigrants' aspirations. Consequently, objectives focused on upward social mobility are often thwarted and may even turn into downward social trajectories for foreign workers or their families. The receiving society has a series of mechanisms that block strategies for socio-professional and educational development of immigrants in Spain.

Projects for social improvement directed at the Dominican Republic may also be thwarted by personal factors, such as spending decisions made by recipients of money transfers, or structural factors such as migratory policies and unemployment. Migration, initially conceived as a short-term project, may be extended and redirected. Consequently, rather invoking an idea of rationality, the notion of a migration "strategy" tends frequently to encompass contradictory situations. The social-mobility project in the country of origin tends to be at odds with the female Dominican immigrant's opportunities for integration and upward social mobility in Spain. If she wishes to improve her living conditions—for instance, by renting a flat or working in live-out domestic service—she will be forced to reduce her saving capacity and send less money back to the country of origin. And not all family members involved in a woman's migratory strategy benefit from upward social mobility to the same degree. The migrants may sacrifice their own social status by taking up work in the Spanish domestic-service sector so that other members of the transnational household, such as husbands, children, and parents, can benefit from upward social mobility at home.

Notes

1. The analytical synopsis of social-mobility strategies comparing female immigration trends in Spain among various nationalities is in Oso 2002. The analysis of female migration with reference to social-mobility strategies is the basis of Oso 2001.

2. Although this research also included a number of interviews with female Dominican sex workers, their social reality makes them worthy of specific consideration. In this chapter, I have opted to focus exclusively on Dominican domestic workers in Spain.

3. *Encuesta de Población Activa,* Instituto Nacional de Estadística, Madrid, 2006.

4. Due to the extraordinary regularization processes established by the Spanish government, no quotas were fixed for 1996, 2000, and 2001.

5. The survey carried out by Colectivo IOE shows that 37 percent of Dominican domestic-service workers did not engage in paid employment in their countries; 21 percent were domestic workers; 12 percent were administrative workers; and 10 percent worked in the retail trade (Colectivo IOE 2001: 289).

6. According to a Ministerial Order dated February 22, 1989 (*Official Spanish Gazette,* March 6, 1989), foreigners who wish to enter Spain are obliged to have sufficient financial resources to enable them to live in the country. Article 2.3 of the Ministerial Order authorizes immigration officers at Spanish border controls to demand proof of financial resources. If a foreigner appears not to possess such resources, he or she can be refused entry into Spain. Article 4.1 of the same order specifies that these controls are to be directed mainly at citizens of those countries that statistically have a greater tendency to engage in illegal immigration to Spain. In addition, the immigration officer at the border control has no liability for these expulsions, as he or she is not required to sign written confirmation of a decision communicated verbally.

7. A large percentage of Dominican immigrants have curly hair. Dominican women are fond of straightening their hair, which requires specific treatments using creams (some of which have to be imported) that generally are not available in Spanish hairdressing salons. Hairdressing is therefore one of the most popular types of businesses owned by Dominicans.

References

Anuario estadístico de extranjería. 1993. Madrid: Ministerio del Interior.
Anuario estadístico de extranjería. 1995. Madrid: Ministerio del Interior.
Anuario estadístico de extranjería. 1999. Madrid: Ministerio del Interior.
Colectivo IOE. 2001. *Mujer, inmigración y trabajo.* Madrid: Instituto de Mayores y Servicios Sociales, Ministerio de Trabajo y Asuntos Sociales.

Gregorio Gil, Carmen. 1998. *La migración femenina y su impacto en las relacions de género.* Madrid: Narcea.

Gresle, François, Michel Panoff, Michel Perrin, and Pierre Tripier. 1994. *Dictionnaire des sciences humaines.* Paris: Nathan.

Izquierdo Escribano, Antonio. 2000. "Semblanza de las mujeres extranjeras que se hallan en España en situación irregular." In *Mujeres inmigrantes en la irregularidad, pobreza, marginación laboral y prostitución,* ed. Antonio Izquierdo Escribano. Madrid: Instituto de la Mujer, Informe Inédito de Investigación.

Oso, Laura. 1998. *La migración hacia España de mujeres jefas de hogar.* Madrid: Instituto de la Mujer.

Oso, Laura. 2000. "Estrategias migratorias y de movilidad social de las mujeres inmigrantes en situación irregular: Servicio doméstico y prostitución." In *Mujeres inmigrantes en la irregularidad, pobreza, marginación laboral y prostitución,* unpublished research report, ed. Antonio Izquierdo Escribano. Madrid: Instituto de la Mujer, Informe Inédito de Investigación.

Oso, Laura. 2001. "Domestiques, concierges et prostituées: Migration et mobilité sociale des femmes immigrées, espagnoles à Paris, équatoriennes et colombiennes en Espagne." Ph.D. diss., Institut d'Etudes du Developpement Economique et Social, Université de Paris I—Panthéon Sorbonne.

Oso, Laura. 2002. "Stratégies de mobilité sociale des domestiques immigrées en Espagne." *Revue Tiers Monde* 43, no. 170 (April–June): 287–305.

Oso, Laura, ed. 2003. "El empresariado étnico como una estrategia de movilidad social para las mujeres inmigrantes." Instituto de la Mujer, Madrid.

Oso Casas, Laura. 1997. "Les effets de la migration sur le statut socio-économique et sur le rôle des femmes." Pp. 87–144 in *Face aux changements, les femmes du Sud,* ed. Jeanne Bisilliat. Paris: L'Harmattan.

Oso Casas, Laura, and S. Machín Herranz. 1993. "Choque de culturas: El caso de la inmigración dominicana en la Comunidad Autónoma de Madrid." *Sociedad y Utopía,* no. 1: 193–199.

Sorokin, Pitirim A. 1964. *Social and Cultural Mobility.* New York: Free Press.

10

Identity and Kinship

Caribbean Transnational Narratives

MARY CHAMBERLAIN

Introduction

The idea of transnationality as a feature of Caribbean families is not, of course, new. Rosina Brodber-Wiltshire (1986) first coined the term—the transnational family—referring to those bifurcated networks which were a feature of Jamaican/North American families, and has since been remarked upon by observers based both in the Caribbean and in North America, notably in the work on Caribbean migrants in New York by Constance Sutton and Susan Makiesky-Barrow (1994); Paula Aymer (1997); Linda Basch, Nina Glick Schiller, and Christine Szanton Blanc (with their remarkable *Nations Unbound* [1994]); Nina Glick Schiller and Georges Fouron (with their equally remarkable *Georges Woke Up Laughing* [2001]). Denis Conway (1988); Karen Fog Olwig (1993); and Elizabeth Thomas-Hope (1992), to name a few. In the United Kingdom, however, the focus on transnationalism is more recent, not least because Caribbean migration to Britain is itself more recent than that to North America, and scholars are only now beginning to emerge out of the mold of the race-relations approach, which dominated much academic thinking, to address this feature of migratory behavior.[1] Harry Goulbourne (1999) has already drawn attention to it in his contribution to *Changing Britain: Families and Households in the 1990s,* as well as, most recently, in his *Caribbean Transnational Experience* (Goulbourne 2002). My own work (Chamberlain 1997) has also drawn attention to transnationalism as a feature of Caribbean families (notably, those of

Barbados), as has the work by Paul Thompson and Elaine Bauer (2001) on Jamaican families.

This contribution, then, is not offering new insights into either migration or transnationalism. Instead, it will explore the narratives of transnational families—the way transnational peoples describe their lives—as a way to understand the continuing transnational linkages between kin. It will argue that the similarities and repetitions in the accounts of family and migration conform to, and reinforce, "cultural templates": patterns of response through which accounts may be stereotyped, and in which values and priorities are encoded, and transmitted. As such, they provide important clues in understanding the nature and meaning of Caribbean transnational family life.

Migration History and Culture

The contemporary Caribbean was built on waves of free and enforced migrations—to, within, and beyond the region. From the seventeenth century until the twentieth century, the importation of labor continued steadily. A conservative estimate suggests that between the seventeenth century and the nineteenth century,[2] 15 million Africans arrived in the New World, the majority of them destined for the British West Indies (Sheridan 1994 [1974]). This importation was in addition to the Europeans who came in the same period as indentured servants, plantation owners, workers, merchants, professionals, and political prisoners. Between 1838 and 1918, 536,310 immigrants from India and China arrived in the British West Indies (principally in British Guiana, Trinidad, and Jamaica; Look Lai 1993), their numbers augmented by smaller migrations by free and liberated Africans, Portuguese and other Europeans, Syrians, Jews, and Lebanese. In addition, from 1838, and full emancipation, ex-slaves migrated within the region principally, but not exclusively, from the "old" colonies, such as Barbados or Jamaica, to the "new" colonies of Trinidad and Guiana, while some Asian indentured laborers returned to India or migrated elsewhere in the Caribbean region, and beyond (Laurence 1994; Shepherd 1998).[3] The 1873 Emigration Act in Barbados gives an enticing clue to the scope of nineteenth-century migration, listing Demerara, Dominica, Granada, Nevis, Nickerie, St. Kitts, St. Lucia, St. Vincent, Surinam, Tobago, and Trinidad as migratory destinations, while the 1891 census of Trinidad records that in a population of 208,030, 33,071 were immigrants from the British West Indies, and a further 1,259 were from "foreign West Indies" (Chamberlain 2001: 33).

It was not, however, until the latter part of the nineteenth century that Caribbean migration assumed its more familiar, contemporary character as Caribbeans of all races and ethnicities migrated to North, South, and Central America and, in the latter half of the twentieth century, to Europe (and beyond).

The scale of these various migratory waves—of Africans, Indians, and Chinese— to the Caribbean, and of all within and beyond, has meant that few families have been unaffected by migration, and, as we shall see, most live within kinship networks that would locate themselves within transnational social fields. For instance, approximately 45,000 Jamaicans and 42,000 Barbadians left Barbados for Panama between 1904 and 1914 (Newton 1987 [1984]), although Hilary Beckles (1990) calculates that out-migration to Panama was as high as one in four Barbadians. Many of those who left for Panama migrated onward to Cuba and the United States. Others moved south, to Venezuela, Brazil, and Peru (Johnson 1998). By 1890, there were already 19,979 foreign-born black people in the United States, by far the majority of whom were West Indians, a figure which had risen to 73,808 by 1920 and 98,620 by 1930 (Kasinitz 1992). Yet between 1932 and 1937, more West Indians returned to the Caribbean than migrated to the United States (Kasinitz 1992). After World War II, and particu- larly after the McCarran-Walter Act in the United States in 1952, British West Indians migrated to the United Kingdom. Between 1948 and 1966 (when the Immigration Act in Britain effectively halted Commonwealth immigration) the Caribbean-born population stood at approximately 304,070 (Peach 1991), many of whom had already experienced migration to, for instance, Aruba or Curaçao, or to the United States on the H-2 program, which permitted U.S. farmers to import foreign (mainly Caribbean) workers on temporary contracts during the war. Indeed, the regularity of migration has led many scholars (Chamberlain 1997; Richardson 1983; Thomas-Hope 1992) to argue that the Caribbean is characterized by cultures or traditions of migration which see migration as a goal in itself, as well as a means to individual or familial eco- nomic, educational, or social improvement.

From the beginning, however, a number of characteristics emerged that distinguished Caribbean migration. For the most part, despite poor commu- nications, nineteenth- and twentieth-century migrants maintained close links across the oceans and the generations through letters, remittances and return (Chamberlain 1997; Thomas Hope 1992). As a result, the Caribbean remained a constant feature in the lives of migrants, while for those who remained in the region, migration was seen as a link with "foreign," not a severance from home; an opportunity to extend, not disrupt, the family links. In other words, trans- national activity was built into the fabric of migration.

More recently, the trend to return—first noted for Britain by Ceri Peach (1991) for the 1980s—has continued, and it accelerated in the 1990s (Goul- bourne 2002). Return has renewed links with new generations, which continue to replenish family values, models, and behavior and has enabled continuity across generations between family members in Britain, the Caribbean, and else- where. Moreover, family contact has been facilitated by easier and cheaper communications, enabling relatively frequent, if temporary, visits to the Caribbean, or wherever kin may live (notably, North America) by British-based Caribbeans and their children, visits to England from Caribbean (or American-based) kin, or returned residents, supplemented by regular and frequent telephone contact. In addition, aging parents in the Caribbean have heightened the emotional intensity felt by their children and grandchildren in Britain, giving a fresh urgency to the frequency of contact and visits and the desire to flesh out "roots" for younger British-born generations. Visits home, as one Trinidadian informant described, are "important, to see Mum and Dad regularly . . . [and] because I would like my kids to keep in touch with Trinidad and all the relatives there . . . to appreciate the other part of the culture. . . . I think that makes them a better individual."[4]

Such patterns of migration and return are not, however, without pain and are marked, in both cases, by the absence of an older (grandparent) generation. One returnee's daughter felt that "now she's [mother] gone it's like losing my right arm."[5] Her mother, now settled in Trinidad, justified that "it's not far. It's just an eight hours journey to come, so [she] can always come along, or we can always come across."[6] But families, as we will see, are able to withstand the absence of members. The power of this linkage has roots within the family nexus which has been accommodated to migration, rather than disrupted by it, and should be recognized as a central element of Caribbean family culture.

Family Culture

The family nexus contains features which distinguish it from its European and North American counterparts. Contemporary patterns of marriage and family life emerged during slavery (Besson 2002; Higman 1976) and evolved into a peculiarly *Creole* family formation, with an emphasis on consanguinity, patterns of multiple conjugality, inclusiveness of family membership, importance of kinship networks to provide reciprocal support and hospitality, and reverence for elders and ancestors. Kinship, within this system, recognized relatives who could claim a common ancestor, on both paternal and maternal sides of the family, such that this "unrestricted cognatic/nonunilineal [descent] system . . . maximised forbidden kinship lines and scarce land rights" (Besson 2002: 30). It was a system far removed from the European ideal and model which prioritized the conjugal union as the heart of the family.

The descent system and the variety of conjugal systems and patterns found even within a single family network has resulted in a complex web of kin in which notions of "step" and "half" families are not used to describe kin in the West Indies: all are embraced as "full" kin, and relatives from both the paternal and maternal line are equally included, as well as, in many cases, "godparents" and close family friends. As one informant described, "I know my family's not just my brothers and sisters." As we shall see, there was a continuity of family values across all generations, where loyalty and support, obligation and responsibility, overrode the logistics of living arrangements. These were values prided in and of themselves; they also provided practical support. "If," as Jerry (who figures in the second case study) argued, "there is a support network that is needed, you can provide it with knowing who your family members are, so that not only you can provide help, but they can help you as well."[7]

A clue to the power of families as membership support and in the maintenance of transnational ties rests, however, in the narratives and language used by family members to describe themselves and their relationships with kin. This language is couched in a celebratory, rather than problematic, rhetoric (Sutton 2002), in which can be encoded prescriptions for appropriate and approved behavior (Chamberlain 2000). Thus, the rhetoric of the family emphasizes concepts such as closeness, lovingness, and support; applies descriptions of strength and hard work, in particular, to older family members; and embraces an expansiveness of, and knowledge about, kin. Thus, many informants could recall details of family circumstances for all kin, including those distanced genealogically, generationally, or geographically. Such recall confirmed the strength of family linkages and a resilience to breakup or estrangement through migration which might hitherto have been expected to disrupt such patterns. Equally, family narratives stressed the unity of the family nexus, and the pride attached to this. As one young informant commented, "The sense of family, the sense of unity, was much stronger [than English families]. . . . I'm actually really proud of Caribbean families; that was something that we will always retain."[8]

Migration may have been an ancillary factor in the emphasis throughout the Caribbean on kin, reinforced by practices of co-parenting, fostering, or "child shifting" (typically by grandparents or aunts), and by the patterns of migration which relied on kin network for settlement. Family and kinship, in turn, became a metaphor for, and an organizing principle of, social behavior. Phrases such as living "like family," friendships "like sisters," and support "like brothers" indicate the importance of such roles in the early stages of migration, while the use of these similes indicates the vitality of family models, and in particular that of sibling relationships, in the shaping of networks (Chamberlain 1999). "We help each other out" was a common comment; we "trust." Networks provided accommodation and work, companionship and support (including domestic help such as childcare), and financial assistance and replicated a pattern of neighborhood family identified from their childhoods. The physical environment may have changed, but the cultural structures for survival migrated with the migrants. In much the same way, David Owen (1995) indicates that despite the dispersal of black communities in British cities, there remain significant concentrations. Within that, populations from the different islands continue to be concentrated in particular boroughs or areas. The distribution of the Black–Other ethnic group is similar to that of Caribbean-born people, suggesting strongly that migrant children continue to live close to, or even with, parents and other kin and in areas which contain facilities (such as shops, community centers, supplementary schools, churches, restaurants, and travel agencies) which support the Caribbean and Black–Other community. As Jerry described it, "Instinctively we didn't want to go too far away from each other. . . . You're all there, within reach of each other. . . . It's as if we're carrying on a tradition that we're not even fully aware of."[9]

The following case studies explore how two families (both originating in Jamaica) accommodate and utilize their transnational family networks, and participate in a shared rhetoric of belonging and reciprocity.

Family 1

The first family migrated from Jamaica to Britain during the 1950s and 1960s. Lloyd migrated first in 1957 and was "received" into Britain by his wife's cousin. Two years later, he was joined by his wife, Hyacinth, who left their five children in Jamaica under the care of her sister and other kin. In time, those five children were brought over to join their parents and two more British-born siblings. Lloyd's migration to Britain paralleled other family members who migrated to the United States, Canada, and, unusually, Japan.

Hyacinth's mother, Lucretia, had married twice; she had four children from the first marriage, and two from her second. Hyacinth and her brother were from the second marriage, but their father died when she was two. Lucretia's first husband, a Chinese man (from China), had also died when his children were small. Lucretia supported all of her children from her earnings as a laundress and lived close to her mother (Hyacinth's grandmother) and her mother's six uncles and aunts (another uncle had migrated to Panama). This grandmother was a "beauty" who

> used to love me so much and love all the grandchildren. She would hold at least six, seven, eight of us on her knees. She used to be so good . . . she used to be so sweet. Everybody say I look like her sometimes. But her hair was like satin. Like satin. When you plait her hair, it just flicks up, soft, soft soft.[10]

Hyacinth's maternal grandfather died when she was small, although she remembers that he "work hard" and "loved children, love his family."[11] She grew up "very, very, very, very, very, very close" to her siblings,[12] with no distinction made between fathers and, in this case, mixed-race siblings. She remains close to all of the family, "up to the fourth cousin" ("I've got cousins is no different from my sister," she said[13]), despite the fact that most of her siblings and cousins are now dispersed around the world. Indeed, she maintains regular contact with

> all the family, everywhere, everyone ... because the way we grow up, our family was so loving and people know us to be so loving and kind and everything else. Why shouldn't you want to know them?[14]

Leaving her children behind in Jamaica, was, therefore, full of anguish.

> Can you believe it, when I said that I had to leave my children? I went bonkers! I tell you! But I never used to smoke and when I came here, and saw the situation, and it's so cold, and my children left behind. I know that they're well-looked after, but I couldn't bear to know that I have to leave them. And I start smoking. I smoke till I turn stupid. I smoked till all my lips stripped. . . . I was dead. I was gone.[15]

She found work and saved hard and "in no time" had saved sufficient money to bring four of her children to England to join her and her husband and to send a fifth child, the eldest, to cousins in Canada. Her son Jerry was eleven when he joined his parents in 1966. He was six when his mother left, and although he lived with his aunt in a tenement yard in Kingston,

> The extended family that we came from, everybody shared in what we did, you know, we could stay with uncle this or auntie that, or what have you, so everybody had a responsibility to bring up everybody else's children. They weren't restricted to any one particular pair.[16]

The first- and second-hand memories of his grandparents are strong. His paternal grandmother—with whom he lived for a year as a toddler—was, as he recalls, "a very strong woman" and is still in his memory. His paternal grandfather was equally "strong," but whereas his grandmother's "strength" refers in part to her disciplinarian character ("very strict"), that of his grandfather referred to his physical stature and his standing in the local community. Although Jerry never knew his maternal grandparents, from family stories his mother "has taken a lot from her, from the way she's spoken of by other members of the family."[17] In particular, the family legend recalls his grandmother as "such a strong woman. And one of the things she taught her kids was 'Always be there for each other, no matter what.'"[18] Significantly, therefore,

The way that my mother has kept us all together . . . is identical . . . [to the] family unit there [in Jamaica]. . . . That's the same sort of thing that my parents, especially my mother, has tried to maintain. . . . So each of the siblings that's gone off ha[s] . . . kept like the family thing going. . . . It's so much instinctive. . . . We're spiritual people . . . and our history is more of somebody telling you what's happened, and you never forget it. It's not a case of, "Oh, I can't remember." It's there with you all the time. . . . It's sort of passed down, which is good. It's nice because . . . especially living in this country, where there's a lot of pressures . . . especially because we're an ethnic minority, the family unit provides the type of solace, stability, that is needed to go ahead. . . . We're always looking out, or thinking about the other one, or the two that's not here, or the three that's not here. . . . It's as if we're carrying on a tradition that we're not even fully aware of.[19]

As a result, in England, the family members live close to each other in South London.

When Jerry was sixteen, his mother went to the United States to visit her sister-in-law who was looking after three nieces from Jamaica, "keeping those children, school them and everything in America."[20] Hyacinth's mother-in-law, who suffered from diabetes and high blood pressure, was also staying in the United States with this sister. In the course of the visit, the sister-in-law became ill and required hospitalization. Without hesitation, Hyacinth called her husband and informed him that she would be staying. She looked after the children until her sister-in-law was better, then cared for her mother-in-law until her death, then, as her sister-in-law suggested (and with her help), Hyacinth got a job while her husband took care of their children in England. She stayed for three years, sending over money and goods, and had planned to stay long enough to earn the right to live and work in the United States. However, she learned that her sixteen-year-old daughter was pregnant, and Jerry, too, age nineteen, was fathering a child. She returned home immediately "after I spoke my piece, what could I do . . . but love them? Let them know that I'm their grandmother."[21]

Hyacinth did more than love them. She allowed Jerry and his girlfriend to live in her home until they were able to live independently, and helped bring up this grandchild along with her existing—and subsequent—grandchildren. She now has fifteen and has played an active role in their upbringing. "I don't mind at all. . . . If I only have the strength and the help that I need, financially, I don't mind at all. I love it."[22] The help is both practical and symbolic, as she recounts to them stories of Jamaica and their family and acculturates them with their origins and values. As she says, "We are the grandparents; we know we are West Indians. We are not white English, so they have to have a background of their own."[23]

Significantly, however, it was not only Hyacinth who contributed to the care of Simon, Jerry's child. Simon's paternal grandfather was influential in his childhood, as was his maternal grandmother, from St. Vincent, who helped out with his child care, as did Jerry's sisters. "The extended family" as Jerry described "that's been there. You know, if it wasn't my side, it was [my partner's], so, you know, it didn't really matter."[24] Simon, now twenty-two, lives with his maternal grandmother in a neighborhood filled with both maternal and paternal kin ("we're a close knit family," he said[25]) and is as preoccupied with the importance of family as his father and grandmother, traveling back to Jamaica and St. Vincent and to North America to meet relatives. He has inherited a wide kinship network from his father and from his mother—"another family tree. Very big.... I went to Canada to visit my grandfather, my mum's dad, ... and my auntie and uncle."[26] In this, he mirrors his father, who traveled regularly back to Jamaica and who insisted that Simon's mother revisit St. Vincent before he would marry her "to be at peace with herself, settle some of the memories she had from home, instead of just thinking about it, the way I found whatever it was I was looking for at home ... get to know her family ... [and] her father's side of the family."[27] Jerry, however, has three sons, one of whom is an "outside" child. Although Simon is not close to this brother, "He's still my brother.... He's still part of me, he's still blood, at the end of the day, you know."[28]

In this family, the family values, which actively incorporated wider kin within the socialization of children, have been translated across the ocean and inherited through the generations. "What's helped [my sons] more than anything else," Jerry argues, "is this network that we've got, the family network. It's given them stability, because they know they've got us to fall back on, should they fall by the wayside in any way.... Whatever happened to them out there may affect them more than it would have done, had they not had this."[29]

Thus, Lucretia's dictum to stay together has been an ethos inherited across the generations. Or, as Jerry puts it, "I've got a saying: 'Your kids will always be your kids, but you can have an ex-wife and ex-girlfriends.'"[30] More particularly, the importance of the Caribbean, and of the family in the Caribbean, in providing a sense of identity is a further ethos which ran through the generations, and was well articulated by Jerry:

I see myself as a human being first, and as a black person of Afro-Caribbean descent. I've become a British person through rules and regulations, but I can never be English. Not even my sons, who were born here. They might be English on paper, but they will not ... be regarded as such. They will always be Afro-Caribbean, or West Indian. ...

And this is why I'm insistent about them learning about where their parents are from. . . . I always thought that we've got this escape hatch in the back of our minds, those of us who are not born here, where we can always go back to. But those who are born here haven't got that, it's just stories to them, you know. But they're always being portrayed as being from somewhere else. Now, if you keep telling a young black kid that he's a West Indian when he was born here, I mean, how does he feel? What sort of things are happening to his head all his life? To be apart from the society that he's grown up in? . . . The one thing they will feel, having gone back [to the Caribbean] . . . is that they realize, for the first time, that they are part of something . . . part of something else. . . . [The Caribbean] will always be there for them as part of something that is their heritage.[31]

Family 2

Benson was seventeen when he and his siblings migrated from Jamaica to England in 1966 to join his parents. His father (now deceased) also had a number of "outside" children both before and after marriage to Benson's mother, all of whom were integral to Benson's definitions of family. Benson's family, like many in the Caribbean, was built on the migrations of successive generations. His maternal grandfather went to Panama, and then to Cuba (where he died), supporting the family, until his death, on the remittances returned. His father had migrated to the United States prior to migrating to England. Benson has one sister in Jamaica, two sisters in Canada, and a brother in Germany. As a result, transnational kinship was an integral dynamic of this—and other—families.

Benson's father was in England for five years before Benson's mother joined him, leaving the children in Jamaica under the care of her mother, her brother, and a family friend. As with Jerry's family, this was a common pattern of support given to migrants who, in turn, were expected to support the family back home. The family (including the "outside" siblings) lived in close proximity, and the neighborhood provided a context of both support and supervision, and both were implicated necessarily in the transnational endeavor:

In those days . . . you have to respect your elders. If you see somebody coming . . . who is older than you, you had to show respect. You can't do nothing, you know, for them to see, otherwise they might give you a smack, or they might go and tell your parents, then you get another one on top of it! Take, for instance, you see somebody, an adult person . . . and you don't say "Good morning" or "Good afternoon," . . . They'll call you, "Don't you see me?" "Don't you have any manners?"[32]

In time, Benson and his siblings joined their parents in England. Perhaps because part of his childhood was spent apart from his parents (as, indeed, were the childhoods of his own parents), family unity was paramount:

> To me, family is like a religion. . . . You've got that belief . . . which is very important to you, in your life . . . it's something to pass onto the next generation . . . the children . . . see how everyone lives, so obviously they'll emulate them, try and do the same, try and be close knit, all stick together. . . . Blood is thicker than water, so families always come first. . . . We share and share. . . . That's the way I was brought up.[33]

Identity, and family, are of far greater significance to Benson than the accumulation of material wealth or social status. "I'm not that kind of a person."[34] Blood, as he says, is thicker than water, a belief created partly from his upbringing, and partly from his own experience of separation from his parents ("I didn't want that to happen to my children,"[35] and his continuing separation from some of his siblings. He has been married twice and has two children from each marriage. His first wife subsequently had a third child, although she no longer lives with the father of that child. Nevertheless, according to his eldest daughter, Juliette (from the first marriage), Benson does not discriminate between his children and their half-sibling. Equally, Juliette "gets on fine" with her former stepfather. "Something that my dad's always told me, you know, friends are for, like, now, but family's forever. . . . My family's always been important to me, and always will be."[36] Juliette is equally close to her maternal kin, particularly her maternal grandmother, whom she calls "Nan," and her maternal step-grandfather "my Nan's husband is the only grandfather that I know."[37]

This grandfather has family living in America, the Cayman Islands, and the Virgin Islands and "likes to go on holidays, at least once a year, to visit them and keep in contact."[38] It is behavior which Juliette lauds. Equally, she is close to her brother, her half-brother, her two half-sisters, and

> my little brother's father, he's got two daughters as well, two older daughters . . . and my mum said they're my sisters, even though they're half-sisters or whatever, so I've got a very extended family . . . we're very close.[39]

Juliette does not feel disadvantaged by her parent's divorce. On the contrary, her half-brother's father was a constant presence in her childhood, as was her own father, and the reconfiguration of both of her parent's families of creation has extended her own network of step- and half-siblings and their kin. God-parents, and family friends, were also brought into the ambit of "family," repli-cating as far as possible her father's concept of neighborhood family which he cherished from his childhood in Jamaica. It was this aspect of Jamaica which Juliette, on one of her visits to the island, found so appealing. It made her feel

> comfortable. Everybody was so friendly, and they'd walk past you and say "Good morning." The people just don't do that here.... If you walked past them and you said "hello" or "good morning," they'd look at you as if you were crazy. [It was] just the sheer friendliness of it.[40]

As a result, if the opportunity arose, she would settle in Jamaica. "I would. I'd definitely go." Her cousin had already returned a few years ago. In terms of identity, Juliette considers herself both British and Jamaican, although 'the only connection I've got with being British is the fact that I was born here and grew up here, but all of the time [I felt I was] Jamaican."[41]

Her experience and her model of family is extensive and inclusive, embrac-ing kin on equal terms regardless of locality or genealogy. Like her father, she feels that it is of vital importance to maintain the links with her family in Jamaica as well as in North America, for "the family's here forever, whereas friends come and go."[42] The inclusive definition of family and the strength of kinship ties may be seen as both cause and effect of this transnational Carib-bean family. Like her father, she feels that it is of vital importance to maintain the links with her family in Jamaica as well as in North America and would wish to transmit that inheritance to her own children when she has them "defi-nitely, definitely. It's really important."[43] Benson, in time, plans to return to the Caribbean, where the direct links with another generation will begin and the cycle will continue.

Conclusion

The case studies articulate how the practices and rhetoric of family served to link its members dispersed around the world. Both, clearly, were families in which, as Jerry put it, "There's always somebody going abroad to foreign."[44] Indeed, both are microcosms of the Caribbean's migratory history, with family members, over several generations, moving around the Caribbean to North and South America, to Britain, and to a wider Europe. In both cases, family mem-bers maintained contact over the years, despite the difficulty of communica-tions, particularly in the early part of the twentieth century. These migrations were enabled, in both families, by the willingness of kin to take care of children while one, or both, parents migrated abroad and an assumption that child rearing was the responsibility not solely of the parents, but of the wider family. Indeed, in many cases in this research, individuals reported being "grown" (reared) by other family members or, in turn, "growing" a child for another (often a sibling). Both families demonstrated the practicality of chain migration, as individuals were "received" into England by kin who had preceded them.

The language in which family members, in these examples and elsewhere, spoke about family was equally indicative. Repetitions and replications of sentiments and experiences emerged across the family narratives, suggesting the existence of cultural templates (Chamberlain 2000), ways in which values and prescriptions for behavior were encoded and transmitted, and acted as passports into the lives of kinsfolk across borders. The repetitions of phrases such as "closeness" signal these values; but so, too, are other indicators repeated across the narratives, of which we have examples here—"strong" grandfathers, Hyacinth's grandmother with her hair "like satin," knowing family to the "fourth generation," Jerry's "spirituality" and so forth. Such descriptions and metaphors recur frequently in the narratives, hinting not at the autonomy of the individual, but at their collectivity: individuality through identification *through* family, rather than *from* family, a sense of identification with and through lineage, even rebirth of ancestors in a new generation. "I was a grandmother child," commented one informant, "I feel her presence even now." "We were all full of my grandmother," the Trinidadian Dionne Brand wrote in her short story "Photograph":

> She had left us full and empty of her. We dreamed in my grandmother, and we woke up in her, bleary-eyed and gesturing for her arms, her elbows, her smell. We jockeyed with each other, lied to each other, quarrelled with each other, and with her for the boon of lying close to her, sculpting ourselves around the roundness of her back. Braiding her hair and oiling her feet. . . . She had left us empty and full of her. (Brand 1989: 180)

"When you are looking at me," another Jamaican woman born in 1935 remarked, "you're looking at my mother." "I was never lonely," another informant said (about her migration to England). "I carried my family within me." Yet another Jamaican woman commented simply on her family, "Is them me get me blessing from."

Knitted into the narratives are, therefore, powerful identifications with the family and the intimacy of their lives together. These identifications emerged as key components in narratives of belonging and identity in which "family" stood for identifiable beliefs and values, expectations, and behaviors. If this was symbolic, it also contained practical elements. Both families regarded the world's assets as resources to be utilized. While Hyacinth brought over four of her children to England, a fifth was sent to family in Canada, suggesting that this child's placement was a strategic move to benefit the family, a move enabled by the confidence placed in kin over there to "grow" the next generation. At the same time, reciprocity was expected. Other families in the study demonstrated similar family strategies. A Trinidadian family in our sample, for instance, sent one child to an aunt in North America and one, Leonard, to Britain so that they could take advantage of the opportunities there to improve the chances of other family members. In old age, Leonard used up his retirement savings to pay for his brother in Trinidad to come to England for a serious of operations for cancer:

> But we said it's a life and we couldn't let him die. . . . We paid for every-thing. . . . If my mother and my parents hadn't sent me to England, I would not have been in the position to do what we have done. So it stems back from the original attitude of my parents, their unselfishness, the sacrifice they have made to send me here.

Loyalty, as members of a shared lineage, could be assumed and trust guar-anteed. As another, British-born informant remarked:

> At any stage or any time of your life . . . when you're fed up or want a change, or you want to move or you want to go somewhere else, so it's very important to keep connection with your family and get to know them well. That is very important. It's like anything [happens] and you want somewhere to run to, or you need to flee and go somewhere and you don't know nobody, then you're doomed. So that's best to know and keep in contact, then you say, you can write, or you phone and you say, "Listen, it's hell going on in England," you know. "I'm coming home. I cannot stay here one more year." . . . So in that sense, it's good to keep in contact, you know?[45]

Both families in the case studies here operated within a global context where national borders were no barrier to family connectedness. Members of a transnational family—of close transnational networks—were provided with opportunities to utilize those networks to enhance their material or occupa-tional world, to broaden their experience, or to provide support when required.

Hyacinth flew across the Atlantic to support her sister-in-law, and she, in turn, provided Hyacinth with employment in America as recompense. This employment then helped Hyacinth's children in England. Arguably, the spreading and dispersal of material and emotional resources throughout the transnational trajectories of families provided them with diversity and security, strength and opportunity. At the same time, when the family was both the source of belonging and the resource for survival, then identity was both portable and secure.

The emphasis on closeness extends the meaning of the narratives by encoding values and prescriptions for loyalty, love, and "living good." They are particular ways of talking about particular relationships. These narratives link families across the oceans and the generations. They strengthen family membership and ties that have very practical implications in enabling migration, and facilitating return. But they are also increasingly powerful as expression of, and foci for, a Caribbean cultural identity abroad and in the Caribbean. As Caribbean family patterns in Britain continue to conform to those identified in the Caribbean, and as transnational links continue to affirm the influence of the Caribbean, the idea of family and the meanings attached to it have emerged as key elements in the narratives of belonging and identity. Moreover, the idea of family as a *Caribbean* family centered the sense of identity for its individual members and was an inheritance passed down to, and accepted by, younger generations of British-born Caribbeans. It is not just that you come from Jamaica (or Trinidad or Barbados) but that you come from a particular Jamaican (Trinidadian, Barbadian) *family* which stands for identifiable beliefs and values, and which represents a formidable network of kin whose loyalty—as members of a shared lineage—can be taken on trust:

> We have a family reunion now ... in New York.... Two years ago ... [it was] in Canada.... The one before that was in Jamaica.... Every two years, yes.... Every year it become bigger ... a few hundred I would say.... How many tables it was? About 30![46]

Indeed, as Constance Sutton (2002) has argued, family reunions, as rituals, provide a public expression of what is normally considered a private world and are visible affirmations of family identity that override all other affiliations. What links the family is kinship and lineage, neither of which relies on place for meaning. The longevity of migration as a feature of Caribbean life has arguably reinforced the sense of kinship and lineage as unifying features of family life and as a distinguishing feature of Caribbean diasporic communities.

The rhetorical bank in which this capital of family was deposited emphasized love and support, and its access was guaranteed by the password of closeness. In both families represented here, men and women shared the rhetoric of belonging and passed this on to their children. Caribbean families have often been marked as "matrifocal," with the assumption that men play a marginal role in the support and nurture of their children and, more generally, in family life. While the processes of family formation may expose women as single and sometimes sole supporters of their families, as we have seen, men can and do play an important role in family maintenance, even when they may not cohabit with their children, or their children's mothers (Barrow 1998). Benson, for instance, included as "family" his father's "outside" children, and could insist that his daughter embrace as kin individuals linked by subsequent partnerships of his own and her mother, his former partner. Both Jerry and Benson subscribed fully to the rhetoric of closeness and taught it to their children. At the same time, many women were able to (and in the context of the Caribbean, expected to) contribute independently toward the maintenance of their families. Both Benson's and Jerry's mothers migrated and worked equally hard to reunite their families; Hyacinth planned to stay in the United States. In the event, Hyacinth returned to contribute toward the care of her grandchildren and to continue to impart to them the family values and sense of lineage and belonging which had stood the test of time in this, as in other, transnational families.

Notes

This chapter is based on research by Harry Goulbourne and Mary Chamberlain, "Living Arrangements, Social Change and Family Structure of Caribbeans," a project funded by the Economic and Social Research Council as part of its Research Programme on Population and Household Change (Project No. L315253009). The author and publisher gratefully acknowledge permission from the original publishers to reproduce this essay, previously printed in Jean Besson and Karen Fog Olwig, eds., *Narratives of Belonging* (New York: Palgrave, 2006).

1. The British-based Economic and Social Research Council's Research Programme on Transnational Communities, 1998–2002, under the directorship of Steve Vertovec, was a major attempt to define the nature of contemporary transnational activity in a range of fields, including migration.

2. Britain made the transatlantic slave trade illegal in 1807. Slavery in the British West Indies was abolished in 1834, although a period of apprenticeship followed. Full emancipation of the slaves was achieved in 1838.

3. Some Chinese re-migrated to California, participating in the building of the Pacific railroad and the California Gold Rush.

4. Economic and Social Data Service (ESDS) Qualidata, University of Essex, TB018 (codes refer to country of origin, family, generation, recording number, and transcript page number). Pseudonyms are used throughout.

5. ESDS Qualidata, TR038.

6. Ibid., TR097.
7. Ibid., JF022.
8. Ibid., JC011.
9. Ibid., JF022.
10. Ibid., JF020/1/1/1/13.
11. Ibid., JF020/1/1/2/16.
12. Ibid., JF020/1/1/2/17.
13. Ibid., JF020/1/1/18.
14. Ibid.
15. Ibid., JF020/1/1/1/10.
16. Ibid., JF022/2/1/1/6.
17. Ibid.
18. Ibid., JF022/2/1/1/15.
19. Ibid., JF022/2/1/1/10–11.
20. Ibid., JF020/1/2/31.
21. Ibid., JF020/1/2/1/38.
22. Ibid., JF020/1/1/2/26.
23. Ibid., JF020/1/2/1/42.
24. Ibid., JF022/2/2/2/32.
25. Ibid., JF021/1/1/6.
26. Ibid., JF021/1/1/10–11.
27. Ibid., JF022/1/2/36–37.
28. Ibid., JF021/1/2/1.
29. Ibid., JF022/2/2/41.
30. Ibid., JF022/2/2/2/40.
31. Ibid., JF022/2/2/2/42–43.
32. Ibid., JG025/2/1/1/16.
33. Ibid., JG025/2/1/1/11.
34. Ibid., JG025/2/1/2/20.
35. Ibid., JG025/2/1/2/32.
36. Ibid., JG023/3/1/1/6.
37. Ibid., JG023/3/1/1/13.
38. Ibid., JG023/3/1/1/14.
39. Ibid.
40. Ibid., JG023/3/1/2/26.
41. Ibid., JG023/3/2/1/33.
42. Ibid., JG023/3/2/1/35.
43. Ibid., JGO23/3/2/1/33.
44. Ibid., JF022/1/1/4.
45. Ibid., JN049/2/2/2/52.
46. Ibid., JL0351(b).

References

Aymer, Paula. 1997. *Uprooted Women: Migrant Domestics in the Caribbean.* Westport, Conn.: Praeger.

Barrow, Christine. 1998. "Caribbean Masculinity and Family: Revisiting 'Marginality' and 'Reputation.'" In *Caribbean Portraits: Essays on Gender Ideologies and Identities,* ed. Christine Barrow. Kingston: Ian Randle Publishers.

Basch, Linda, Nina Glick Schiller, and Christina Szanton Blanc. 1994. *Nations Unbound: Transnational Projects, Postcolonial Predicaments and Deterritorialized Nation-States.* Langhorne, Penn.: Gordon and Breach.

Beckles, Hilary. 1990. *The History of Barbados.* Cambridge: Cambridge University Press.

Besson, Jean. 2002. *Martha Brae's Two Histories. European Expansion and Caribbean Culture-Building in Jamaica.* Chapel Hill and London: University of North Carolina Press.

Brand, Dionne. 1989. "Photograph." In *Her True-True Name: An Anthology of Women's Writing from the Caribbean.* London: Heinemann.

Chamberlain, Mary. 1997. *Narratives of Exile and Return.* Warwick University Caribbean Studies. Oxford: Macmillan.

Chamberlain, Mary. 1999. "The Family as Model and Metaphor in Caribbean Migration to Britain." *Journal of Ethnic and Migration Studies* 25, no. 2: 251–266.

Chamberlain, Mary. 2000. "Praise Songs of the Family: Lineage and Kinship in the Caribbean Diaspora." *History Workshop Journal* 50: 114–128.

Chamberlain, Mary. 2001. "Migration, the Caribbean and the family." In *Caribbean Families in Britain and the Transatlantic World,* ed. Harry Goulbourne and Mary Chamberlain. Warwick University Caribbean Studies. Oxford: Macmillan.

Glick Schiller, Nina, and Georges Fouron. 2000. *Georges Woke Up Laughing: Long Distance Nationalism and the Search for Home.* Durham, N.C.: Duke University Press.

Goulbourne, Harry. 1999. "The Transnational Character of Caribbean Kinship in Britain." In *Changing Britain: Families and Households in the 1990s*, ed. Susan McRae. Oxford: Oxford University Press.

Goulbourne, Harry. 2002. *Caribbean Transnational Experience*. London: Pluto.

Higman, Barry W. 1976. *Slave Population and Economy in Jamaica, 1807–1834*. Cambridge: Cambridge University Press.

Johnson, Howard. 1998. "Barbadian Migrants in the Putumayo District of the Amazon, 1904–1911." In *Caribbean Migration: Globalised Identities*, ed. Mary Chamberlain. London: Routledge.

Kasinitz, Philip. 1992. *Caribbean New York: Black Immigrants and the Politics of Race*. Ithaca, N.Y.: Cornell University Press.

Laurence, K. O. 1994. *A Question of Labour. Indentured Immigration into Trinidad and British Guiana, 1875–1917*. Kingston: Ian Randle Publishers.

Look Lai, Walton. 1993. *Indentured Labor, Caribbean Sugar: Chinese and Indian Migrants to the British West Indies, 1838–1918*. Baltimore: Johns Hopkins University Press.

Newton, Velma. 1987. *The Silver Men: West Indian Labour Migration to Panama, 1850–1914*. Kingston: University of the West Indies, Institute of Social and Economic Research.

Olwig, Karen Fog. 1993. "The Migration Experience: Caribbean Women at Home and Abroad." In *Women and Change in the Caribbean*, ed. Janet H. Momsen. London: James Currey.

Owen, David W. 1995. "Mapping the Caribbean Population in Britain." Unpublished working paper W2/95, Living Arrangements, Family Structure and Social Change of Caribbeans Project, Economic and Social Research Council, Swindon.

Peach, Ceri. 1991. "The Caribbean in Europe: Contrasting Patterns of Migration and Settlement in Britain, France and the Netherlands." Research Paper in Ethnic Relations no. 15, Centre for Research in Ethnic Relations, University of Warwick.

Richardson, Bonham C. 1983. *Caribbean Migrants: Environment and Human Survival on St. Kitts and Nevis*. Knoxville: University of Tennessee Press.

Shepherd, Verene A. 1998. "Indians, Jamaicans and the Emergence of a Modern Migration Culture." In *Caribbean Migration: Globalised Identities*, ed. Mary Chamberlain. London: Routledge.

Sheridan, Richard B. 1994 (1974). *Sugar and Slavery: An Economic History of the British West Indies, 1623–1775*. Kingston: University of the West Indies, Canoe Press.

Sutton, Constance. 2002. "Celebrating Ourselves: Keeping Kin Connections Alive. Family Reunions in the Afro-Caribbean Diaspora." Paper presented at the Gender and Transnational Families Conference, Amsterdam, May–June 2002.

Sutton, Constance, and Susan Makiesky-Barrow. 1994. "Migration and West Indian Racial and Ethnic Consciousness." In *Caribbean Life in New York City: Sociocultural Dimensions*, ed. Constance Sutton and Elsa Chaney. New York: Center for Migration Studies of New York.

Thomas-Hope, Elizabeth. 1992. *Explanation in Caribbean Migration*. London: Macmillan.

Thompson, Paul, and Elaine Bauer. 2001. "Recapturing Distant Caribbean Childhoods and Communities: The Shaping of Memory in the Testimonies of Jamaican Migrants in Britain and North America." Paper presented at the Annual Conference of the Association of Caribbean Historians, Trinidad.

Wiltshire-Brodber, Rosina. 1986. *The Transnational Family*. St. Augustine, Trinidad: Institute of International Relations, University of the West Indies.

About the Contributors

Elizabeth Aranda is an Associate Professor of Sociology at the University of South Florida. She has written about Puerto Rican migration, Latinos in the United States, and race and ethnic relations. She is the author of *Emotional Bridges to Puerto Rico* (2006) and is currently writing a book about Latinos in South Florida.

Margarita Cervantes-Rodríguez is a Visiting Research Scholar at the Center for Migration and Development at Princeton University. She is the author of *International Migration in Cuba: Accumulation, Imperial Designs and Transnational Social Fields* (forthcoming). She specializes in international migration and transnational processes and is currently conducting research on issues pertaining to immigration and health as part of a research project sponsored by the Robert Wood Johnson Foundation.

Mary Chamberlain is a Professor of Caribbean History at Oxford Brookes University. She is the author of *Narratives of Exile and Return* (1997, 2004), *Family Love in the Diaspora: Migration and the Anglo-Caribbean Experience* (2006), and the editor of *Caribbean Migration: Globalised Identities* (1997) and *Caribbean Families in Britain and the Transatlantic World* (with Harry Goulbourne; 2001). She is currently working on *Culture, Migration and Nationhood: Barbados and Empire, 1937–1966.* She is a fellow of the Royal Historical Society, and has served on a number of advisory and editorial boards.

Michel Giraud is a sociologist and researcher at the Centre National de la Recherche Scientifique of France, which is affiliated with the Centre de Recherche sur les Pouvoirs Locaux dans la Caraïbe of the Université des Antilles et de la Guyane. He is the author of books and articles on the French Caribbean societies and their diasporas in continental France, including "The Antillese in France: Trends and Prospects" in a special issue of *Ethnic and Racial Studies* on the Caribbean diaspora (2004).

Nina Glick Schiller is a Professor of Social Anthropology and director of the Research Institute of Cosmopolitan Cultures at the University of Manchester. Her research interests and publications address transnational migration, migration theory, methodological nationalism, and cities. Her books include *Nations Unbound: Transnational Projects, Postcolonial Predicaments, and the Deterritorialized Nation-State* (1993) and *Georges Woke Up Laughing: Long Distance Nationalism and the Search for Home* (2001).

Ramón Grosfoguel is an Associate Professor of Ethnic Studies at the University of California, Berkeley, and Senior Research Associate of the Maison des Sciences de l'Homme in Paris. He has published on the political economy of the world system and on Caribbean migrations to Western Europe and the United States. He is the author of *Colonial Subjects: Puerto Ricans in a Global Perspective* (2003). Most recently, he was co-editor, with Eric Mielants, of a special issue of the *International Journal of Comparative Sociology* on minorities, racism, and cultures of scholarship.

Lisa Maya Knauer is an Assistant Professor of Anthropology and African/African American Studies at the University of Massachusetts, Dartmouth. She has written several articles and book chapters about Afro-Cuban music and religion in New York and Havana. She is the co-editor of *Contested Histories in Public Space: Memory, Race, and Nation* (forthcoming) and *Memory and the Impact of Political Transformation in Public Space* (2004).

John R. Logan is a Professor of Sociology and director of the research initiative on Spatial Structures in the Social Sciences at Brown University. He continues his research on immigrants and minorities in U.S. cities, including a new project using data from the late nineteenth century. He is the co-author, with Harvey Molotch, of *Urban Fortunes: The Political Economy of Place*, which was recently republished in a twentieth-anniversary edition.

Eric Mielants is an Associate Professor of Sociology in the College of Arts and Sciences at Fairfield University. He has written articles and essays on racism, social theory, and contemporary migration issues. Most recently, he is the author of *The Origins of Capitalism and the Rise of the West* (Temple University Press, 2008).

Monique Milia-Marie-Luce is a Maître de Conférences in Contemporary History at the University of the French Guyana and the French West Indies. She has written articles on comparative migration between Puerto Ricans and French West Indians and on sport and identity in Martinique.

Laura Oso Casas is a Senior Lecturer in the Faculty of Sociology at the University of Coruña. She has worked as a consultant for various international organizations, including the Organization for Economic Cooperation and Development, the European Union, and the United Nations International Research and Training Institute for the Advancement of Women. Her research has focused mainly on gender and migration in Spain and Spanish migration to France. She is the author of *La migración hacia España de mujeres jefas de hogar* (1998) and *Españolas en París: Estrategias de ahorro y consumo en las migraciones internacionales* (2004).

Livio Sansone is an Associate Professor of Anthropology at the Federal University of Bahia and head of the Graduate Program in Ethnic and African Studies, as well as of the Factory of Ideas Program. He has published extensively in the fields of race relations, globalization, youth culture, and work or unemployment among lower-class people in Suriname, the Netherlands, England, Italy and Brazil. He is the author of *Blackness without Ethnicity: Creating Race in Brazil* (2003).

Charles (Wenquan) Zhang is an Assistant Professor of Sociology at Texas A&M University. His research interests include migratory patterns and adaptation experiences of recent immigrants and the application of GIS and Spatial Econometrics in modeling spatial inequality. He has published in the areas of suburbanization processes and the development of ethnic enclave clusters for major minority groups in large metropolitan regions of the United States. His recent projects deal with racial and ethnic neighborhood transition and innovative measurements of residential segregation.

Index